BUDDHA AND HIS PHILOSOPHY

Buddha *and his* Philosophy

Dr. S. L. Misra

Mahaveer & Sons
(Publishers & Distributors)
New Delhi-110002

Buddha *and his* Philosophy

First Published 2011

ISBN 978-81-8377-299-0

Published by :

MAHAVEER & SONS

(Publishers & Distributors)

H-2/16, Ansari Road, Darya Ganj,
(Near Shiv Mandir) New Delhi-110002
E-mail : mahaveersonspub@rediffmail.com
Ph. 011 23242069, Mob. 09899608339

PRINTED IN INDIA

Published by Mahaveer & Sons, Publishers & Distributors, H-2/16 Ansari Road, Near Shiv Mandir, Daryaganj, New Delhi-110002, Printed at Himanshu Printers, Delhi.

Preface

GAUTAMA BUDDHA, the founder of Buddhism, lived in Northern India in the 6th century B.C. His personal name was Siddhartha, and his family name was Gautama. He was called the 'Buddha' after He attained Enlightenment and realized the ultimate Truth. 'Buddha' means the *'Awakened' ox* the *'Enlightened One'*. He generally called Himself the *Tathagata,* while His followers called Him *Bhagava,* the Blessed One. Others spoke of Him as Gautama or Sakyamuni.

He was born a prince who seemed to have everything. He had a luxurious upbringing and His family was of pure descent on both sides. He was the heir to the throne, extremely handsome, inspiring trust, stately and gifted with great beauty of complexion and a fine presence. At sixteen He married His cousin named Yasodhara. She was majestic, serene and full of dignity and grace.

Despite all this, Prince Siddhartha felt trapped amidst the luxury like a bird in a golden cage. During His visits outside the palace, He saw what was known as the 'Four Sights', that is, an old man, a sick man, a dead man, and a holy recluse. When He saw the sights, one after another, the realization came to Him that, 'Life is subject to old age and death'.

Content

1

NATURE OF LIFE THE BUDDHA

GAUTAMA BUDDHA, the founder of Buddhism, lived in Northern India in the 6th century B.C. His personal name was Siddhartha, and his family name was Gautama. He was called the 'Buddha' after He attained Enlightenment and realized the ultimate Truth. 'Buddha' means the *'Awakened' ox* the *'Enlightened One'*. He generally called Himself the *Tathagata,* while His followers called Him *Bhagava,* the Blessed One. Others spoke of Him as Gautama or Sakyamuni.

He was born a prince who seemed to have everything. He had a luxurious upbringing and His family was of pure descent on both sides. He was the heir to the throne, extremely handsome, inspiring trust, stately and gifted with great beauty of complexion and a fine presence. At sixteen He married His cousin named Yasodhara. She was majestic, serene and full of dignity and grace.

Despite all this, Prince Siddhartha felt trapped amidst the luxury like a bird in a golden cage. During His visits outside the palace, He saw what was known as the 'Four Sights', that is, an old man, a sick man, a dead man, and a holy recluse. When He saw the sights, one after another, the realization came to Him that, 'Life is subject to old age and death'. He asked, 'Where is the realm of life in which there is neither old age nor death?' The sight of the recluse, who was calm after having given up the craving for material life, gave Him the clue that the first step in His search for Truth was Renunciation. This means realizing that worldly possessions cannot bring the ultimate happiness people crave for.

Determined to find the way out of these universal sufferings, He decided to leave home to find the cure not for Himself only, but for all mankind. One night in His twenty-ninth year, He bade His sleeping wife and son a silent farewell, saddled His great white horse, and rode off toward the forest.

His renunciation is unprecedented in history. He left at the height of youth, from pleasures to difficulties; from certainty of material security to austerities; from a position of wealth and power to that of a wandering ascetic who took shelter in caves and forests, with His ragged robe as the only protection against the blazing sun, rain and winter winds. He renounced His position, wealth, promise of prestige and power, and a life filled with love and hope in exchange for the difficult search for Truth which no one had found although many in India had sought for thousands of years.

For six long years, He laboured to find this Truth. What was the truth He sought? It was to understand truly the nature of existence and to find the ultimate, unchanging happiness. He studied under the foremost masters of the day, and learned everything these religious teachers could teach Him. When He found that they could not teach Him what He was seeking for, He decided to find the Truth through His own efforts. A band of five ascetics joined Him and together they practised severe austerities in the belief that if the body was tortured then the soul would be released from suffering. Siddhartha was a man of energy and will power and He outdid other ascetics in every austerity they practised. While fasting, He ate so little that when He took hold of the skin of His stomach, He actually touched His spine. He pushed Himself to do superhuman feats of self-torture so that He would have certainly died. But He realised the futility of self-mortification, and decided to practise moderation instead.

On the full moon night of the month of Vesakha, He sat under the Bodhi tree at Gaya, wrapped in deep meditation. It was then that His mind burst the bubble of the material universe and realised the true nature of all life and all things. At the age of 35 years, He was transformed from an earnest truth seeker into the Buddha, the Enlightened One.

For nearly half a century following the Enlightenment, the Buddha walked on the dusty paths of India teaching the Dharma so that those who heard and practised could be ennobled and free. He founded an order of monks and nuns, challenged the caste system, raised the status of women, encouraged religious freedom and free inquiry, opened the gates of deliverance to all, in every condition of life, high or low, saint or sinner, and ennobled the lives of criminals like Angulimala and courtesans like Ambapali. He freed humanity from religious slavery, religious dogma and blindfaith.

He towered in wisdom and intellect. Every problem was analysed into component parts and then reassembled in logical order with the meaning made clear. None could defeat Him in dialogue. He is an unequalled teacher even until today. He still is the foremost analyst of the mind and phenomena. For the first time in history, He gave human beings the power to think for themselves, raised the worth of mankind, and showed that human beings can reach to the highest knowledge and supreme Enlightenment by their own efforts. He encouraged people to open their minds and think without bias nor preconceived notions to understand the reality of life and the universe.

Despite His peerless wisdom and royal lineage, He was never removed from the simple villagers. Surface distinctions of class and caste meant little to Him. No one was too little or low for Him to help. Often when an outcaste, or poor and dejected person came to Him, his or her self-respect was restored and turned from the ignoble life to that of a noble being.

The Buddha was full of compassion *(karuna)* and wisdom *(panna),* knowing how and what to teach individuals according to their level of understanding. He was known to have walked long distances to help one single person to show him or her the correct Path.

He was affectionate and devoted to His disciples, always inquiring after their well being and progress. When staying at the monastery, He paid daily visits to the sick wards. His compassion for the sick can be seen from His advice: 'He who attends the sick, attends on me.' The Buddha kept order and discipline on the basis of mutual respect. King Pasenadi Kosala could not understand how the Buddha maintained such order and discipline in the community of monks when he, as a king with the power to punish, could not maintain it as well in his court. The Buddha's method was to make people act from an inner understanding rather than make them behave by imposing laws and threatening them with punishment.

Many miraculous powers were attributed to Him, but He did not consider any kind of supernatural powers important. To Him, the greatest miracle was to explain the Truth and make a cruel person to become kind through realisation. A teacher with deep compassion, He was moved by human suffering and determined to free people from their fetters by a rational system of thought and way of life.

The Buddha did not claim to have 'created' worldly conditions, universal phenomena, or the Universal Law which we call the 'Dharma'. Although described as *lokavidu* or 'knower of the worlds', He was not regarded as the sole custodian of that Universal Law. He freely acknowledged that the Dharma, together with the working of the cosmos, is timeless; it has no creator and is independent in the absolute sense. Every conditioned thing that exists in the cosmos is subject to the operation of Dharma. What the Buddha did (like all the other Buddhas before Him) was to *rediscover* this infallible Truth and make it known to mankind. In discovering the Truth, He also found the means whereby one could ultimately free oneself from being subjected to the endless cycle of conditioning, with its attendant evils of unsatisfactoriness.

After forty-five years of ministry, the Buddha passed away *(attained Parinirvana)* at the age of eighty at a place called Kusinara, leaving behind numerous followers, monks and nuns, and a vast treasure store of Dharma Teaching. The impact of His great love and dedication is still felt today.

In the *Three Greatest Men in History,* H.G. Wells states:

'In the Buddha you see clearly a man, simple, devout, alone, battling for light, a vivid human personality, not a myth. He too gave a message to mankind universal in character. Many of our best modern ideas are in closest harmony with it. All the miseries and discontents of life are due, he taught, to selfishness. Before a man can become serene he must cease to live for his senses or himself. Then he merges into a greater being. Buddhism in a different language called men to self-forgetfulness 500years before Christ. In some ways he was nearer to us and our needs. He was more lucid upon our individual importance in service than Christ and less ambiguous upon the question of personal immortality.'

His Renunciation

The renunciation of Prince Siddhartha was the boldest step that a man has ever taken.

It was night. Siddhartha could no longer find peace. He strode through the halls of the palace and finally went to the king. He bowed and said to him:

'Father, grant the request I have to make. Permit me to leave the palace to follow the path to deliverance, for all earthly things are changing and of short duration. So we must part, father.'

'Son, give up this idea. You are still too young for a religious calling. It is rather for me to embrace religion. The time has come for me to leave the palace. I abdicate, O my son!'

'Promise me four things, O father, and I shall not leave your house and repair to the woods.'

'What are they?' asked the king.

'Promise me that my life will not end in death, that sickness will not impair my health, that age will not follow my youth, that misfortune will not destroy my prosperity.'

'I cannot promise them, son, for they are inevitable.'

'Then do not hold me back. O father, my mind is fixed. All earthly things are transitory.'

Thus the prince resolved to accomplish the Great Renunciation that very night.

At the age of 29 years, Siddhartha was a full blooded, young man in the prime of life. As it was, the temptation not to abandon all He had known and loved was great. He knew the effort to seek the truth must have been formidable. During His final moments in the palace, He visited His bedroom and looked at His slumbering wife and their newborn child. The great impulse to remain and abandon His plan must have caused Him intense agony. Contrary to present day materialist values, in those days in India, it was considered a noble thing for a person to forsake home and loved ones to become an ascetic to lead a holy life. It was considered a sacrifice which was spiritually praiseworthy. All things considered, therefore, it would seem that Siddhartha was right in boldly and quickly carrying out His plan.

Two thousand five hundred years after His renunciation, some people criticise Him for His action. They say it was cruel for Him to run away from the palace without even telling His wife. They condemn Siddhartha for His manner of leaving home and Kingdom. Some describe it as a 'callous abandonment of wife and family'. Yet what would have happened if He had not left so quietly and had approached His loved ones for a formal farewell? They would, of course, have implored Him to change His mind. The scene would have been hysterical, and quite possibly the little domain of His father Rajah Suddhodana would have been thrown into turmoil. His intention to seek the Truth would have had to be aborted by His father and wife who would have disagreed with His renunciation plans although He had discussed with His father and His wife about His intentions of renunciation. Because of His departure on that day, today, five hundred million human beings follow Him. If He had stayed without 'running away' only

His wife and son would have run after Him. His wife, however, did not accuse Him of desertion when she realised the purpose of His renunciation. Instead, she gave up her luxurious life to lead a simple life as a mark of respect. Earlier, when He discussed His renunciation with His wife she came to know that there was no way for her to stop His renunciation. She then requested Him to have a son before Him. That is why He decided to renounce the very day the son was born.

He renounced the world not for His own sake or convenience but for the sake of suffering humanity. To Him the whole of mankind is one family. The renunciation of Prince Siddhartha at that early age was the boldest step that a man could have ever taken.

Detachment is one of the most important factors for the attainment of Enlightenment. The attainment of Enlightenment is by way of non-attachment. Most of life's troubles are caused by attachment. We get angry; we worry; we become greedy and complain bitterly. All these causes of unhappiness, tension, stubbornness and sadness are due to attachment. When we investigate any trouble or worry we have, the main cause is always attachment. Had Prince Siddhartha developed His attachment towards His wife, child, kingdom and worldly pleasures, He would never have been able to discover the remedy for suffering mankind. Therefore, He had to sacrifice everything including worldly pleasures in order to have a concentrated mind free from any distractions, in order to find the Truth that can cure humanity from suffering. Consider this, if the prince had not gone forth, humanity would today still be entrapped in fear, ignorance and misery, with no real understanding of the human condition.

In the eyes of this young Prince, the whole world was burning with lust, anger, greed and many other defilements which ignite the fire of our passions. He saw each and every living being in this world, including His wife and father, suffering from all sorts of physical and mental ailments. So determined was He to seek a solution for the eradication of suffering amongst suffering humanity, that He was prepared to sacrifice everything.

Here is how a poet saw the renunciation of the Buddha:

'T'was not through hatred of children sweet, T'was not through hatred of His lovely wife, Thriller of hearts— not that He loved them less, But Buddhahood more, that He renounced them all.'

Nature of the Buddha

As long, brethren, as the moon and sun have not arisen in the world, just as long is there no shining forth a great light of great radiance. There prevails gross darkness, the darkness of bewilderment. Night is not distinguishable from the day, nor the month, the half-moon and the seasons of the years from each other.'

'But, brethren, when the moon and sun arise in the world, then a great light of great radiance shines forth. Gross darkness, the darkness of bewilderment, is no more: Then are months and the half-moon and the seasons of years.'

'Just so, brethren, as long as a Buddha, who is an Arahant, a Buddha Supreme, arises not, there is no shining forth a great light of great radiance. But gross darkness, the darkness of bewilderment, prevails. There is no pro-claiming, no teaching, no showing forth, no setting up, no openingup, no analysis, no makingclear of the Four Noble Truths.'

'What Four? The Noble Truth of Suffering, the Arising of Suffering, the Ceasing of Suffering, and the Approach to the Ceasing of Suffering.'

'Wherefore, brethren, do you exert yourselves to realize "This is suffering; this is the arising of suffering; this is the ceasing of suffering; this is the approach to the ceasing of suffering".'

The above words give us a clear picture of the great value of the arising of the Buddha to the world. The Buddha arose at a time when Western Philosophy as developed by the Greeks, was led by Heraclites who gave a new interpretation to the early religions of the Olympian gods. It was a time when Jeremiah was giving a new message among the Jews in Babylon.

It was a time when Pythagoras was introducing a doctrine of reincarnation in Greece. It was a time when Confucius was esta-blishing his ethics of conduct in China.

It was a time when India's social fabric was heavily encrusted with priestcraft, Brahmanical dominance, self-mortification, caste distinctions, corrupt feudalism and subjugation of women.

It was at such a time that the Buddha, the most fragrant flower of the human race, appeared in the land where saints and sages dedicated their lives to the search for truth.

He was a great man who wielded an extraordinary influence on others even during His lifetime. His personal magnetism, moral prestige and radiant confidence in His discovery, made Him a popular success. During His active life as a Teacher, the Buddha enlightened many who listened to Him. He attracted the high and low, rich and poor, educated and illiterate, men and women, householders and ascetics, nobles and peasants. He went in search of the vicious to teach, while the pure and virtuous came in search of Him to learn. To all, He gave the gift of the Truth that He had discovered. His disciples were kings and soldiers, merchants and millionaires, beggars, courtesans, religious, criminal-minded as well as deluded people. When people were fighting, He made peace between them. When they were deluded, He enlightened them. When they were inflamed with rage and lust, He gave them the cooling water of Truth. When they were forsaken and wretched, He extended to them the infinite love of His compassionate heart. All people were one in the eyes of the Buddha.

He was *'Lokavidu*—'The knower of the world'. Having

himself lived a life of luxury He knew the world too well to have any illusions about its nature, or to believe that its laws could be completely refashioned to suit the desires of human beings. He knew that the world does not only exist for their pleasure. He knew about the nature of worldly conditions. He realised the vicissitude of worldly life. He knew the futility of human imagination or day-dreaming about the world.

He did not encourage wishful-thinking in terms of establishing a worldly Utopia. He did not set out to remould the world. Rather, He told of the Way by which one could conquer one's own world — the inner subjective world that is everyone's private domain. In simple language, He told us that the whole world is within us and it is led by the mind and that mind must be trained and cleansed properly. The external material world could be controlled and cease to create anguish if our inner world is under control.

His Teaching was basically simple and meaningful: 'To put an end to evil; to fulfil all good; to purify the mind. This is the advice of all the Buddhas.' (DHAMMAPADA 183)

He taught the people how to eradicate ignorance. He encouraged them to maintain freedom in the mind to think freely.

By every test of what He said and did, He demonstrated that He was the pre-eminent man of His day. He declared a faith of service, a ministry of sacrifice and achievement. He advised us to start each day as if it was the beginning of a life. We must not waste time and energy in searching the beginning of life. We should fulfil our endless responsibilities and duties of daily existence here and now without depending on others to do it for us. In other words, He taught us to be self-reliant.

He gave mankind a new explanation of the universe.

He gave a new vision of eternal happiness, the achievement of perfection in Buddhahood. He pointed out the way to the permanent state beyond all impermanence, the way to Nirvana, the final deliverance from the misery of existence.

His time was more than 2,500 years ago. Yet, even today this great Teacher is honoured not only by all religious-minded people. He is also honoured by atheists, historians, rationalists and intellect-uals, free thinkers, scientists and psychologists all over the world who freely acknowledge Him as the Enlightened, most liberal minded and compassionate Teacher.

The Buddha was a unique human being who was self Enlightened. He had no one whom He could regard as His teacher. Through His own efforts, He practised to perfection the ten Paramitas—supreme qualities of generosity, discipline, renunciation, wisdom, energy, endurance, truthfulness, deter-mination, goodwill and equanimity. Through His mental puri-fication, He opened the doors to all knowledge. He knew all things to be known, cultivated all things to be cultivated, and destroyed all things to be destroyed. Indeed, it is difficult to compare other religious teachers to Him in terms of cultivation of the mind, mental purity and supreme wisdom.

So special was He and so electrifying His message, that many people asked Him ' 'What (not so much Who) He was'. The question of 'Who He was' would be with respect to His name, origin, ancestry, etc., while 'What He was' referred to the order of beings to which He belonged. So 'godly' and inspiring was He that even during His time, there were numerous attempts by others to turn Him into a god or a reincarnation of a god. He never agreed to be regarded as such. In the Anguttara Nikaya, He said: 'I am indeed not a deva nor any other form of divine being; neither am I an ordinary human being. Know ye that I am the Buddha, the Awakened One.' After Enlightenment, the

Buddha could no longer be classified even as a 'manusya' or an ordinary human being. He belonged to the Buddha wangsa, a special class of enlightened beings, all of whom are Buddhas.

Buddhas appear in this world from time to time. But some people have the mistaken idea that it is the same Buddha who is reincarnated or appears in the world over and over again. Actually, they are not the same person, because then there would be no scope for others to attain to Buddhahood. Buddhists believe that anyone can become a Buddha if he develops his qualities to perfection and is able to remove his ignorance completely through his own efforts. After Enlightenment, however, all Buddhas become identical in their attainment and experience of Nirvana.

In India, the followers of many orthodox religious groups tried to condemn the Buddha because of His liberal and rational teachings which revolutionised Indian society at that time. Many regarded Him as an enemy as His teachings contradicted their age-old religious traditions but more intellectuals as well as people from all ranks of society began to follow Him and accept His teaching. Some tried to reduce His stature by introducing Him as a reincarnation of one of their gods. This way they could absorb Buddhism into their religion. To a certain extent, this strategy worked in India since it had, through the centuries, contributed to the decay and the subsequent uprooting of Buddhism from the land of its origin.

Even today there are certain religious groups who try to absorb the Buddha into their faiths as a way of gaining converts to their religion from among Buddhists. Their basis for doing so is by claiming that the Buddha Himself had predicted that another Buddha would appear in this world, and that the latest Buddha will become even more popular. One group even claims that Jesus Christ who lived 600 years after Gautama the Buddha is the latest Buddha. Another group says that the next Buddha had arrived in Japan in the 13th century. Yet another group believes that their founder came from the lineage of great teachers like Gautama and Jesus. These groups advise Buddhists to give up their "old" Buddha and follow the so-called new Buddha. While it is good to see them giving the Buddha the same status as their own religious teachers, we feel that these attempts to absorb Buddhists into another faith by misrepresenting the truth are in extreme bad taste.

Those who claim that the new Buddha had already arrived are obviously misrepresenting what the Buddha had said. Although the Buddha predicted the coming of the next Buddha, He mentioned some conditions which had to be met before this can be possible. It is the nature of Buddhahood that the next Buddha will not appear as long as the dispensation of the current Buddha still exists. He will appear only when the Four Noble Truths and the Eightfold Path have been completely forgotten. The people living then must be properly guided in order to understand the same Truth taught by the previous Buddhas. We are still living within the dispensation of Gautama the Buddha. Although the moral conduct of the people has, with very few exceptions, deteriorated, the future Buddha will only appear after some incalculable period when the Path to Nirvana is completely lost to mankind and when people are again ready to receive Him.

Some people have already started to erect the image of the future Buddha and have started to worship and pray just because of that belief. They have moulded the image and features of that Buddha according to their own imagination.

THE Buddha was the embodiment of all the virtues that He preached. During His successful and eventful ministry of 45 years, He translated all His words into actions. At no time did He ever show any human frailty or any base passion. The Buddha's moral code is the most perfect the world has ever known.

For more than 25 centuries, millions of people have found inspiration and solace in His Teaching. His greatness still shines today like a sun that outshines the glow of lesser lights. His Teachings still beckon the weary pilgrim to the security and peace of Nirvana. No other person has sacrificed so much worldly comfort for the sake of suffering humanity.

The Buddha was among the first religious leaders in human history to admonish against animal sacrifice for any reason and to appeal to people not to harm any living creature.

To the Buddha, religion was not a contractual agreement between a divinity and man but a way to enlightenment. He did not want followers with blind faith; He wanted followers who could think freely and wisely and work out their own salvation.

The entire human race has been blessed with His presence.

There was never an occasion when the Buddha expressed any unfriendliness towards a single person. Not even to His opponents and worst enemies did the Buddha express any unfriendliness. There were a few prejudiced minds who turned against the Buddha and who tried to kill Him; yet the Buddha never treated them as enemies. The Buddha once said, 'As an elephant in the battlefield endures the arrows that are shot into him, so will I endure the abuse and unfriendly expressions of others. In the annals of history, no man is recorded as having so consecrated himself to the welfare of all living beings as the Buddha did. From the hour of His Enlightenment to the end of His Life, He strove tirelessly to elevate mankind. He slept only two hours a day. Though 25 centuries have gone since the passing away of this great Teacher, His message of love and wisdom still exists in its pristine purity. This message is still decisively influencing the destinies of humanity. He was the most Compassionate One who illuminated this world with loving-kindness.

After attaining Nirvana, the Buddha left a deathless message that is still with us. Today we are confronted by the terrible threat to world peace. At no time in the history of the world is His message more needed than it is now.

The Buddha was born to dispel the darkness of ignorance and to show the world how to get rid of suffering and disease, decay and death and all the worries and miseries of living beings.

According to some other beliefs, a certain god will appear in this world from time to time to destroy wicked people and to protect the good ones. The Buddha did not appear in this world to destroy wicked people but to show them the correct path.

In the history of the world, did we ever hear of any religious teacher who was so filled with such all absorbing compassion and love for suffering humanity as the Buddha was? We have heard of some wise men in Greece: Socrates, Plato and Aristotle and many others who lived at about the same time as the Buddha. But they were only philosophers and great thinkers and seekers after truth; they lacked any inspiring love for the suffering multitudes.

The Buddha's way of liberating mankind was to teach them how to find complete freedom from physical and mental suffering. He was not interested in alleviating a few chance cases of physical or mental distress. He was more concerned with revealing a Path that all people could follow.

Let us take all the great philosophers, psychologists, thinkers, scientists, rationalists, social workers, reformers and other religious teachers and compare, with an unbiased mind, their greatness, virtues, services and wisdom with the Buddha's virtues, compassion and Enlightenment. It is not difficult to see where the Buddha stands amongst all those great intellectuals.

Historical Evidences of the Buddha

Relevance of the Historical Evidence for Buddha to Christianity:

The historical evidence for the life of Buddha will be briefly discussed in order to provide the reader with another example of documentation for a religious figure in the ancient world in addition to Jesus. As the reader will probably conclude, the historical documentation for the life and teachings of Jesus is far greater than the historical documentation for the life of Buddha, provided that the reader possesses a general understanding of the historical documentation available for the life and teachings of Jesus.

Historical Evidence for the Life and Teachings of Buddha:

1. Buddha, or Siddhartha Gautama, was born in North India sometime around 563 B.C.E. and presumably lived a long life, perhaps being about eighty years old when he died 2. "So far as we are aware, he didn't commit anything to writing. Thus, all we know of Buddha's teaching has come down to us from others. From the very beginning, though, both an oral tradition and a written tradition developed"

3 · "Although **the oldest available *written Buddhist texts* are *relatively late,* tradition** assures us that the texts known as *Nikayas* contain an early and reliable record of the Buddha's actual teachings, for immediately after the Buddha's death a council of monks was summoned to recall and collect these teachings".

4 · "Unfortunately, very little is known about Shakyamuni Buddha that we could call historical fact. Historical record keeping was not much practiced in those days, and his followers were far more concerned about preserving his teaching than with the details of his life-and, of course, that's what really matters" .

5 · "I want to emphasize this point: Commonly repeated stories about the life of Buddha are the stuff of legend, not history" .

6 · "Various ancient sources give us information about the life of Buddha. The oldest and most important document is the Pali Canon. Committed to writing in the first century B.C.E., the Pali Canon is a carefully assembled collection of the then-existing scriptural works and traditions regarding Buddha. The accounts in the Pali Canon, however, are really nothing more than two commentaries that deal with two different parts of Buddha's life. They give us only some basic facts".

7 · " **The first complete biography of the Buddha was written in the first century C.E.** by the poet Ashvaghosha. This work, known as the *Buddha-Charita,* is unreservedly mythical; the author was not interested in historical veracity. Many of the legends about Shakyamuni Buddha's life are derived from the *Buddha-Charita*".

· "Approximately *four centuries* **after Buddha's death,** the *first* great effort was made to gather together the existing sources and determine, insofar as was possible,

the true record of Buddha's life and teaching. This scholarly and thoroughgoing work came to be known as the Pali Canon" .

"Again, the story of Buddha's life is much more the stuff of legends than of history. But it's well worth surveying, however briefly. As you might expect, **there are numerous variations to the legends**".

GAUTAMA the Buddha is not a mythical figure but an actual, historical personality who introduced the religion known today as Buddhism. Evidences to prove the existence of this great religious Teacher are to be found in the following facts:-

1. The testimonies of those who knew Him personally. These testimonies are recorded in the rock-inscriptions, pillars and pagodas made in His honour. These testimonies and monuments to His memory were created by kings and others who were near enough to His time to be able to verify the story of His life.

2. The discovery of places and the remains of buildings that were mentioned in the narratives of His time.

3. The Sangha, the holy order which He founded, has had an unbroken existence to the present day. The Sangha possessed the facts of His life and Teachings which have been transmitted from generation to generation in various parts of the world.

4. The fact that in the very year of His death, and at various times subsequently, conventions and councils of the Sangha were held for the verification of the actual Teachings of the Founder. These verified Teachings have been passed on from teacher to pupil from His time to the present day.

5. After His passing away, His body was cremated and

the bodily relics were divided among eight kingdoms in India. Each king built a pagoda to contain his portion of the relics. The portion given to King Ajatasatthu was enshrined by him in a pagoda at Rajagriha. Less than two centuries later, Emperor Asoka took the relics and distributed them throughout his empire. The inscriptions enshrined in this and other pagodas confirm that those were the relics of Gautama the Buddha. Some of these relics which were not touched by Emperor Asoka were discovered only as recently as one hundred years ago, with inscriptions to prove their authenticity.

6. 'The Mahavamsa', the best and authentic ancient history known to us gives detailed particulars of life as well as details of the life of Emperor Asoka and all other sovereigns related to Buddhist history. Indian history has also given a prominent place to the Buddha's life, activities, Buddhist traditions and customs.

7. The records which we can find in the Buddhist countries where people received Buddhism a few hundred years after the Buddha's passing away such as Sri Lanka, Myammar, China, Tibet, Nepal, Korea, Mongolia, Japan, Thailand, Vietnam, Cambodia and Laos show unbroken historical, cultural, religious, literary and traditional evidence that there was a religious teacher in India known as Gautama the Buddha. Many of these records are widely separated in time and space and yet they say exactly the same things about the Buddha—this proves that they could not have invented these stories independently.

8. The Tripitaka, an unbroken record of His 45 years of Teaching is more than sufficient to prove that the Buddha really lived in this world because no other religious leader has ever said anything like what the Buddha has taught.

9. The accuracy and authenticity of the Buddhist texts is supported by the fact that they provide information for

historians to write Indian history during the 5th and 6th century B.C. The texts, which represent the earliest reliable written records in India, provide a profound insight into the socio-economic, cultural and political environment and conditions during the Buddha's lifetime as well as into the lives of His contemporaries, such as King Bimbisara.

In the Original Teachings of the Buddha, there is no such thing as 'saving others'. According to the method introduced by the Buddha, each and every person must make the effort to train and purify him or herself to attain his or her own salvation by following the guidance given by the Buddha.

The belief that everyone must strive to become a Buddha in order to attain salvation cannot be found in the original Teachings of the Buddha. This belief is just like asking every person to become a doctor in order to cure other people and himself of diseases. This advice is most impractical. If people want to cure themselves of their sicknesses they can get medical advice from a qualified doctor. This they can do without waiting until they are all doctors before curing themselves. Nor is there any need for each and every person to be a doctor.

Of course, those who wish to become doctors can do so. But they must have intelligence, courage and the means to study medicine. Likewise, it is not compulsory for everyone to become a Buddha to find salvation. Those who wish to become Buddhas can do so. However, they need the courage and knowledge to sacrifice their comforts and practise all kinds of renunciations in order to attain Buddhahood. Even if we are not prepared to aim for Buddha-hood, we must aim to become perfect ones, called Arahantas.

To attain Arahantahood, one has to eradicate all greed and selfishness. This implies that while relating with others, an Arahant will act with compassion and try to inspire others to go on the Path leading to Liberation. The Arahant is living proof of the good results that accrue to a person who follows the method taught by the Buddha. The attainment of Nirvana is not possible if one acts with a selfish motive. Therefore, it is baseless to say that striving to become an Arahant is a selfish act.

Buddhahood is indisputably the best and the noblest of all the three ideals (of becoming a Supreme Buddha, Silent Buddha or an Arahant). But not everyone is capable of achieving this highest ideal. Surely all scientists cannot be Einsteins and Newtons. There must be room for lesser scientists who nevertheless help the world according to their capabilities.

Arahantas also impart the Dhamma taught by the Buddha for the benefit of others to find their own salvation by following the advice given by these Arahantas.

Not only arahantas preached the Dharma taught by the Buddha. Some other disciples also preached the Dharma from time to time. One of the chief disciples of the Buddha, Sariputta, attained sotapanna, the first stage of sainthood after listening to one Buddha word from Venerable Assaji, the youngest among the first five disciples of the Buddha and later attained Arantahood by following the Buddha. Emperor Asoka who introduced Buddhism in many parts of the world became a Buddhist after listening to the Dharma from a novice monk named Nigrodha.

BUDDHAHOOD is not reserved only for chosen people or for supernatural beings. Anyone can become a Buddha. This is unique because no founder of any other religion ever said that his followers have the opportunity or potential for the same attainment as theirs.

However, attaining Buddhahood is the most difficult task a person can achieve in this world. One must work hard by sacrificing one's worldly pleasures. One has to develop and purify one's mind from all evil thoughts in order to obtain this Enlightenment. It will take innumerable births for a person to purify and to develop the mind in order to become a Buddha. Long periods of great effort are necessary in order to complete the high qualification of this self-training. The course of this self-training which culminates in Buddhahood, includes self-discipline, self-restraint, superhuman effort, firm determination, and willingness to undergo any kind of suffering for the sake of other living beings in this world.

This clearly shows that the Buddha did not obtain supreme Enlightenment by simply praying, worshipping, or making offerings to some supernatural beings. He attained Buddhahood by the purification of His mind and heart. He gained Supreme Enlighten-ment without the influence of any external, supernatural forces but by the development of His own insight. Thus only a man who has firm determination and courage to overcome all hindrances, weaknesses and selfish desires can attain Buddhahood.

Prince Siddhartha did not attain Buddhahood overnight simply by sitting under the Bodhi tree. No supernatural being appeared and revealed anything by whispering into His ear while He was in deep meditation under the Bodhi tree. Behind His Supreme Enligh-tenment there was a long history of previous births. Many of the Jataka stories tell us how He worked hard by sacrificing His life in many previous births to attain His Supreme Buddhahood. No one can attain Buddhahood without devoting many lifetimes practising the ten perfections or *Paramita?*. The great period of time needed to develop these ten perfections explains why a Supreme Buddha appears only at very long intervals of time.

Therefore, the Buddha's advice to His followers is that in order to find their salvation it is not necessary for each and every person to wait until Buddhahood is gained.

Aspirants can also find their salvation by becoming Pacceka Buddhas (Silent Buddhas) or Arahantas – (Perfected Ones). Pacceka Buddhas appear in this world during the period when there is no supreme Enlightened Buddha. They are also Enlightened. Although their degree of perfection is not similar to that of the Supreme Buddha, they experience the same Nirvanic bliss. Unlike the Supreme Buddha, however, they do not preach to the masses. They lead a life of solitude.

Arahantas can also experience the same Nirvanic bliss as the Buddhas do. There is no discrimination or status in Nirvana. The only difference is that Arahantas do not have the Supreme Enligh-tenment to be able to enlighten others in the same way as the Buddhas can. Arahantas have overcome all their desires and other human weaknesses. They can appreciate the Dharma which was discovered and taught by the Buddha. They also have some ability to show others the Path to salvation.

*I*N Mahayana philosophy, the personality of the Buddha is given elaborate treatment. According to this philosophy, the Buddhas have three "bodies" *(trikaya),* or three aspects of personality: the Dharma-kaya, the Sambhoga-kaya, and the Nirmana-kaya.

After a Buddha has attained Enlightenment, He is the living embodiment of wisdom, compassion, happiness and freedom. Two thousand five hundred years ago, there was only one Buddha in the Buddhist tradition. He is the historical Sakyamuni the Buddha. However, even during His lifetime, He made the distinction between

Himself as the enlightened, historical individual, on one hand, and Himself as the Embodiment of Truth, on the other. The enlightened personality was known as the 'Rupakaya' (Form-body) or 'Nirmana-kaya' (Manifestation-body). This was the physical body of the Buddha who was born as Siddharta Gautama among men, attained

Enlightenment, preached the Dharma and attained Maha Parinirvana. The Manifestation-body or physical body of Buddhas are many and differ from one another. On the other hand, the principle of Enlightenment which is embodied in Him is known as Dharma-kaya or Truth-body. This is the essence of Buddhahood and is independent of the person realising it. 'Dharma' in this context means 'ultimate universal Truth', and does not refer to the verbal teachings which were recorded down in the scriptures. The teaching of the Buddha also emanates from this 'Essence' or 'Truth'. So the real, essential Buddha is Truth or the principle of Enlightenment. This idea is clearly stated in the original Pali texts of the Theravada. The Buddha told vasettha that the Tathagata (the Buddha) was Dharma-kaya, the 'Truth-body' or the 'Embodiment of Truth', as well as Dharmabhuta, 'Truth-become', that is, 'One who has become Truth' (DIGHA NIKAYA). On another occasion, the Buddha told Vakkali: 'He who sees the Dharma (Truth) sees the Tathagata; he who sees the Tathagata sees the Dharma' (SAMYUTTA NIKAYA). That is to say, the Buddha is equal to Truth, and all Buddhas are one and the same, being no different from one another in the Dharma-kaya, because Truth is one.'

In the Buddha's lifetime, both the *Nirmana-kaya* and the *Dharma-kaya* were united in Him. However, after His *Parinirvana,* the distinction became more pronounced, especially in Mahayana philosophy. His Manifestation-body died and after cremation was enshrined in the form of relics in stupas: His Dharma-body is eternally present.

Later, the Mahayana philosophy developed the *'Sambhoga-kaya',* the Enjoyment of—Bliss-body. The *Sambhoga-kaya* can be considered as the body or aspect through which the Buddha rejoiced in the Dharma, in teaching the Truth, in leading others to the realisation of the Truth, and in enjoying the company of good, noble people. This is a selfless, pure, spiritual enjoyment, not to be confused with sensual pleasure. This 'Enjoyment-body' or 'Body of Bliss' is not categorically mentioned in Theravada texts although it can be appreciated without contradiction if understood in this context. In Mahayana, the Enjoyment-body of the Buddha, unlike the imper-sonal, abstract principle of the *Dharma-kaya,* is also represented as a person, though not a human, historical person.

Although the terms *Sambhoga-kaya* and *Dharma-kaya* found in the later Pali works come from Mahayana and semi-Mahayana works, scholars from other traditions did not show hostility towards them. Venerable Buddhaghosa in his *Visuddhi Magga* referred to the bodies of the Buddha thus:

'The Buddha is possessed of a beautiful *rupakaya* adorned with eighty minor and thirty-two major signs of a great man, and possessed of a *Dharma-kaya* purified in every way and glorified by *Sila, Samadhi, Panna,* full of splendour and virtue, incomparable and fully enlightened.'

Though Buddhaghosa's conception was realistic, he was not immune to the religious bias of attributing superhuman power to the Buddha. In the *Atthasallini,* he said that during a three months' absence of the Buddha from the physical world, when He was engaged in preaching the *Abhidharma* to His mother in the *Tusita* heaven, He created some *Nimmitta-buddhas* as exact replicas of Himself. These *Nimmitta-buddhas* could not be distinguished from the Buddha in voice, words and even the rays of light that issued forth from His body. The 'created Buddha' could be detected only by the gods of the higher realms of existence and not by ordinary gods or men. From this description, it is clear that the early Therava-dins conceived Buddha's *Rupakaya* or *Sambhoga-kaya* as that of a human being, and His *Dharma-kaya* as the collection of His Dharma, that is, doctrines.

2

Message for All

*B*UDDHISM is one of the oldest religions still being prac-tised in the world today. While the names of many other religions which existed in India have been forgotten, the teachings of the Buddha, (better known as the Dharma) are still relevant to the needs of today's society. This is because the Buddha always considered Himself as a *human* religious teacher whose message was meant to promote freedom, happiness and wellbeing of others. The Buddha's primary concern was to help His followers to live a normal life without going to the extremes of either self-denial or totally surrendering to sensual desires.

The practical nature of the Buddha's teaching is revealed in the fact that not everyone is expected to attain exactly the same goal in one lifetime, since the mental impurities are rooted differently in individuals. Some people are spiritually more advanced than others and they can proceed to greater heights according to their state of development. But every single human being has the ultimate potential to attain the supreme goal of Buddhahood if he or she has the determination and will to do so.

Even now does the soothing, sweet voice of the Buddha ring in our ears. And sometimes we perhaps feel a little ashamed because we do not understand Him fully. Often we only praise His Teaching and respect Him, but do not try to practise what He preached. The Buddha's Teaching and message have had their effect on all people for thousands of years whether they believe in any religion or not. His message is for all.

Though the Buddha, the flower of mankind, is no longer in this world, the sweet fragrance and exquisite aroma of His Teachings have spread far and wide. Its balmy, diffusing fragrance has calmed and soothed millions. Its ambrosial perfume has heartened and cheered every nation which it has penetrated. The reason that His Teachings have captured millions of hearts is because they were introduced not by weapons or political power but by love and compassion for humanity. Not a drop of blood stains its pure path. Buddhism wins by the warm touch of love, not by the cold claws of fear. Fear of the supernatural and the doctrine of everlasting hell-fire have no place in Buddhism.

During the last 25 centuries since the appearance of the Buddha, many changes have taken place in this world. Kingdoms have risen and fallen; nations have prospered and perished. And the world today has forgotten many of these past civilisations. But the name of the Buddha remains alive and fresh in the minds of millions of people today. The Kingdom of Righteousness that He built is still strong and steady. Although many temples, pagodas, images, libraries and other religious symbols erected in His honour were destroyed by religious fanatics from time to time, His untainted Noble Name and the message He gave remain in the minds of understanding people.

The Buddha taught that the greatest of conquests was not the subjugation of others but of the self. He taught in the DHAMMAPADA, 'Even though a man conquers ten thousand men in battle, he who conquers but himself is the greatest of conquerors'.

Perhaps the best example of how the gentle message of the Compassionate One could rehabilitate the most savage of men is the case of the Emperor Asoka. About two hundred years after the Buddha, this king waged fierce battles across India and caused great anguish and fear. But when he embraced the Dharma, he regretted the evil that he had done. We remember and honour him today because after his conversion to the path of peace, he embarked on another battle: a battle to bring peace to humanity. He proved without doubt that the Buddha was right when He asserted that true greatness springs from love, not hatred, from humility, not pride; from compassion, not cruelty.

The Emperor Asoka's conversion from cruelty to kindness was so complete that he forbade even the killing of animals in his kingdom. He realised that his subjects stole because of want and he set out to reduce want in his kingdom. But above all, he instructed the followers of the Buddha to remember the Master's teaching never to force their beliefs on others who were loyal to other reli-gious leaders. In other cases we have heard of kings who, upon conversion, diverted their thirst for blood by spreading their new religion by the sword! Only Buddhism can take pride in a king who has never been equaled in such greatness before or ever since.

The Buddha's Teachings were introduced in order that societies could be cultured and civilized and live in peace and harmony. All of life's most difficult problems can be better understood if we but try to learn and practise His teachings. The Buddha's approach to the problems and suffering of mankind is straightforward and direct.

The Buddha was the greatest conqueror the world has ever seen. He conquered the world with His infallible weapons of love and truth. His Teaching illuminates the Way for mankind to cross from a world of darkness, hatred, and suffering, to a new world of light, love and happiness.

Power of Miraculous

IN every religion we know of miracles being performed by either the founders of these religions or by some of their disciples. In the case of the Buddha, miracles occurred from the day of His birth until His passing away into *Nirvana.* Many of the psychic powers of the Buddha were attained through His long and intense training in meditation. The Buddha meditated and passed through all the highest stages of contemplation that culminated in pure self-possession and wisdom. Such attainments through meditation are considered nothing miraculous but fall within the psychic power of any trained ascetic.

using meditation on the night of His Enlightenment, there arose within the Buddha a vision of His previous births, the many existences with all their details. He remembered His previous births and how He had made use of these births to gain His Enlightenment. Then the Buddha had a second and wider vision in which He saw the whole universe as a system of Karma and Rebirth. He saw the universe made up of beings that were noble and wicked, happy and unhappy. He saw them all continually 'passing away according to their good and bad deeds', leaving one form of existence and taking shape in another. Finally, He understood the nature of Suffering, the Cessation of Suffering and the Path that leads to the Cessation of Suffering. Then a third vision arose within the Buddha. He realised that He was completely free from all bondages, human or divine. He realised that He had done what had to be done. He realised He had no more rebirth to go through because He had eradicated all craving and He was living with His final body. This knowledge destroyed all ignorance, all darkness, and light arose within Him. Such is the psychic power and the wisdom that arose within the Buddha as He sat meditating under the Bodhi tree.

The Buddha had a natural birth; He lived in a normal way. But He was an extraordinary man, as far as His Enlightenment was concerned. Those who have not learnt to appreciate His Supreme Wisdom try to explain His greatness by peeping into His life and looking for miracles. However, the Buddha's Supreme Enlighten-ment is more than enough for us to understand His greatness. There is no need to show His greatness by introducing miraculous powers. Miracles have little relation to seeing things as they are.

The Buddha knew of the power that could be developed by training the human mind. He also knew that His disciples could acquire such powers through mental development. Thus the Buddha advised them not to exercise such psychic power in order to convert less intelligent people. He was referring to the 'miraculous' power to walk on water, to exorcise spirits, raise the dead and perform the so-called supernormal practices. He was also referring to the 'miracles of prophesy' such as thought-reading, sooth-saying, fortune-telling, and so on. When the uneducated believers see the performance of such powers, their faith deepens. But the nominal converts who are attracted to a religion because of these powers embrace a faith, not because they realise the Truth, but because they harbour hallucinations. Besides, some people may pass remarks that these miracles are due to certain charms or tricks. In drawing people to listen to the Dharma, the Buddha appealed to their reasoning power.

The following story illustrates the Buddha's attitude towards miraculous powers. One day the Buddha met an ascetic who sat by the bank of a river. This ascetic had practised austerities for 25 years. The Buddha asked him what he had attained for all his labour. The ascetic proudly replied that, now at last, he could cross the river by walking on the water. The Buddha pointed out that this gain was insignificant compared to all the years of labour, since anyone could cross the river using a ferry for one penny!

In certain religions, a man's miraculous performance can help him to be declared a saint. But in Buddhism, miracles can be a hindrance for a person to attain sainthood, which is a gradual personal attainment and individual concern resulting in completely eradicating defilements from the mind. Each person himself must work for his sainthood through self-purification and no one else can make another person a saint.

The Buddha says that a person can gain miraculous power with-out developing spiritual power. He teaches us that if we first gain spiritual power, then we automatically receive the miraculous or psychic powers too. But if we develop miraculous powers without spiritual development, then we are in danger. We can misuse this power for worldly gain (Pataligama-Udana). There are many who have deviated from the right path by using their miraculous powers without having any spiritual development. Many people who are supposed to have obtained some miraculous powers succumbed to

the vain glory of obtaining some worldly gain. Even worse, people with miraculous powers but without spiritual development can be deluded into thinking that they have divine power.

Many so-called miracles talked about by people are merely imagi-nations and hallucinations created by their own minds due to a lack of understanding of things as they truly are. All these miracles remain as miracles only for as long as people fail to know what these powers really are.

The Buddha also expressly forbade His disciples to use miracles to prove the superiority of His teachings. On one occasion He said that the use of miracles to gain converts was like using dancing girls to tempt people to believe something. Anyone with the proper mental training can perform miracles because these are simply an expression of the superiority of mind over matter.

According to the Buddha, the miracle ofrealisation of the Truth is the only miracle. When a murderer, thief, terrorist, drunkard, or adulterer is made to realise that what he had been doing is wrong and gives up his bad, immoral and harmful way of life, this change can be regarded as a miracle. The change for the better arising from an understanding of Dharma universal law or natural occurrences is the highest miracle that any person can perform.

THE scriptures mention a few occasions when the Bud-dha remained silent to metaphysical and speculative questions posed to Him. Some scholars, owing to their misunderstanding of the Buddha's silence, came to the wrong conclusion that the Buddha was unable to answer these questions.

When the Buddha knew that the questioner was not in a position to understand the answer because of its profundity, or if the questions themselves were wrongly put in the first place, the Blessed One remained silent. Some of the questions to which the Buddha remained silent are:

1. Is the universe eternal?
2. Is it not eternal?
3. Is the universe finite?
4. Is it infinite?
5. Is soul the same as the body?
6. Is the soul one thing and the body another?
7. Does the Tathagata exist after death?

8. Does He not exist after death?

9. Does He both (at the same time) exist and not exist after death?

10. Does He both (at the same time) neither exist nor not exist?

The Buddha who had truly realised the nature of these issues observed noble silence. An ordinary person who is still unen-lightened might have a lot to say, but all would be sheer conjecture based on his or her imagination.

The Buddha's silence on these issues is more significant than attempting to deliver thousands of discourses on them. The paucity of our human vocabulary which is built upon relative experiences cannot hope to convey the depth and dimensions of Reality which a person has not experienced through Insight. On several occasions, the Buddha had very patiently explained that human language is too limited and cannot describe the ultimate Truth. If the ultimate Truth is absolute, then it does not have any point of reference for worldlings with only mundane experiences and relative under-standing to fully comprehend it. When they try to do so with their limited mental capacities, they misunderstand the Truth like the seven blind men and the elephant. A listener who has not realised the Truth cannot fathom the explanation given, just like a man who was blind since birth will have no way of visualising the colour of the sky.

The Buddha did not attempt to give answers to all the questions put to Him. He was under no obligation to respond to meaningless questions which reflected gross misunderstanding on the part of the questioner and which in any case had no relevance to one's spiritual development. He was a practical Teacher, full of compassion and wisdom. He always spoke to people fully understanding their temperament, capability and capacity to comprehend.

When a person asked questions not with the intention to learn how to lead a religious life but simply to create an opportunity for splitting hairs, the Blessed One did not answer these questions. Questions were answered to help a person towards self-realisation, not as a way of showing His towering wisdom.

According to the Buddha, there are several ways of answer-ing various types of questions. The first type of question is one that requires a definite answer, such as a 'yes' or 'no'. For example, the question, 'Are all conditioned things impermanent?' is answered with a 'Yes'. The second type of question is one requiring an analytical answer. Suppose someone says that Angulimala was a murderer before he became an 'Arahant' and is it possible for any murderer to become an arahant? This question should be analysed before you can say 'Yes' or 'No'. Otherwise, it will not be answered correctly and comprehensively. You would need to analyse what conditions make it possible for a murderer to become a saint within one lifetime.

The third type of question is one where it is necessary to ask a counter question to help the questioner to think the problem through. If you ask, 'Why is it wrong to kill other living beings?' the counter question is, 'How does it feel when others try to kill you?' The fourth kind of question is one that should be dropped. It means that you should not answer it. These are the questions which are speculative in nature, and any answer to such questions will only create more confusion. An example of such a question is, 'Does the universe have a beginning or not?' People can discuss such questions for years without coming to a conclusion. They can only answer such questions based on their imagination, not on real understanding.

Some answers which the Buddha gave have close parallels to the kind of responses found in nuclear science.

According to Robert Oppenheimer, "If we ask, for instance, whether the position of the electron remains the same, we must say 'no'; if we ask whether the electron is at rest, we must say 'no'; if we ask whether it is in motion, we must say 'no'. The Buddha has given such answers when interrogated as to the conditions of a man's self after his death; but they are not familiar answers in accordance with the tradition of seventeenth and eighteenth century science".

It is important to note however that the Buddha did give answers to some of these questions to His most intellectually developed disciples after the questioner had left. And in many cases, His explanations are contained in other discourses which show us why these questions were not answered by the Buddha merely to satisfy the inquisitive but undeveloped minds of the questioners.

The Buddha's Attitude towards Worldly Knowledge

Worldly knowledge is useful for worldly ends. With such knowledge, mankind learns how to use the earth's resources to improve the standard of living, grow more ORLDLY knowledge is useful for worldly ends. With such knowledge, mankind learns how to use the earth's resources to improve the standard of living, grow more food, generate power to run factories and to light up streets and houses, manage factories and businesses, cure sickness, build flats and bridges, cook exotic dishes, and so on. Worldly knowledge can also be used for harmful purposes such as building missiles with nuclear warheads, manipulating the stock market, cheating 'legally', and inflaming political anxiety and hatred. Despite the rapid expansion of worldly knowledge, especially in the twenty-first century, mankind has been brought no nearer to the solution to human problems and eradicating pervasive unsatisfactoriness. In all likelihood, it never will solve human beings' universal problems and bring peace and happiness because of the premises on which such knowledge, discoveries and inventions are built.

While Buddhism can bring greater understanding on how to lead a good worldly life, its main focus is how to gain liberation through the development of wisdom, mental culture and purity. For ordinary human beings, there is no end to the search for worldly knowledge, which in the final analysis does not really matter. For as long as we are ignorant about the Dharma, we will forever be trapped in Samsara, the repeated cycle of birth and death. According to the Buddha:

'For a long time, Brothers, have you suffered the death of a mother; for a longtime, the death of a father; for a longtime, the death of a son; for a longtime, the death of a daughter; for a long time, the death of brothers and sisters; for a long time have you undergone the loss of your goods; for a long time have you been afflicted with disease. And because you have experienced the death of a mother, the death of a father, the death of a son, the death of a daughter, the death of brothers and sisters, the loss of goods, the pangs of disease, company of the undesired, you have truly shed more tears upon this long way—hastening from birth to death, from death to birth—than all the waters that are held in the four great seas.' (Anguttara Nikaya)

Here the Buddha was describing the Suffering of continuous births and deaths in the world. He wanted to show people the Way out of all these Sufferings.

Why did the Buddha speak in this manner to His disciples? And why did He not make an attempt to solve the problems as to whether the world is eternal or not, whether it is finite or not? Such problems might be exciting and stimulating to those who have the curiosity. But in no way would the answers to these problems help a person to overcome Suffering. That is why He ignored questions like these because they were futile and the knowledge about such things would not contribute to one's spiritual wellbeing.

The Buddha knew that to speak on things which were of no practical value and beyond the power of comprehension, was a waste of time and energy. He foresaw that to advance hypotheses about such things only served to divert thoughts from their proper chan-nel and hinder spiritual development.

Worldly knowledge and scientific research should be comple-mented and balanced with religious and spiritual values. Otherwise such worldly knowledge does not in any way contribute to one's progress in leading a pure, religious life. Human beings have come to the stage where their minds fed by the instruments and fruits of technological advancements, have become obsessed with egoism, craving for power, and greed for material wealth. Without religious values, worldly knowledge and technological advancement can lead to their downfall and destruction. These will only inflame their greed which will take on new and terrifying dimensions. On the other hand, when worldly knowledge is harnessed for moral ends, it can bring maximum benefit and happiness for humanity.

The Last Message of the Buddha

THREE months before His passing away the Buddha addressed His disciples and said; 'I have delivered sermons to you during these forty-five years. You must learn them well and treasure them. You must practise them and teach them to others. This will be of great use for the welfare of those living now and for the welfare of those who come after you'.

'My years are now full ripe; the life span left is short. I will soon attain Parinirvana. You must be earnest. O monks, be mindful and of pure virtue! Whoever untiringly pursues the Teaching, will go beyond the cycle of birth and death and will make an end of Suffer-ing.'

When Ananda asked the Buddha what would become of the Order after He passed away, the Buddha replied, 'What does the Order expect of me, Ananda? I have preached the Truth without any distinction; for in regard to the Truth, there is no clenched fist in the Teachings of the Buddha... It may be, Ananda, that to some among you, the thought will come 'The Master's words will soon end; soon we will no longer have a Master.' But do not think like this, Ananda. When I am gone, my Teaching and the disciplinary code shall be your Master.'

The Buddha further explained: 'If there is anyone who thinks, 'It is I who will lead the brotherhood', or 'The Order is dependent on me, it is I who should give instructions', the Buddha does not think that he should lead the Order or that the Order is dependent on him. I have reached the end of my days. Just as a worn-out cart can only be made to move with much additional care, so my body can be kept going only with much additional care. Therefore, Ananda, be a lamp and refuge unto yourselves. Look for no other refuge. Let the Truth be your lamp and your refuge. Seek no refuge elsewhere.'

At the age of eighty, on His birthday, He passed away without displaying any supernatural powers. He showed the real nature of component things even in His own life.

When the Buddha passed away into Nirvana, one of His dis-ciples remarked, 'All must depart—all beings that have life must shed their compounded forms. Yes, even a Master such as the Bud-dha, a peerless being, powerful in Wisdom and Enlightenment, must pass away.'

3
AFTER THE BUDDHA

WHEN a group of ascetics asked the same question to certain disciples of the Buddha, they could not get a satisfactory answer from them. Anuradha, a disciple, approached the Buddha and reported to Him about their conversation. Considering the understanding capacity of the questioners, the Buddha usually observed silence at such questions.

However in this instance, the Buddha explained to Anuradha in the following manner:

'O Anuradha, what do you think, is the form *(rupa)* permanent or impermanent?'

'Impermanent, Sir.'

'Is that which is impermanent, painful or pleasant?'
'Painful, Sir.'

'Is it proper to regard that which is impermanent, painful and subject to change as: 'This is mine; this is I, this is my soul or permanent substance?'

'It is not proper, Sir.'

'Is feeling permanent or impermanent?'

'Impermanent, Sir.'

'Is that which is impermanent, painful or pleasant?'

'Painful, Sir.'

'Is it proper to regard that which is impermanent, painful and subject to change as 'This is mine, this is I, this is my soul'?' 'It is not proper, Sir.'

'Are perception, formative tendencies and consciousness, per-manent or impermanent?' 'Impermanent, Sir.'

'Is that which is impermanent, painful or pleasant?' 'Painful, Sir.'

'Is it proper to regard that which is impermanent, painful and subject to change as: 'This is mine, this is I, this is my soul'?' 'It is not proper, Sir.'

'Therefore whatever form, feeling, perception, formative tenden-cies, consciousness which have been, will be and is now connected with oneself, or with others, gross or subtle, inferior or superior, far or near; all forms, feelings, perceptions, formative tendencies and consciousness should be considered by right knowledge in this way: 'This is not mine; this is not I; this is not my soul.' Having seen thus, a noble, learned disciple becomes disenchanted with the form, feel-ing, perception, formative tendencies and consciousness. Becoming disenchanted, he controls his passion and subsequently discards them.'

'Being free from passion he becomes emancipated and insight arises in him: 'I am emancipated.' He realizes: 'Birth is destroyed, I have lived the holy life and done what had to be done. There is no more birth for me.'

'What do you think, Anuradha, do you regard the form as a Tathagata?'

'No, Sir.'

'O Anuradha, what is your view, do you see a Tathagata in the form?'

'No, Sir.'

'Do you see a Tathagata apart from form?' 'No, Sir.'

'Do you see a Tathagata in feeling, perception, formative tenden-cies, and consciousness?'

'No, Sir.'

O Anuradha, what do you think, do you regard that which is without form, feeling, perception, formative tendencies and con-sciousness as a Tathagata?'

No, Sir.'

Now, Anuradha, since a Tathagata is not to be found in this very life, (because physical body is not Tathagata)* is it proper for you to say: 'This noble and supreme one has pointed out and ex-plained these four propositions:

A Tathagata exists after death;

A Tathagata does not exist after death;

A Tathagata exists and yet does not exist after death;

A Tathagata neither exists nor does not exist after death?'

'No Sir.'

Well and good, Anuradha. Formerly and now also I expound and point out only the truth of Suffering and the cessation of Suffering.' (ANURADHA SUTTA - SAMYUTTA NIKAYA)

* See the section entitled 'Trikaya - The Three Bodies of The Buddha'.

The above dialogue between the Buddha and Anuradha may not be satisfactory to many, since it does not satisfy the inquiring mind of the people looking for answers from a materialist point of view. Absolute Truth (the Dharma) is such that it does not give satisfaction to the emotion and intellect. Truth happens to be the most difficult thing for people to comprehend. It can only be fully comprehended by Insight which transcends logic. Buddhahood is the embodiment of all the great virtues and supreme enlighten-ment. That is why Buddhas who could enlighten others are very rare in this world.

A Successor to the Buddha

Many people ask why the Buddha did not appoint a successor. But can any one appoint another to take the place of the Supreme Enlightened One? Attaining Buddhahood is the highest of all achievements that only one who has gained supreme wisdom can reach. To attain this highest position, one must excel in every endeavour such as self-training, self-discipline, moral background, supreme knowledge, and extraordinary compassion towards every living being. Therefore, a person must make the effort to be prepared in order to attain Buddhahood. For example, a doctor cannot appoint even his own son as a doctor unless the son has qualified himself professionally. A lawyer cannot appoint another person as a lawyer unless that person obtains the necessary qualifications. A scientist cannot appoint another person as a scientist unless that person possesses the knowledge of a scientist. If He had done so, the successor, lacking the supreme qualities of Buddhahood, would have misused His authority or distorted the teaching. According to the Buddha each individual must develop understanding and insight by him or herself by using the Teachings as a guide (ehi *passiko).* A "successor" of the Buddha would only have created an organised religion or church with dogmas and commands and blind faith. We only have to study world history to see the kind of abuse that can take place when authority is placed in the hands of spiritually undeveloped persons. Therefore, the Buddha did not appoint a successor.

W hen the Buddha was about to pass away, venerable Ananda and many other disciples wept. The Buddha said, 'Enough, Ananda. Do not allow yourself to be troubled. Do not weep. Have I not already told you that it is in the very nature of things that they must pass away. We must be separated from all that is near and dear to us. The foolish person conceives his idea of Self; the wise man sees there is no ground on which to build the Self. Thus the wise man has a right conception of the world. He will realise that all component things will be dissolved again; but the Truth will always remain.'

The Buddha continued: 'Why should I preserve this body when the body of the excellent law will endure? I am resolved. I have accomplished my purpose and have attended to the work set by me. Ananda, for a long time you have been very near to me in thoughts, words and acts of much love beyond all measure. You have done well, Ananda. Be earnest in effort and you too will soon be free from bondages! You will be free from sensuality, from delusion, and from ignorance.' Suppressing his tears, Ananda said to the Buddha, 'Who shall teach us when You are gone?' And the Buddha advised him to regard His Teaching as the Master.

The Buddha continued again: 'I am not the first Buddha to come upon earth; nor shall I be the last.* In due time, another Buddha will arise in this world, a Holy One, a Supremely Enlight-ened One, endowed with wisdom, in conduct auspicious, knowing the universe, an incomparable leader of men, a master of devas and men. He will reveal to you the same Eternal Truths which I have taught you. He will proclaim a religious life, wholly perfect and pure; such as I now proclaim.'

'How shall we know him?', asked Ananda. The Buddha replied, 'He will be known as *Maitreya* which means kindness or friendli-ness.'

Buddhists believe that those people who at present are doing meritorious deeds by leading a religious life will have a chance to be reborn as human beings in the time of *Maitreya Buddha* and will obtain *Nirvana* identical with that of Gauṭama Buddha. In this way they will find salvation through the guidance of His Teaching. His Teaching will become a hope of the remote future for every-body. However, according to the Buddha devout religious people can gain this Nirvanic bliss at any time if they really work for it irrespective of whether a Buddha appears or not.

4

TIMELESS TRUTH OF THE BUDDHA

BUDDHISM is a beautiful gem of many facets, attracting people of diverse personalities. Every facet in this gem has time tested methods and approaches that can benefit the Truth seekers with their various levels of understanding and spiritual maturity.

The Buddha Dharma is the fruit resulting from a most intensive search conducted over a long period of time by a compassionate noble man whose mission was to help suffering humanity. Despite being surrounded by all the wealth and luxuries normally showered on a crown prince, He renounced His luxurious life and voluntarily embarked on a tough journey to seek the Truth and to find a panacea to cure the sickness of the worldly life with its attendant suffering and unsatisfactoriness. He was bent on finding a solution to alleviate all suffering. In His long search, the prince did not rely on or resort to divine guidance or traditional beliefs as was fashionable in the past. He did an intensive search with a free and open mind, guided solely by His sincerity of purpose, noble resolution, inexhaustible patience, and a truly compassionate heart with the ardent wish to relieve suffering. After six long years of intensive experiment, of trial and error, the noble prince achieved His aim—He gained Enlightenment and gave the world His pristine teachings known as Dharma or Buddhism.

The Buddha once said, 'Monks, the lion, king of beasts, at eventide comes forth from his lair. He stretches himself. Having done so, he surveys the four quarters in all directions. Having done that, he utters thrice his lion's roar. Having thrice uttered his lion's roar, he sallies forth in search of prey.'

'Now, monks, whatever animals hear the sound of the roaring of the lion, king of beasts, for the most part, they are afraid; they fall to quaking and trembling. Those that dwell in holes seek them; water-dwellers make for the water; forest-dwellers enter the forest; birds mount into the air.'

'Then whatsoever ruler's elephants in village, town or palace are tethered with stout leather bonds, they burst out and rend those bonds asunder and in panic run to and fro. Thus potent is

the lion, king of beasts, over animals. Of such mighty power and majesty is he.' Just so, monks, is it when a Buddha arises in the world, an Arahant, a Perfectly Enlightened One, perfect in wisdom and in conduct, wayfarer, Knower of the worlds, the unsurpassed trainer of those who can be trained, teacher of gods and men, a Buddha, an Exalted One. He teaches the Dharma: "Such is the nature of concept of Self; this is the way leading to the ending of such a Self!"

'Whatsoever gods there be, they too, on hearing the Dharma of the *Tathagata,* for the most part are afraid: they fall to quaking and trembling, saying: 'We who thought ourselves permanent are after all impermanent: that we who thought ourselves stable are after all unstable: not to last, though lasting we thought ourselves. So it seems that we are impermanent, unstable, not to last, compassed about with a Self.' Thus potent is a *Tathagata* over the world of gods and men.'

What is Buddhism?

What is Buddhism? This question has puzzled many people who often enquire if Buddhism is a philosophy, a religion, or a way of life. The simple answer is that Buddhism is too vast and too profound to be neatly placed in any single mundane category. Of course, Buddhism includes philosophy and religion and a way of life. But Buddhism goes beyond these categories.

The categories or labels given to Buddhism are like signboards that indicate the contents of what is available. If we compare Buddhism to a medicine shop, it will be clear that the signboard on the medicine shop does not cure a person of sickness. You take the medicine to heal yourself without being attached to the label for the medicine. Likewise, if the Teaching of the Buddha is effective, then use it and do not be attached to the label or signboard. Buddhism cannot be forced into any single category or limited under any signboard.

People living at different times and in different places have given various labels and interpretations to Buddhism. To some people, Buddhism might appear to be only a mass of superstitious practices. To another group of people, Buddhism might be a convenient label to be used for temporal gains. To another group, it is old fashioned.

To yet another group, Buddhism is a significant system of thought appealing to intellectuals only. To some others, it is a scientific discovery. To the pious and devout Buddhist, Buddhism encompasses his or her entire life, the fulfillment of all material and spiritual aspirations. In this sense we can say that Buddhism is a noble way of life.

Some intellectuals see Buddhism as a product of its Indian environment or as an outgrowth of another kind of Indian religious teaching. This assessment is not wholly accurate. Buddhism is nothing but the Absolute Noble Truth. It is an intellectual approach to reality. However, the Buddha's realisation of universal problems did not come through a purely intellectual or rational process but through mental development and purification. The intellectual stance reminiscent of the scientific attitude, surely makes the Buddha absolutely unique among religious teachers of all time. Of course, the high standard of intellectual inquiry and ethical endeavour prevailing at the time in India were prime conditions for the re-emergence of the light of the Dharma from the darkness of oblivion. Thousands of years of religious and philosophical develop-ment had left on the intellectual soil of India a rich and fertile deposit of ideas and ideals which formed the best possible environ-ment from which the seed of the Dharma could sprout and flourish. Greece, China, Egypt and Babylonia, for all their loftiness of thought, had not attained the same quality of vision as the forest and mountain-dwelling sages of India. The germ of Enlightenment which had been borne, like a winged seed from distant fields, from worlds in space and time infinitely remote from ours—this very germ of Enlightenment found growth and development in the north-eastern corner of India. This very germ of Enlightenment found its full expression in the experience of the man, Gautama Buddha. The fountainhead of all Buddhism is this experience which is called 'Enlightenment'. With this experience of Enlightenment, the Buddha began His Teaching not with any dogmatic beliefs or mysteries, but with a valid, universal experience, which He gave to the world as universal truth. Therefore, the closest definition of Buddhism is NOBLE TRUTH. Remember that the Buddha did not teach from theories. He always taught from a practical standpoint based on His understanding, His Enlightenment, and His realisation of the Truth. He constantly urged His followers to see 'things-as-they-really-are'.

Buddhism began with the right understanding embodied over 2500 years ago in the person of Siddharta Gautama. When the Buddha introduced His teachings, His intention was not to develop the concept of self in people's minds and create more craving for eternal life and sense pleasure. Rather, His intention was to point out the futility of the worldly life and to show the correct, practical Path to salvation that He discovered.

The original Teachings of the Buddha revealed with sharp accuracy the true nature of life and the world. However, a distinction must be made between the Buddha's original Teaching (often called the Dharma or the Buddha Word) and the religion that developed based on His Teachings, which is popularly called 'Buddhism'.

The Teachings of the Buddha not only started a religion, but inspired the blossoming of a whole civilisation. These Teachings became a great civilizing force that moved through the history of many a culture and nation. Indeed, Buddhism inspired some of the greatest civilisations that the world has ever known. It has a wonderful history of achievement in the fields of literature, art, philosophy, psychology, ethics, architecture and culture. In the course of centuries, countless social educational institutions were established in the various nations that were dedicated to the Buddha's Teaching. The history of Buddhism was written in golden letters of brotherhood and goodwill. The Buddhist way of life and practices turned into a rational, scientific and practical religious way of life for spiritual development from the day the Buddha preached His Teaching and showed the real purpose and meaning of life and religion. All this is because people had the opportunity to open their minds freely.

Impact of Buddhism on Civilization

Today Buddhism remains as a great civilizing force in

the modern world. As a civilizing force, Buddhism awakens the self-respect and feeling of self-responsibility of countless people and stirs up the energy of many a nation. It fosters spiritual progress by appealing to the thinking powers of human beings. It promotes in people the sense of tolerance by remaining free from religious and national narrowness and fanaticism. It tames the wild and refines the citizens to be clear and sober in mind. In short, Buddhism produces the feeling of self-reliance by teaching that the whole destiny of humanity lies in their own hands, and that they themselves possess the faculty of developing their own energy and insight in order to reach the highest goal.

For over two thousand years, Buddhism has satisfied the spiritual needs of nearly one-fifth of mankind. Today the appeal of Buddhism is as strong as ever. The Teachings of the Buddha remain among the richest spiritual resources of mankind because they lift the horizon of human effort to a higher level beyond a mere dedication to man's insatiable needs and appetites. Owing to its breadth of per-spective, the Buddha's vision of life has a tendency to attract intellectuals who have exhausted their individual quest for meaning. However, the fruit of the Buddha's vision is something more than intellectual gymnastics or solace for the intellectually effete. Buddhism does not encourage verbal speculation and argument for its own sake.

Buddhism is practical, rational and offers a realistic view of life and of the world. It does not entice people into living in a fool's paradise, nor does it frighten and agonize people with all kinds of imaginary fears and guilt-feelings. It does not create religious fanatics to disturb the followers of other religions. The Buddhist attitude to other religions is remarkable. Instead of converting the followers of other religions into Buddhism, Buddhists can encourage them to practise their own religions because Buddhists never think the followers of other religions are bad people. Buddhism tells us exactly and objectively what we are and what the world around us is, and shows us the way to perfect freedom, peace, tranquility and happiness.

If humanity today is to be saved from reacting against the moral standards taught by religions, Buddhism is a most effective vehicle. Buddhism is the religion of humanity, whose founder was a human being who sought no divine revelation or intervention in the formulation of His Teachings. In an age when human beings are overwhelmed by their success in the control of the material universe, they might like to look back and take stock of the achievements they have made in controlling the most difficult of all phenomena: their own selves. It is in this quest that the modern human beings will find in Buddhism an answer to their numerous problems and doubts.

Today, Buddhism appeals to the West because it has no dogmas, and it satisfies both the reason and the heart alike. It insists on self-reliance coupled with tolerance for others. It embraces modern scientific discoveries if they are for constructive purposes. Buddhism points to man alone as the creator of his present life and as the sole designer of his own destiny. Such is the nature of Buddhism. This is why many modern thinkers who are not themselves Buddhist have described Buddhism as a religion of freedom and reason.

The Buddha's message of peace and compassion radiated in all directions and the millions who came under its influence adopted it very readily as a new way of religious life.

Buddhist Contribution to Humanity

Buddhism as a religion has served the hopes and aspirations of humanity well; it has fostered within the social organism a commendable way of life and a communal spirit marked by endeavours towards peace and contentment. It has been in the forefront of human welfare.

Even in politics it was acknowledged on many occasions as a significant break-through in fair treatment, democratic procedures and regard for basic, moral values. Buddhism has given a distinct flavour to the cultures of the Orient. Buddhism has supplied fine and ethical basic attitudes amongst the people who adopted it in one form or another.

Indeed, the immense potential of Buddhism has not been realised by many people who have adopted it only to a limited extent. The capacity of the Buddha's teaching to enhance an individual's personal and general potential has been overshadowed by the contributions of Buddhism to art and literature. But one aspect of Buddhism which has remained of paramount importance throughout its history is its clear Rationalism. Reason, though often overruled to everyone's regret, is something that belongs to humanity, to civilize them, no matter how obscured it may be by the other facets of human nature such as emotions. Buddhism will continue to exhort man to be a rational being, ruled by the head, but giving due consideration to the heart as well.

The Buddha's contribution to the social and spiritual progress of mankind was so remarkable that His message which spread all over the world won the love and affection of the people with a devotion that was unprecedented. It is well worth considering that Buddhism does not choose people by following them to convert them with promises of heaven. It is the people who choose Buddhism.

The Ultimate Truth

The unconventional Truth discovered by the Buddha is called the Ultimate Truth. BUDDHISM recognises two kinds of Truth, the apparent conventional truth concerning mundane matters and the real or ultimate Truth concerning the supramundane. The ultimate Truth can be realized only by developing the mind through meditation, and not by theorising or speculation.

The Buddha's Teaching is about the ultimate Truth regarding the world. Buddhism, however, is not a revealed or an organised religion. It is the first example of the purely scientific approach applied to questions concerning the ultimate nature of existence. This timeless Teaching was discovered by the Buddha Himself without the help of any divine agency. This same teaching is strong enough to face any challenge without changing the basic principles of the doctrine. Any religion that is forced to change or adjust its original Teachings to suit the modern world, is a religion that has no firm foundation and no ultimate truth in it. Buddhism can maintain the Truth of the original Teaching of the Master even under the difficult conditions prevailing in the modern world. It can face any challenge posed by the most rigorous method of scientific inquiry. The Buddha did not introduce certain personal or worldly practices which have no connection with morality or religious observances. To the Buddha, such practices have no religious value. We must make the distinction between what the Buddha taught and what people preach and practise in the name of Buddhism.

Every religion consists of not only the teachings of the founder of that religion but also the rites and ceremonies which have grown up around the basic core of the teachings. These rituals and ceremonies have their origins in the cultural practices of the people who accepted the religion. Usually the founders of the great religions do not lay down precise rules about the rituals to be observed. But religious leaders who come after them formalize the religion and set up exacting codes of behaviour which the followers are not allowed to deviate from. As we discussed earlier, this is one of the reasons why the Buddha did not appoint a successor.

Even the religion which we call 'Buddhism' today is very different in its external practices from what the Buddha and His early followers carried out. Centuries of cultural and environmental influence have made the Myanmar, Thai, Chinese, Tibetan, Sri Lankan, Japanese and Korean Buddhist way of life different. But these practices are not in conflict, because the Buddha taught that while the Truth remains absolute, the physical manifestation of this truth can differ according to the way of life of those who profess it.

Thus the modern religion we see in many countries is the product of normal human beings living in a country and adjusting to various social and cultural environments. However, Buddhism as a religion did not begin as a super-worldly system that came down from heaven. Rather it was born and evolved through a long historical process. In its process of evolution, many people slowly moved away from the original Teachings of the founder and started different new schools or sects. All the other existing religions also face the same situation.

A few hundred years after His passing away, the disciples of the Buddha organized a religion around the Teachings of the Master. While organising the religion, they incorporated, among other concepts and beliefs, various types of miracles, mysticism, fortune-telling, charms, talismans, mantras, prayers and many rites and rituals that were not found in the original Teaching. When these extraneous religious beliefs and practices were introduced, many people neglected to develop the most important practices found in the original Teaching: self-discipline, self-restraint, cultivation of morality and spiritual development. Instead of practising the original Teaching, they gave more of their attention and effort to protection from evil spirits and became more interested in discovering ways and means of getting rid of the so-called misfortunes or bad influences of stars, black magic, and sickness. In this manner, through time the religious practices and beliefs degenerated, being confined to worldly pursuits. Even today, many people believe that they can get rid of their difficulties through the influence of external powers.

People still cling to these beliefs. Hence they neglect to cultivate the strength of their will-power, intelligence, understanding and other related humane qualities. In other words, people started to abuse their human intelligence by following those beliefs and practices in the name of Buddhism. They also polluted the purity of the sublime teaching of the Buddha.

One should therefore not come to a hasty conclusion either to judge the validity of a religion or to condemn it simply by observing what people perform in the name of that religion. To understand and evaluate the real nature of a religion one must study and investigate the original Teachings of the founder of that religion.

In the face of the profusion of ideas and practices which were later developments, it is useful for us to return to the positive and timeless Dharma taught by the Buddha. Whatever people believe and practise in the name of Buddhism, the basic Teachings of the Buddha still exist in the original Buddhist texts.

Two Main Schools of Buddhism

Afew hundred years after the Buddha's passing away, there arose eighteen different schools or sects all of which claimed to represent the original Teachings of the Buddha. The differences between these schools were basically due to various interpretations of the Teachings of the Buddha. Over a period of time, these schools gradually merged into two main schools: Theravada and Mahayana. Today, the majority of the followers of Buddhism are divided into these two schools.

Basically Mahayana Buddhism grew out of the Buddha's teaching that each individual carries within himself the potential for Buddhahood.*

Theravadins say that this potential can be realised through individual effort. Mahayanists, on the other hand, believe that they can seek salvation through the intervention of other superior beings called Bodhisatvas. According to them, Bodhisatvas are future Buddhas who, out of compassion for their fellow human beings, have delayed their own attainment of Buddhahood until they have helped others towards liberation. In spite of this basic difference, however, it must be stressed that doctrinally there is absolutely no disagreement concerning the Dharma as contained in the sacred Tripitaka texts. Because Buddhists have been encouraged by the Master to carefully inquire after the truth, they have been free to interpret the scriptures according to their understanding. But above all, both Mahayana and Theravada are one in their acceptance of the Buddha and His teachings as the only method to attain the supreme bliss of Nirvana.

The areas of agreement between the two schools are as follows:

1. Both accept Sakyamuni Buddha as the Teacher.

2. The Four Noble Truths are exactly the same in both schools.

3. The Eightfold Path is exactly the same in both schools.

4. The *Pattica-Samuppada* or teaching on Dependent Origination is the same in both schools.

5. Both reject the idea of a supreme being who created and governed this world.

6. Both accept *karma* as taught by the Buddha.

7. Both accept *Anicca, Dukkha, Anatta* and *Sila, Samadhi, Panna* without any difference.

8. Both reject the belief in an eternal soul.

9. Both accept rebirth after death.

10. Both accept Devaloka and Brahmaloka.

11. Both accept Nirvana is the final goal or salvation

Some people are of the view that Theravada is selfish because it teaches that people should seek their own salvation. But how can a selfish person gain Enlightenment? Both schools accept the three *Yana* or *Bodhi* and consider the Bodhisatva Ideal as the highest. The Mahayana has created many mystical Bodhisatvas, while the Theravada believes that a Bodhisatva is not a supernatural living being but a person amongst us who devotes his or her entire life for the attainment of perfection, and ultimately becomes a fully Enlightened Buddha for the well-being and happiness of the world.

The terms Hinayana (Small Vehicle) and Mahayana (Great Vehicle) are not known in the Theravada Pali literature. They are not found in the Pali Canon *(Tripitaka)* or in the Commentaries on the *Tripitaka.*

Theravada Buddhists generally follow orthodox religious traditions that prevailed in India two thousand five hundred years ago. They perform their religious services in the Pali language. They also expect to attain the final goal *(Nirvana)* by becoming a Supreme Enlightened Buddha, a Pacceka Buddha, or an Arahant. The majority of them prefer the Arahantahood. Buddhists in Sri Lanka, Myammar, and Thailand belong to this school. Their practices are in accordance with the customs and traditions of the countries where they live. Mahayanists perform their religious services in their mother tongue. They expect to attain the final goal *(Nirvana)* by becoming Buddhas. Hence, they honour both the Buddha and Bodhisatva (one who is destined to be a Buddha) with the same respect. Buddhists in China, Japan and Korea belong to this school.

Most of those in Tibet and Mongolia follow another school of Buddhism which is known as vajrayana. According to Buddhist scholars this school inclines more towards the Mahayana sect.

It is universally accepted by scholars that the terms *Hinayana* and *Mahayana* are later innovations. Historically speaking, the *Theravada* already existed long before these terms came into being. That *Theravada*, considered to include the original teaching of the Buddha, was introduced to Sri Lanka and established there in the 3rd century B.C., during the time of Emperor Asoka of India. At that time there was nothing called *Mahayana*. *Mahayana* as such appeared much later, about the beginning of the Christian Era. Buddhism that was introduced to Sri Lanka, with its Tripitaka and Commentaries, in the 3rd Century B.C., remained there intact as *Theravada*, and did not become involved in the *Hinayana – Mahayana* dispute that developed later in India. It seems therefore not legitimate to include *Theravada* in either of these two categories. However, after the inauguration of the World Fellowship of Buddhists in 1950, well-informed people, both in the East and in the West, use the term *Theravada*, and not the term *Hinayana*, with reference to Buddhism prevalent in South-east Asian countries. There are still outmoded people who use the term *Hinayana*. In fact, the *Samadhi Nirmorcana* Sutra (a Mahayana Sutra) clearly says that it is

Sravakayana – Theravada and the *Mahayana* constitute one *Yana (ekayana)* and that they are not two different and distinct 'vehicles'.

It must be emphasised here that although different schools of Buddhism held different opinions on the teaching of the Buddha, they never had any violence or bloodshed and have co-existed peacefully for more than two thousand years. Certainly neither party conducted a religious war or any other kind of aggression against the other throughout history. This is the uniqueness of Buddhist tolerance.

5

BASIC DOCTRINES

The Tripitaka was compiled and arranged in its present form by those Arahants who had immediate contact with the Master Himself. The Buddha has passed away, but the sublime Dharma which He unreservedly bequeathed to humanity still exists in its pristine purity.

Although the Master left no written records of His Teachings, His distinguished disciples preserved them faithfully by committing to memory and transmitting them orally from generation to generation.

Immediately after the passing away of the Buddha, 500 distinguished Arahants held a convention known as the First Buddhist Council to rehearse the Doctrine taught by the Buddha. venerable Ananda, the faithful attendant of the Buddha who had the special privilege of hearing all the discourses the Buddha uttered recited the Dharma, whilst the venerable upali recited the vinaya, the rules of conduct for the Sangha.

One hundred years after the First Buddhist Council, during the time of King Kalasoka, some disciples saw the need to change certain minor rules. The orthodox monks said that nothing should be changed while the others insisted on modifying some disciplinary rules *(Vinaya)*. Finally, the formation of different schools of Buddhism germinated after this council. And in the Second Council, only matters pertaining to the vinaya were discussed and no controversy about the Dharma was reported.

In the 3rd Century B.C. during the time of Emperor Asoka, the Third Council was held to discuss the differences of opinion held by the Sangha community. At this Council the differences were not confined to the vinaya but were also connected with the Dharma. At the end of this Council, the President of the Council, ven. Moggaliputta Tissa, compiled a book called KATHAvATTHu refuting the heretical, false views and theories held by some disciples. The teaching approved and accepted by this Council was known as *Theravada* or *'The Way of The Elders'*. The ABHIDHARMA PITAKA was discussed and included at this Council. The Fourth Council was held in Sri Lanka in 80 B.C. under the patronage of the pious King Vattagamini Abhaya. It was at this time in Sri Lanka that the *Tripitaka* was committed to writing for the first time in the world.

It must be emphasised that while the writings were continued, the basic tradition has always remained oral. Every aspect of the teaching was maintained and venerated in the memory rather than in the written record. That is why the disciples were known as *Sravaka* listeners. By reciting and listening they maintained the teaching in the oral tradition for over 2500 years.

The *Tripitaka* consists of three sections of the Buddha's Teachings. They are the Discipline (VINAYA PITAKA), the Discourse (SUTRA PITAKA), and Absolute Doctrine (ABHIDHARMA PITAKA).

The *Vinaya Pitaka* mainly deals with the disciplinary code of the Order of monks *(Bhikkhus)* and nuns *(Bhikkhunis)*. It describes in detail the gradual development of the *Sasana (Dispensation)*. It also gives an account of the life and ministry of the Buddha. Indirectly it reveals some useful information about ancient history, Indian customs, arts, sciences, etc.

For nearly twenty-years since His Enlightenment, the Buddha did not lay down rules for the control of the Sangha. Later, as the occasion arose and the number of monks increased, the Buddha promulgated rules for the future discipline of the Sangha.

This Pitaka consists of the five following books:

1. PARAJIKA PALI (Major Offences)
2. PACITTIYA PALI (Minor Offences)
3. MAHAVAGGA PALI (Greater Section)
4. CULLAVAGGA PALI (Smaller Section)
5. PARIVARA PALI (Epitome of the Vinaya)

Sutra Pitaka

The SUTRA PITAKA consists chiefly of discourses delivered by the Buddha Himself on various occasions. There are also a few discourses delivered by some of His distinguished disciples, such as the Venerables Sariputta, Ananda, Moggallana, and famous female Venerables like Khema, Uttara, Visakha, etc., included in it. It is like a book of prescriptions, as the sermons embodied therein were expounded to suit the different occasions and the temperaments of various persons. There may be seemingly contradictory statements, but they should not be misconstrued as they were opportunely uttered by the Buddha to suit a particular purpose. Therefore morals, ethics, discipline, duties, responsibilities, obligations and humane qualities can be found in the sutra pitaka.

This *Pitaka* is divided into five *Nikayas* or collections, viz:

1. DIGHA NIKAYA (Collection of Long Discourses)

2. MAJJHIMA NIKAYA (Collection of Middle-length Discourses)

3. SAMYUTTA NIKAYA (Collection of Kindred Sayings)

4. ANGUTTARA NIKAYA (Collection of Discourses arranged in accordance with number)

5. KHUDDAKA NIKAYA (Smaller Collection)

The fifth is subdivided into fifteen books:

1. KHUDDAKA PATHA (Shorter Texts)
2. DHAMMAPADA (The Way of Truth)
3. UDANA (Heartfelt sayings or Paeans of Joy)
4. ITI VUTTAKA ('Thus said' Discourses)
5. SUTRA NIPATA (Collected Discourses)
6. VIMANA VATTHU (Stories of Celestial Mansions)
7. PETA VATTHU (Stories of Petas)
8. THERAGATHA (Psalms of the Brethren)
9. THERIGATHA (Psalms of the Sisters)
10. JATAKA (Birth Stories)
11. NIDDESA (Expositions)
12. PATISAMBHIDA (Analytical Knowledge)
13. APADANA (Lives of Saints)
14. BUDDHAVAMSA (The History of Buddha)
15. Cariya Pitaka (Modes of Conduct)

Abhidharma Pitaka

The *Abhidharma* is, to a deep thinker, the most important and interesting collection, as it contains the profound philosophy and psychology of the Buddha's teaching in contrast to the illuminating but conventional discourses in the SUTRA PITAKA.

In the SUTRA PITAKA one often finds references to individual, being, etc., but in the Abhidharma, instead of such conventional terms, we meet with ultimate terms, such as aggregates, mind, matter, etc.

in the Sutra is found the *Vohara Desana* (Conventional Teaching), whilst in the ABHIDHARMA is found the *Paramattha Desana* (Ultimate Doctrine). In the ABHIDHARMA everything is analysed and explained in detail, and as such it is called *analytical doctrine (Vibhajja Vada).*

Four ultimate, supramundane subjects *(Paramattha)* are enumerated in the ABHIDHARMA. They are *Citta,* (Consciousness), *Cetasika* (Mental concomitants), *Rupa* (Matter) and *Nirvana.*

The so-called being is microscopically analysed and its component parts are minutely described. Finally the ultimate goal and the method to achieve it is explained with all necessary details.

The ABHIDHARMA PITAKA is composed of the following works:

1. DHAMMA-SANGANI (Enumeration of Phenomena)

2. VIBHANGA (The Book of the Treatises)

3. KATHA VATTHU (Point of Controversy)

4. PUGGALA PANNATTI (Description of Individuals)

5. DHATU KATHA (Discussion with reference to Elements)

6. YAMAKA (The Book of Pairs)

7. PATTHANA (The Book of Relations)

According to another classification, mentioned by the Buddha Himself, the whole Teaching is ninefold, namely— 1. *Sutra,* 2. *Geyya,* 3. *Yeyyakarama,* 4. *Gatha,* 5. *Udana,* 6. *Itivuttaka,* 7. *Jataka,* 8. *Abbhutadhamma,* 9. *Vedalla.*

1. *Sutra*—These are the short, medium, and long discourses expounded by the Buddha on various occasions, such as MANGALA SUTRA (Discourse on Blessings), RATANA SUTRA (The Jewel Discourse), METTA SUTRA (Discourse on Goodwill), etc. According to the Commentary the Vinaya is also included in this division.

2. *Geyya*—These are discourses mixed with *Gathas* or verses, such as the SAGATHAVAGGA of the SAMYUTTA NIKAYA.

3. VEYYAKARANA —Lit. exposition. The whole ABHIDHARMA PITAKA, discourses without verses, and everything that is not included in the remaining eight divisions belong to this class.

4. GATHA—These include verses found in the DHAMMAPADA (Way of Truth), THERAGATHA (Psalms of the Brethren), THERIGATHA (Psalms of the Sisters), and those isolated verses which are not classed amongst the *Sutra.*

5. UDÀNA—These are the 'Paeans of Joy' found in the UDANA, one of the divisions of the KHUDDAKA NIKAYA.

6. ITIVUTTAKA—These are the 112 discourses which commence with the phrase—'Thus the Blessed One has said'. ITIVUTTAKA is one of the fifteen books that comprise the KHUDDAKA NIKAYA.

7. JATAKA—These are the 547 birth-stories related by the Buddha in connection with His previous births.

8. ABBHUTA DHAMMA—These are the few discourses that deal with wonderful and marvellous things, as for example the ACCHARIYA-ABBHUTA DHAMMA SUTRA of the MAJJHIMA NIKAYA *(No. 123)*

9. VEDALLA—These are the pleasurable discourses, such as CHULLA VEDALLA, MAHA VEDALLA (M.N. Nos *43, 44*), SAMMA DITTHI SUTRA (M.N. No. *9*), etc. In some of these discourses, the answers given to certain questions were put with a feeling of joy.

What is Abhidharma?

The ABHIDHARMA PITAKA contains the profound moral psychology and philosophy of the Buddha's teaching in contrast to the moral discourses in the SUTRA PITAKA.

The knowledge gained from the *Sutra* can certainly help us in overcoming our difficulties, as well as in developing our moral conduct and training the mind. Having such knowledge will enable one to lead a life which is peaceful, respectable, harmless and noble. By listening to the discourses, we develop understanding of the Dharma and can mould our daily lives accordingly. The concepts behind certain words and terms used in the SUTRA PITAKA are, however, subject to changes and should be interpreted within the context of the social environment prevailing at the Buddha's time. The concepts used in the *Sutra* are like the conventional words and terms lay people use to express scientific subjects. While concepts in the Sutra are to be understood in the conventional sense, those used in the *Abhidharma* must be understood in the ultimate sense. The concepts expressed in the *Abhidharma* are like the precise scientific or technical words and terms used by scientists to prevent misinterpretations. It is only in the *Abhidharma* that explanations are given on how and at which mental beats a person can create good and bad *karmic* thoughts, according to his or her desires and other mental states. Clear explanations of the nature of the different mental faculties and precise analytical interpretations of the elements can be found in this important collection of discourses.

understanding the Dharma through the knowledge gained from the *Sutra* is like the knowledge acquired from studying the prescriptions for different types of sicknesses. Such knowledge when applied can certainly help to cure certain types of sicknesses. On the other hand, a qualified physician, with precise knowledge, can diagnose a wider range of sicknesses and discover their causes. This specialized knowledge provides a better position to prescribe more effective remedies. Similarly, a person who has studied the *Abhidharma* can better understand the nature of the mind and analyse the mental attitudes which cause a human being to commit mistakes and develop the will to avoid evil.

The *Abhidharma* teaches that the egoistic beliefs and other concepts such as *'I'*, *'you'*, *'person'* and 'the *world'*, which we use in daily conversation, do not adequately describe the *real* nature of existence. The conventional concepts do not reflect the fleeting nature of pleasures, uncertainties, impermanence of every component thing, and the conflict among the elements and energies intrinsic in all animate or inanimate things. The *Abhidharma* doctrine gives a clear exposition of the ultimate nature of human beings and brings the analysis of the human condition further than other studies known to them.

The *Abhidharma* deals with realities existing in the ultimate sense, or *paramattha dhamma* in Pali. There are four such realities:

1. *Citta,* mind or consciousness, defined as 'that which knows or experiences' an object. *Citta* occurs as distinct momentary states of consciousness.

2. *Cetasika,* the mental factors that arise and occur along with the *citta.*

3. *Rupa,* physical phenomenon or material form.

4. *Nirvana,* the unconditioned state of bliss which is the final goal.

Citta, the *cetasika,* and *rupa* are conditioned realities. They arise because of conditions, and will disappear when the conditions sustaining them cease to continue to do so. They are impermanent states. *Nirvana,* on the other hand, is an unconditioned reality. it does not arise and, therefore, does not fall away. These four realities can be experienced regardless of the names we may choose to give them. Other than these realities, everything—be they within ourselves or without, whether in the past, present or future, whether coarse or subtle, low or lofty, far or near—is a concept and not the ultimate reality.

Citta, cetasika, and *Nirvana* are also called *nama. Nirvana* is an unconditioned *nama.* The two conditioned *nama,* that is, *citta* and *cetasika,* together with *rupa* (form), make up psychophysical organisms, including human beings. Both mind and matter, or *nama-rupa,* are analysed in *Abhidharma* as though under a microscope. Events connected with the process of birth and death are explained in detail. The *Abhidharma* clarifies intricate points of the Dharma and enables the arising of an understanding of reality, thereby setting forth in clear terms the Path of Emancipation. The realization we gain from the *Abhidharma* with regard to our lives and the world is not to be understood in a conventional sense, but is an absolute reality.

The clear exposition of thought processes found in the *Abhidharma* cannot be found in any other psychological treatise either in the east or west. Consciousness is defined, while thoughts are analysed and classified mainly from an ethical standpoint. The composition of each type of consciousness is set forth in detail. The fact that consciousness flows like a stream, a view propounded by psychologists like William James, becomes extremely clear to one who understands the *Abhidharma*. in addition, a student of *Abhidharma* can fully comprehend the *Anatta (No-soul)* doctrine, which is important both from a philosophical as well as ethical standpoint.

The *Abhidharma* explains the process of rebirth in various planes after the occurrence of death without anything to pass from one life to another. This explanation provides support to the doctrine of *Karma* and Rebirth. It also gives a wealth of details about the mind, as well as the units of mental and material forces, properties of matter, sources of matter, relationship of mind and matter.

In the ABHIDHAMMATTHA SANGAHA, a manual of *Abhidharma,* there is a brief exposition of the 'Law of Dependent Origination', followed by a descriptive account of the Causal Relations which finds no parallel in any other study of the human condition anywhere else in the world. Because of its analytics and profound expositions, the *Abhidharma* is not a subject of fleeting interest designed for the superficial reader.

To what extent can we compare modern psychology with the analysis provided in the *Abhidharma?* Modern psychology, limited as it is, comes within the scope of *Abhidharma* in so far as it deals with the mind—with thoughts, thought processes, and mental states. The difference lies in the fact that *Abhidharma* does not accept the concept of a psyche or a soul.

The analysis of the nature of the mind given in the *Abhidharma* is not available through any other source. Even modern psychologists are very much in the dark with regards to subjects like mental impulses or mental beats *(Javana Citta)* as discussed in the *Abhidharma.* Dr. Graham Howe, an eminent Harley Street psychologist, wrote in his book, THE INVISIBLE ANATOMY:

In the course of their work many psychologists have found, as the pioneer work of C.G. Jung has shown, that 'we are near to [the] Buddha. To read a little Buddhism is to realise that the Buddhists knew two thousand five hundred years ago far more about our modern problems of psychology than they have yet been given credit for. They studied these problems long ago, and found the answers too. We are now rediscovering the Ancient Wisdom of the East.'

Some scholars assert that the *Abhidharma* is not the teaching of the Buddha, but it grew out of the commentaries on the basic teachings of the Buddha. These commentaries are said to be the work of great scholar monks. Tradition, however, attributes the nucleus of the *Abhidharma* to the Buddha Himself.

Commentators state that the Buddha, as a mark of gratitude to His mother who was born as a deva in a celestial plane, preached the *Abhidharma* to her together with other devas continuously for three months. The principal topics *(matika)* of the advanced teaching, such as moral states *(kusala dharma)* and immoral states *(akusala dharma),* were then repeated by the Buddha to Venerable Sariputta Thera, who subsequently elaborated them and later compiled them into six books.

From ancient times there were controversies as to whether the

Abhidharma was really taught by the Buddha. "While this discussion may be interesting for academic purposes, what is important is for us to experience and understand the realities described in the *Abhidharma.* One will realize for oneself that such profound and consistently verifiable truths can only emanate from a supremely enlightened source—from a Buddha. Much of what is contained in the *Abhidharma* is also found in the SUTRA PITAKA, and such sermons had never been heard until they were first uttered by the Buddha. Therefore, those who claim that the Buddha was not the source of the *Abhidharma* would have to say the same thing about the *Sutra*. Such a statement, of course, cannot be supported by evidence.

According to the Theravada tradition, the essence, fundamentals and framework of the *Abhidharma* are ascribed to the Buddha although the tabulations and classifications may have been the work of later disciples. "What is important is the essence. It is this that we would try to experience for ourselves. The Buddha Himself clearly took this stand of using the knowledge of the *Abhidharma* to clarify many existing psychological, metaphysical and philosophical problems. Mere intellectual quibbling about whether the Buddha taught the *Abhidharma* or not will not help us to understand reality.

The question is also raised whether the *Abhidharma* is essential for Dharma practice. The answer to this will depend on the individual who undertakes the practice. People vary in their levels of under-standing, their temperaments and spiritual development. ideally, all the different spiritual faculties should be harmonized, but some people are quite contented with devotional practices based on faith, while others are keen on developing penetrative insight. The *Abhidharma* is most useful to those who want to understand the Dharma in greater depth and detail. it aids the development of insight into the three characteristics of existence—impermanence, unsatisfactoriness, and non-self. it is useful not only for the periods devoted to formal meditation, but also during the rest of the day when we are engaged in various mundane chores. We derive great benefit from the study of the *Abhidharma* when we experience absolute reality. in addition, a comprehensive knowledge of the *Abhidharma* is useful for those engaged in teaching and explaining the Dharma. in fact the real meaning of the most important Buddhist terminologies such as *Dharma, Karma, Samsara, Sankhara, Paticca Samuppada* and *Nirvana* cannot be understood without a knowledge of *Abhidharma.*

Mind and Matter *(Nama-Rupa)*

According to Buddhism, life is a combination of mind *(nama)* and matter *(rupa)*. Mind consists of the combination of sensations, perceptions, volitional activities and consciousness. Matter consists of the combination of the four elements of solidity, fluidity, motion and heat.

Life is the co-existence of mind and matter. Decay is the lack of co-ordination of mind and matter. Death is the separation of mind and matter. Rebirth is the recombination of mind and matter. After the passing away of the physical body *(matter)*, the mental forces *(mind)* recombine and assume a new combination in a different material form and condition another existence.

The relation of mind to matter is like the relation of a battery to an engine of a motor car. The battery helps to start the engine. The engine helps to charge the battery. The combination helps to run the motor car. in the same manner, matter helps the mind to function and the mind helps to set matter in motion.

Buddhism teaches that life is not the property of matter alone, and that the life-process continues or flows as a result of cause and effect. The mental and material elements that compose sentient beings from amoeba to elephant and also to man, existed previously in other forms.

Although some people hold the view that life originates in matter alone, the greatest scientists have accepted that mind precedes matter in order for life to originate. in Buddhism, this concept is called 'relinking consciousness'.

Each of us, in the ultimate sense, is mind and matter, a compound of mental and material phenomena, and nothing more. Apart from these realities that go to form the *nama-rupa* compound, there is no self, or soul. The mind part of the compound is what experiences an object. The matter part does not experience anything. "When the body is injured, it is not the body that feels the pain, but the mental side. When we are hungry it is not the stomach that feels the hunger but the mind. However, mind cannot eat the food to ease the hunger. The mind and its factors, make the body digest the food. Thus neither the *nama* nor the *rupa* has any efficient power of its own. One is dependent on the other; one supports the other. Both mind and matter arise because of conditions and perish immediately, and this is happening every moment of our lives. By studying and experiencing these realities we will get insight into: (1) what we truly are; (2) what we find around us; (3) how and why we react to what is within and around us; and (4) what we should aspire to reach as a spiritual goal.

To gain insight into the nature of the psycho-physical life is to realise that life is an illusion, a mirage or a bubble, a mere process of becoming and dissolving, or arising and passing away. "Whatever exists, arises from causes and conditions. "When the causes and conditions cease to be, the thing will cease to exist.

Four Noble Truths

Why are we here? Why are we not happy with our lives? What is the cause of our unsatisfactoriness? How can we see the end of unsatisfactoriness and experience eternal peace?

*T*HE Buddha's Teaching is based on the Four Noble Truths. To realise these Truths is to realise and penetrate into the true nature of existence, including the full knowledge of oneself. When we recognise that all phenomenal things are transitory, are subject to suffering and are void of any essential reality, we will be convinced that true and enduring happiness cannot be found in material possessions and worldly achievement, that true happiness must be sought only through mental purity and the cultivation of wisdom.

The Four Noble Truths are a very important aspect of the Buddha's teaching. The Buddha has said that it is because we fail to understand the Four Noble Truths that we continue to go round in the cycle of birth and death. The very first sermon of the Buddha, the DHARMACHAKRA SUTRA, which He gave to the five monks at the Deer Park in Sarnath was on the Four Noble Truths and the Eightfold Path. The Four Noble Truths are:

The Noble Truth of *Dukkha*

The Noble Truth of the Cause of *Dukkha*

The Noble Truth of the End of *Dukkha*

The Noble Truth of the Path leading to the End of *Dukkha*

There are many ways of understanding the Pali word '*Dukkha*'. It has generally been translated as 'suffering' or 'unsatisfactoriness', but this term as used in the Four Noble Truths has a deeper and wider meaning. *Dukkha* contains not only the ordinary meaning of suffering, but also includes deeper ideas such as imperfection, pain, impermanence, disharmony, discomfort, irritation, or awareness of incompleteness and insufficiency. By all means, *Dukkha* includes physical and mental suffering: birth, decay, disease, death, to be united with the unpleasant, to be separated from the pleasant, not to get what one desires. However, many people do not realise that even during the moments of joy and happiness, there is *Dukkha* because these moments are all impermanent states and will pass away when conditions change. Therefore, the truth of *Dukkha* encompasses the whole of existence, in our happiness and sorrow, in every aspect of our lives. As long as we live, we are very profoundly subjected to this truth.

Some people may have the impression that viewing life in terms of *Dukkha* is a rather pessimistic or negative way of looking at life. This is not a pessimistic but a realistic way. if one is suffering from a disease and refuses to recognise the fact that one is ill, and as a result, refuses to seek treatment, we will not consider such a mental attitude as being optimistic, but merely as being foolish. Therefore, by being either optimistic or pessimistic, one does not really understand the nature of life, and is therefore unable to tackle life's problems in the right perspective. The Four Noble Truths begin with the recognition of the prevalence of *Dukkha* and then proceed to analyse its cause and find its cure. Had the Buddha stopped at the Truth of *Dukkha,* then one may say Buddhism has identified the problem but has not given the cure; if such is the case, then the human situation is hopeless. However, not only is the Truth of *Dukkha* recognised, the Buddha proceeded to analyse its cause and the way to cure it. How can Buddhism be considered to be pessimistic if the cure to the problem is known? in fact, it is a teaching which is filled with hope.

in addition, even though *Dukkha* is a noble truth, it does not mean that there is no happiness, enjoyment and pleasure in life. There is, and the Buddha has taught various methods with which we can gain more happiness in our daily life. However, in the final analysis, the fact remains that the pleasure or happiness that we experience in life is impermanent. We may enjoy a happy situation, or the good company of someone we love, or we enjoy youth and health. Sooner or later, when these states change we experience suffering. Therefore, while there is every reason to feel glad when one experiences happiness, one should not cling to these happy states or be side-tracked and forget about working one's way to complete Liberation.

if we wish to cure ourselves of suffering, we must first identify its cause. According to the Buddha, craving or desire *(tanha* or *raga)* is the cause of suffering. This is the Second Noble Truth. People crave for pleasant experiences, crave for material things, crave for eternal life, and when disappointed, crave for eternal death. They are not only attached to sensual pleasures, wealth and power, but also to ideas, views, opinions, concepts, beliefs. And craving is linked to ignorance, that is, not seeing things as they really are, or failing to understand the reality of experience and life. Under the delusion of Self and not realising that personality is *Anatta* (non-Self), a person clings to things which are impermanent, changeable, perishable. The failure to satisfy one's desires through these things causes disappointments and suffering.

The Danger of Selfish Desire

Craving is a fire which burns in all beings: every activity is motivated by desire. They range from the simple physical desire of animals to the complex and often artificially stimulated desires of civilised people. To satisfy desire, animals prey upon one another, and human beings fight, kill, cheat, lie and perform various forms of unwholesome deeds. Craving is a powerful mental force present in all forms of life, and is the chief cause of the ills in life. It is this craving that leads to repeated births in the cycle of existence.

Once we have realised the cause of suffering, we are in a position to put an end to suffering. So, how do we put an end to suffering? Eliminate it at its root by the removal of craving in the mind. This is the Third Noble Truth. The state where craving ceases is known as *Nirvana.* The word *Nirvana* is composed of *'ni'*and *vana '*, meaning the departure from or end of craving. This is a state which is free from suffering and rounds of rebirth. This is a state which is not subjected to the laws of birth, decay and death. This state is so sublime that no human language can express it. *Nirvana* is Unborn, unoriginated, uncreated, unformed. if there were not this unborn, this unoriginated, this uncreated, this unformed, then escape from the conditioned world is not possible.

Nirvana is beyond logic and reasoning. We may engage in highly speculative discussions regarding *Nirvana* or ultimate reality, but this is not the way to really understand it. To understand and realise the truth of *Nirvana,* it is necessary for us to walk the Eightfold Path, and to train and purify ourselves with diligence and patience. Through spiritual development and maturity, we will be able to realise the Third Noble Truth. But first we must begin with *sraddha,* the confidence or faith that the Buddha is truly competent to lead the way.

The Noble Eightfold Path is the Fourth Noble Truth which leads to *Nirvana.* it is a way of life consisting of eight factors. By walking on this Path, it will be possible for us to see an end to suffering. Because Buddhism is a logical and consistent teaching embracing every aspect of life, this noble Path also serves as the finest possible code for leading a happy life. its practice brings benefits to oneself and others, and it is not a Path to be practised by those who call themselves Buddhists alone, but by each and every understanding person, irrespective of his or her religious beliefs.

The Noble Eightfold Path — The Middle Way

This is the Path for leading a pure religious life without going to extremes *an* outstanding aspect of the Buddha's

Teaching is the Eightfold Path, which is to be adopted as a noble way of life. Another name for the Eightfold Path is the Middle Path. The Buddha advised His followers to follow this Path so as to avoid the extremes of sensual pleasures and self-mortification. The Middle Path is a right-eous way of life that does not advocate the acceptance of decrees given by someone outside oneself. A person practises the Middle Path, the guide for moral conduct, not out of fear of any supernatural agency, but out of recognising the intrinsic value in following such an action. He or she chooses this self-imposed discipline with a definite end in view: self-purification.

The Middle Path is a planned course of inward culture and progress. A person can make real progress in righteousness and insight by following this Path even without engaging in external worship and prayers. According to the Buddha, anyone who lives in accordance with the Dharma will be guided and protected by that very universal Law. "When a person lives according to Dharma, he or she will also be living in harmony with the universal law.

Every Buddhist is encouraged to mould his or her life according to the Noble Eightfold Path as taught by the Buddha. One who adjusts one's life according to this noble way of living will be free from miseries and calamities both in this life-time and hereafter. One will also be able to develop the mind by restraining from evil and observing morality.

The Eightfold Path can be compared to a road map. Just as a traveller will need a map to reach a destination, we all need the Eightfold Path which shows us how to attain Nirvana, the final goal of human life. To attain the final goal, there are three aspects of the Eightfold Path to be developed by the devotee. One has to develop *Sila*

(Morality), *Samadhi* (Mental Culture) and *Panna* (Wisdom). While the three must be developed simultaneously, the intensity with which any one area is to be practised varies according to a person's own spiritual development. A devotee must first develop morality, that is, his or her actions should bring good to other living beings. One does this by faithfully adhering to the precepts of abstaining from killing, slandering, stealing, becoming intoxicated or being lustful. As one develops one's morality, the mind will become more easily controlled, enabling one to develop one's powers of concentration. Finally, with the development of concentration, wisdom will arise.

Gradual Development

With His infinite wisdom, the Buddha knew that not all humans have the same ability to reach spiritual maturity at once. So He expounded the Noble Eightfold Path for the gradual development of the spiritual way of life in a practical way. He knew that not all people can become perfect in one lifetime. He said that *Sila, Samadhi,* and *Panna,* must and can be developed over many lifetimes with diligent effort. This Path finally leads to the attainment of ultimate peace where there is no more unsatisfactoriness.

Righteous Life

The Eightfold Path consists of the following eight factors:

Sila Right Speech Right Action Right Livelihood Morality

Samadhi Right EffortRight Mindfulness Right Concentration Mental culture

Panna Right understanding Right Thoughts Wisdom

What is *Right Understanding?* It is explained as having

the knowledge of the Four Noble Truths. in other words, it is the understanding of things as they really are. Right understanding also means that one understands the nature of what are wholesome *karma* (merits) and unwholesome *karma* (demerits)*, and how they may be performed with the body, speech and mind. By understanding *karma,* a person will learn to avoid evil and do good, thereby creating favourable outcomes in life. "When a person has Right Understanding, he or she also understands the Three Characteristics of Life (that all compounded things are transient, subject to suffering, and without a Self) and understands the Law of Dependent Origination. A person with complete Right understanding is one who is free from ignorance, and by the nature of that enlightenment removes the roots of evil from the mind and becomes liberated. The lofty aim of a practising Buddhist is to develop the mind to gain Right understanding about the self, life and all phenomena.

When a person has Right Understanding, he or she develops *Right Thought* as well. This factor is sometimes known as 'Right Resolution', 'Right Aspirations' and 'Right ideas'. it refers to the mental state which eliminates wrong ideas or notions and promotes the other moral factors to be directed to Nirvana. This factor serves a double purpose of eliminating evil thoughts and developing pure thoughts. Right Thought is important because it is one's thoughts which either purify or defile the mind.

There are three aspects to Right Thought. First, a person should maintain an attitude of detachment from worldly pleasures rather than being selfishly attached to them. One should be selfless and think of the welfare of others. Second, the person should maintain loving-kindness, goodwill and benevolence in the mind, which is opposed to hatred, ill-will or aversion. Third, one should act with thoughts of harmlessness or compassion to all beings, which is opposed to cruelty and lack of consideration for others. As a person progresses along the spiritual path, one's thoughts will become increasingly benevolent, harmless, selfless, and filled with love and compassion.

Right Understanding and Right Thought, which are Wisdom factors, will lead to good, moral conduct. There are three factors under moral conduct: Right Speech, Right Action and Right Livelihood. *Right Speech* involves respect for truth and respect for the welfare for others. it means to avoid lying, to avoid back biting or slander, to avoid harsh speech, and to avoid idle talk. We have often underestimated the power of speech and tend to use little control over our speech faculty. But we have all been hurt by someone's words at some time of our lives, and similarly we have been encouraged by the words of another. it is said that a harsh word can wound more deeply than weapons, whereas a gentle word can change the heart and mind of the most hardened criminal. So to develop a harmonious society, we should control, cultivate and use our speech positively. We speak words which are truthful, bring harmony, and are kind and meaningful. The Buddha once said 'pleasant speech is sweet as honey, truthful speech is beautiful like a flower, and wrong speech is unwholesome like filth'.

The next factor under good, moral conduct is *Right Action.* Right Action entails respect for life, respect for property, and respect for personal relationships. it corresponds to the first three of the Five Precepts to be practised by every Buddhist, that is, abstinence from killing, stealing, and sexual misconduct. Life is dear to all, and all tremble at punishment, all fear death and value life. Hence, we should abstain from taking a life which we ourselves cannot give and we should not harm other sentient beings. Respect for property means that we should not take what is not given, by stealing, cheating, or force. Respect for personal relationships means that we should not commit adultery and should avoid sexual misconduct, which is important for maintaining self respect and the trust of those we love as well as making our society a better place to live in.

Right Livelihood is a factor under moral conduct which refers to how we earn our living in society. it is an extension of the two other factors of Right Speech and Right Action. Right Livelihood means that we should earn a living without violating these principles of moral conduct. Buddhists are discouraged from being engaged in the following five kinds of livelihood: trading in other living beings for slaughtering, trading in weapons, trading in flesh by causing the slaughter of animals, trading in intoxicating drinks and drugs, and trading in poison. Some people may say that they have to follow such an occupation for their living and, therefore, it is not wrong for them to do so. But this argument is entirely baseless. if it were valid, then thieves, murderers, gangsters, thugs, smugglers and swindlers can also just as easily say that they are also doing such unrighteous acts only for their living and, therefore, there is nothing wrong with their way of life.

Some people believe that fishing and hunting animals for pleasure and slaughtering animals for food are not against the Buddhist precepts. This is another misconception that arises owing to a lack of knowledge in Dharma. All these are not decent actions and bring suffering to other beings. But in all these actions, the one who is harmed most of all is the one who commits these unwholesome actions. Maintaining a life through wrong means is not in accordance with the Buddha's teaching. The Buddha once said, 'Though one should live a hundred years immorally and unrestrained, yet it would indeed be better to live one day virtuously and meditatively' (DHAMMAPADA 103). It is better to die as a cultured and respected person than to live as a wicked person.

The remaining three factors of the Noble Eightfold Path are factors for the development of wisdom through the purification of the mind. They are Right Effort, Right Mindfulness, and Right Concentration. These factors, when practised, enable a person to strengthen and gain control over the mind, thereby ensuring that his or her actions will continue to be good and that the mind is being prepared to realise the Truth, which will open the door to Freedom, to Enlightenment.

Right Effort means that we cultivate a positive attitude and have enthusiasm in the things we do, whether in our career, in our study, or in our practice of the Dharma. With such a sustained enthusiasm and cheerful determination, we can succeed in the things we do. There are four aspects of Right Effort, two of which refer to evil and the other two to good. First, is the effort to reject evil that has already arisen; and second, the effort to prevent the arising of evil. Third, is the effort to develop good which has not arisen, and fourth, the effort to maintain the good which has arisen. By applying Right Effort in our lives, we can reduce and eventually eliminate the number of unwholesome mental states and increase and firmly establish wholesome thoughts as a natural part of our mind.

Right Effort is closely associated with *Right Mindfulness.* The practice of mindfulness is important in Buddhism. The Buddha said that mindfulness is the one way to achieve the end of suffering. Mindfulness can be developed by being constantly aware of four particular aspects. These are the application of mindfulness with regard to the body (body postures, breathing and so forth), feelings (whether pleasant, unpleasant or neutral); mind (whether the mind is greedy or not, angry, dispersed or deluded or not); and mind objects (whether there are mental hindrances to concentration, the Four Noble Truths, and so on). Mindfulness is essential even in our daily life during which we act in full awareness of our actions, feelings and thoughts, as well as of our environment. The mind should always be clear and attentive rather than distracted and clouded.

Whereas Right Mindfulness is directing our attention to our body, feelings, mind, or mental object or being sensitive to others, in other words, putting our attention to where we choose *Right Concentration* is the sustained application of that attention on the object without being distracted. Concentration is the practice of developing one-pointedness of the mind on one single object, either physical or mental. The mind is totally absorbed in the object without distractions, wavering, anxiety or drowsiness. Through practice under an experienced teacher, Right Concentration brings two benefits. Firstly, it leads to mental and physical well-being, comfort, joy, calm, tranquility. Secondly, it turns the mind into an instrument capable of seeing things as they truly are, and prepares the mind to attain wisdom.

The Noble Eightfold Path is the most important truth taught by the Buddha. As a competent spiritual physician, the Buddha has identified the disease that afflicts all forms of life, and this is *Dukkha* or unsatisfactoriness. He then diagnosed the cause of the unsatis-factoriness which is selfish greed and craving. He discovered that there is a cure for the disease, *Nirvana,* the state where all unsatisfactoriness ceases. And the prescription is the Noble Eightfold Path. "When a competent doctor treats a patient for a serious illness, the prescription is not only for physical treatment, but it is also psychological. The Noble Eightfold Path, the path leading to the end of suffering, is an integrated therapy designed to cure the disease of *Samsara* through the cultivation of moral speech and action, the development of the mind, and the complete transformation of one's level of understanding and quality of thought. it shows the way to gain spiritual maturity and be released completely from suffering.

'For the good to do what is good is easy, For the bad to do what is bad is easy, For the bad to do what is good is difficult, For the Noble to do what is bad is difficult.'

Everything is Changeable

WE notice how life changes and how it continually moves between extremes and contrasts. We notice rise and fall, success and failure, loss and gain; we experience honour and contempt, praise and blame; and we feel how our hearts respond to happiness and sorrow, delight and despair, disappointment and satisfaction, fear and hope. These mighty waves of emotion carry us up, fling us down, and no sooner do we find some rest, than we are carried by the power of a new wave again. How can we expect a footing on the crest of the waves? "Where shall we erect the building of our life in the midst of this ever-restless ocean of existence?

This is a world where any little joy that is allotted to beings is secured only after many disappointments, failures and defeats. This is a world where scanty joy grows amidst sickness, desperation and death. This is a world where beings who a short while ago were connected with us by sympathetic joy are at the next moment in want of our compassion. Such a world as this needs equanimity. It is the nature of the world that we live with our intimate friends who the next day can become our enemies to harm us.

The Buddha described the world as an unending flux of becoming. All is changeable, continuous transformation, ceaseless mutation, and a moving stream. Everything exists from moment to moment. Everything is a recurring rotation of coming into being and then passing out of existence. Everything is moving from birth to death. Life is a continuous movement of change towards death. The matter or material forms in which life does or does not express itself, are also a continuous movement or change towards decay. This teaching of the impermanent nature of everything is one of the main pivots of Buddhism. Nothing on earth partakes of the character of absolute reality. That there will be no death of what is born is impossible. Whatever is subject to origination is subject also to destruction. Change is the very constituent of reality.

The Buddha reminded us that all existing component things are impermanent. With birth, there is death; with arising, there is dissolving; with coming together, there is separation. How can there be birth without death? How can there be arising without dissolving? How can there be coming together without separation?

In declaring the Law of impermanence or change, the Buddha denies the existence of eternal substances. Matter and spirit are false abstractions that, in reality, are only changing factors *(Dharma)* which are connected and which arise in functional dependence on each other.

Today, scientists have accepted the law of change that was discovered by the Buddha. Scientists postulate that there is nothing substantial, solid and tangible in the world. Everything is a vortex of energy, never remaining the same for two consecutive moments. The whole wide world is caught up in this whirl and vortex of change. One of the theories postulated by scientists is the prospect of the ultimate coldness following upon the death or destruction of the sun. Buddhists are not dismayed by this prospect. The Buddha taught that universes or world cycles arise and pass away in endless succession, just as the lives of individuals do. Our world will most certainly come to an end before other worlds come into existence. it has happened before with previous worlds and it will happen again. it is simply a matter of time.

'The world is a passing phenomenon. We all belong to

the world of time. Every written word, every carved stone, every painted picture, the structure of civilisation, every generation of human beings, will vanish away like the leaves and flowers of forgotten summers. "What exists is changeable and what is not changeable does not exist.'

Thus all gods and human beings and animals and material forms— everything in this universe—is subject to the law of impermanency. Buddhism teaches us that the mind seeks a permanent existence but life creates an impermanent physical body. We take this as life, and then unsatisfactoriness disturbs the mind. This is the source of suffering.

'The body like a lump of foam: The feelings like a water bubble; Perception like a mirage; Volitional activities like a banana tree; And Consciousness like jaggery*.'

What is Karma?

KARMA can be put in the simple language of the child: do good and good will come to you, now, and hereafter. Do bad and bad will come to you, now, or hereafter. In the language of the harvest, *karma* can be explained in this way: if you sow good seeds, you will reap a good harvest. if you sow bad seeds, you will reap a bad harvest.

In the language of science, *karma* is called the law of cause and effect: every cause has an effect. Another name for this is the law of moral causation. Moral causation works in the moral realm just as the physical law of action and reaction works in the physical realm.

In the DHAMMAPADA, *karma* is explained in this manner: the mind is the chief *(forerunner)* of all good and bad states. If you speak or act with a bad mind, then unhappiness follows you just as the wheel follows the hoof of the ox. If you speak or act with a good mind, then happiness follows you like the shadow that never leaves you.

Karma is simply action. Within animate organisms there is a power or force which is given different names such as instinctive tendencies, consciousness, etc. This innate propensity forces every conscious being to move. A person moves mentally or physically. His motion is action. The repetition of actions is habit and habit becomes one's character. in Buddhism, this process is called *karma.*

in its ultimate sense, *karma* means both good and bad, mental action or volition. '*Karma* is volition,' says the Buddha. Thus *karma* is not an entity but a process, action, energy and force. Some interpret this force as 'action-influence'. it is our own doings reacting on ourselves. The pain and happiness a person experiences are the results of his or her own deeds, words and thoughts reacting on themselves. Our deeds, words and thoughts produce our prosperity and failure, our happiness and misery.

Karma is an impersonal, natural law that operates strictly in accordance with our actions. It is a law in itself and does not have any lawgiver. *Karma* operates in its own field without the intervention of an external, independent ruling agency. Since there is no hidden agent directing or administering rewards and punishments, Buddhists do not rely on prayer to some supernatural forces to influence karmic results. According to the Buddha, *karma* is neither predestination nor determinism imposed on us by some mysterious, unknown powers or forces to which we must helplessly submit ourselves.

Buddhists believe that one will reap what one has sown; we are the result of what we were, and we will be the result of what we are. in other words, we are not absolutely what we were, and we will not continue to remain as what we are. This simply means that *karma* is not complete determinism. The Buddha pointed out that if everything is fixed and determined, then there would be no free will and no moral or spiritual life. We would merely be the slaves of our past. On the other hand, if everything is undetermined, then there can be no cultivation of moral and spiritual growth. The Buddha again declared the truth of the Middle Path: that karma is to be understood as neither strict determinism nor absolute indeterminism but as an interaction of both.

Misconceptions Regarding Karma

The misinterpretations or irrational views on *karma* are stated in the ANGUTTARA NIKAYA which suggests that the wise will investigate and abandon the following views:

1. the belief that everything is a result of acts in previous lives;

2. the belief that everything is the result of what is willed by a Supreme Creator; and

3. the belief that everything arises without reason or cause.

if a person becomes a murderer, a thief, or an adulterer, and, if his or her actions are due to past actions, or are caused by the whim of a

Supreme Being, or if it happened by mere chance, then this person could not be held responsible for his or her evil action as everything was predetermined.

Yet another misconception about *karma* is that it operates only for certain people according to their faiths. But the destiny of a person in the next life does not in the least depend on what particular religion he or she chooses. "Whatever one's religion may be, one's fate depends entirely on deeds committed by body, speech and thought. it does not matter what religious label one holds, one is bound to be in a happy world in the next life so long as one does good deeds and leads an unblemished life. One is bound to be born to lead a wretched life if one commits evil and harbours wicked thoughts in the mind. Therefore, Buddhists do not proclaim that they are the only blessed people who can go to heaven after their death. "Whatever religion is professed or without any religious label, karmic thoughts alone determine a person's destiny both in this life and in the next. The teaching of karma does not indicate a post-mortem justice. The Buddha did not teach this law of *karma* to protect the rich and to comfort the poor by promising illusory happiness in an after life.

According to Buddhism *karma* explains the inequalities that exist among mankind. These inequalities are due not only to heredity, environment and nature but also to *karma* or the results of our own actions. indeed *karma* is one of the factors which are responsible for the success and the failure of our lives.

Since *karma* is an invisible force, we cannot see it working with our physical eyes. To understand how *karma* works, we can compare it to seeds: the results of *karma* are stored in the subconscious mind in the same way as the leaves, flowers, fruits and trunk of a tree are stored in its seed. under favourable conditions, the fruits of *karma* will be produced just as with moisture and light, the leaves and trunk of a tree will sprout from its tiny seed. The taste of the fruits also carry forward just like karmic energy creates the effect.

The working of *karma* can also be compared to a bank account: a person who is virtuous, charitable and benevolent in this present life is like a person who is adding to his or her "good *karma*" account. This accumulated good *karma* can be used to ensure a trouble free life. But the person must replace what is taken or else one day, the account will be depleted and that person will be bankrupt. Then who can be blamed for one's miserable state? One can blame neither others nor fate. One alone is responsible. Thus a good Buddhist cannot be an escapist but must confront life as it is and not run away from it. The karmic force cannot be controlled by inactivity. vigorous activity for good is indispensable for one's own happiness. Escapism is the resort of the weak, and an escapist cannot run away from the effects of karmic law.

The Buddha says, 'There is no place to hide in order to escape from karmic results' (DHAMMAPADA 127).

Our own Experience

To understand the law of *karma* is to realise that we ourselves are responsible for our own happiness and our own misery. We are the architects of our *karma.* Buddhism explains that we have every opportunity to mould our own *karma* and thereby influence the direction of our lives. On the other hand, we are not complete prisoners of our own actions; we are not slaves to our *karma.* Nor are we mere machines that automatically release instinctive forces that enslave us. Nor are we mere products of nature. We have within ourselves the strength and the ability to change our *karma.* Our minds are mightier than our *karma* and so the law of *karma* can be made to serve us. We do not have to give up our hope and effort in order to surrender ourselves to our own karmic force. To off-set the reaction of our bad *karma* that we have accumulated previously, we have to do more meritorious deeds; and purify our minds rather than simply rely on worshipping, performing rites or torturing our physical bodies in order to overcome our karmic effects. Therefore, a person can overcome the effect of his or her evil deeds if he or she acts wisely by leading a noble life.

We must use the qualities with which we are endowed to promote our ideal. The cards in the game of life are within us. We do not select them. They are traced to our past *karma;* but we can call as we please, do what suits us and as we play, we either gain or lose, depending on our skill or lack of it.

Karma is equated to the action of a person. This action also creates some karmic results. But each and every action carried out without any purposeful intention, cannot become a *kusala-karma* (skilful action) or *akusala-karma* (unskilful action). That is why the Buddha describes *karma* as volitional activities. That means, whatever good and bad deeds we commit without any purposeful intention, are not strong enough to be carried forward to our next life. However, ignorance of the nature of the good and bad effect of the *karma* is not an excuse to justify or avoid the karmic results if they were committed intentionally. A small child or an ignorant man may commit many evil deeds. Since they commit such deeds with intention to harm or injure, it is difficult to say that they are free from the karmic results. if that child touches a burning iron-rod, the heat element does not spare the child of pain. The karmic energy also works exactly in the same manner. Karmic energy is unbiased; like gravity it is impartial.

The radical transformations in the characters of Angulimala and Asoka illustrate human beings' potential to gain control over karmic forces.

Angulimala was a highway robber who murdered more than a thousand of his fellow men. Can we judge him by his external actions? For within his lifetime through sheer self -effort, he became an Arahanta and thus redeemed his past misdeeds.

Asoka, the Emperor of india, killed thousands and thousands to fight his wars and to expand his empire. Yet after winning the battle, he completely reformed himself and changed his career to such an extent that today, *'Amidst the tens of thousands of names of monarchs that crowd the columns of history, their majesties and royal highnesses and the like, the name of Asoka shines and shines almost alone, as a star,'* says the historian, H.G. Wells.

Other Factors which Support Karma

Although Buddhism says that a person can eventually control his or her karmic force, it does not state that everything is due to *karma.* Buddhism does not ignore the role played by other forces of nature. According to Buddhism there are five orders or processes of natural laws *(niyama)* which operate in the physical and mental worlds:

1. *utu niyama* (seasonal laws) relating to the physical inorganic order e.g., seasonal phenomena of winds and rains, etc.,

2. *bija niyama* (biological laws) relating to the order of germs and seeds,

3. *karma niyama* (karmic law) relating to moral causation or the order of act and result,

4. *dharma niyama* (natural phenomena) relating to electrical forces, movement of tides etc., and

5. *citta niyama* (psychological laws) which govern the processes of consciousness.

Thus *karma* is considered only as one of the five natural laws that account for the diversity in this world.

Can Karma be Changed?

Karma is often influenced by circumstances: beneficent and malevolent forces act to counter and to support this self-operating law. The other forces that either aid or hinder this *karma* are birth, time or conditions, appearances, and effort.

A favourable birth *(gati sampatti)* or an unfavourable birth *(vipatti)* can develop or hinder the fruition of *karma.* For instance, if a person is born to a noble family or in a state of happiness, his fortunate birth will provide an easy opportunity for his good *karma* to operate. An unintelligent person who, by some good *karma,* is born in a royal family, will, on account of his noble parentage be honoured by the people. if the same person were to have a less fortunate birth, he would not be similarly treated.

Good appearance *(upadhi sampatti)* and poor appearance *(upadhi vipatti)* are two other factors that hinder or favour the working of *karma.* if by some good *karma,* a person obtains a good birth, but is born deformed by some bad *karma,* then he or she will not be able to fully enjoy the beneficial results of good karma. Even a legitimate heir to a throne may not perhaps be raised to that high position if he happens to be physically or mentally deformed. Beauty, on the other hand, will be an asset to the possessor. A good-looking son of poor parents may attract the attention of others and may be able to distinguish himself through their influence. Also, we can find cases of people from poor, obscure family backgrounds who rise to fame and popularity as film actors or actresses or beauty queens.

Time and occasion are other factors that influence the working of *karma.* in the time of famine or during the time of war, all people without exception are forced to suffer the same fate. Here the unfavourable conditions open up possibilities for evil *karma* to operate. The favourable conditions, on the other hand, will prevent the operation of bad *karma.*

Effort or intelligence is perhaps the most important of all the factors that affect the working of *karma.* Without effort, both worldly and spiritual progress is impossible. if we do not make the effort to cure our disease, or to save ourselves from difficulties, or to strive with diligence for progress, then evil *karma* will find a suitable opportunity to manifest its due effects. However, if we endeavour to surmount difficulties and problems, our good *karma* will come to help. "When shipwrecked in a deep sea, the *Bodhisatva* during one of his previous births, made an effort to save himself and his old mother, while the others prayed to the gods and left their fate in the hands of these gods. The result was that the *Bodhisatva* escaped while the others were drowned.

Thus the working of *karma* is aided or obstructed by birth, beauty and ugliness, time and personal effort or intelligence. However, people can overcome immediate karmic effects by adopting certain methods. Yet, they are not completely free from such karmic effects if they remain within this *Samsara-cycle* of birth and death. Whenever opportunities arise, the same karmic effects that were suppressed, can affect them again. This is the uncertainty of worldly life. Even the Buddha and Arahantas were affected by certain *karmas,* although they were in their final life.

The time factor is another important aspect of the karmic energy for people to experience the good and bad effects of previous actions. People experience certain karmic effects only within this lifetime while certain karmic effects become effective immediately hereafter in the next birth. And certain other karmic effects follow the doers as long as they remain in this wheel of existence until they stop their rebirth after attaining *Nirvana.* The main reason for this difference is owing to mental impulsion *(Javana Citta)* at the time when a thought arises in the mind to do good or bad.

Impartial Energy

Those who do not believe that there is an energy known

as *karma* should understand that this karmic energy is not a byproduct of any particular religion although Hinduism, Buddhism and Jainism

recognize and explain the nature of this energy. This is an existing universal law which has no religious label. All those who violate this law, have to face the consequences irrespective of their religious beliefs, and those who live in accordance with this law experience peace and happiness in their life. Therefore, this karmic law is unbiased towards each and every person, whether they believe it or not; whether they have a religion or not. It is like any other existing universal law. *Karma* is not the exclusive property of Buddhism.

if we understand *karma* as a force or a form of energy, then we can discern no beginning. To ask where is the beginning of *karma* is like asking where is the beginning of electricity. *Karma* like electricity does not begin. It comes into being under certain conditions. Conventionally we say that the origin of *karma* is volition but this is as much conventional as saying that the origin of a river is a mountain top.

Like the waves of the ocean that flow into one another, one unit of consciousness flows into another and this merging of one thought consciousness into another is called the working of *karma.* in short, every living being, according to Buddhism, is an electric current of life that operates on the automatic switch of *karma.*

Karma being a form of energy is not found anywhere in this fleeting consciousness or body. Just as mangoes are not stored anywhere in the mango tree but, dependent on certain conditions, they spring into being, so does *karma.* *Karma* is like wind or fire. it is not stored up anywhere in the universe but comes into being under certain conditions.

Classification of Karma

Karma is classified in four ways according to:

1. the time in which effects are worked out;
2. function – *Kicca;*
3. the priority of effect; and
4. the place in which the karmic effects transpire.

There are moral and immoral actions which may produce their due effects in this very life. They are called "Immediately Effective – *Dittha Dharma Vediniya Karma*". If they do not operate in this life, they become "ineffective – *Ahosi*".

There are some actions which may produce their effects in a subsequent life. They are termed "Subsequently Effective – *Upapajja Vedaniya Karma*".

They too become ineffective if they do not operate in the second birth.

Those actions which may produce their effects in any life in the course of one's wondering in Samsara, are known as "Indefinitely Effective – *Aparapariya Vedaniya Karma?*

This classification of *karma* is with reference to the time in which effects are worked out.

There are four classes of *karma* according to Function – *Kicca.*

Every birth is conditioned by past good and bad *karma* that predominates at the moment of death. The *karma* that conditions the future birth is called "Reproductive – *Janaka Karma*".

Now another *karma* may step forward to assist or maintain the action of this Reproductive Karma. Just as this *karma* has the tendency to strengthen the Reproductive Karma, some other action which tends to weaken, interrupt, the fruition of the Reproductive Karma may step in. Such actions are respectively termed "Supportive-*Upattham-bhaka Karma*" and "Counteractive- *Upapidaka Karma*".

According to the law of *karma,* the potential energy of the Reproductive Karma could be nullified by a more powerful opposing *karma* of the past, which, seeking an opportunity, may quite unexpectedly operate, just as a powerful opposing force can check the path of the flying arrow and bring it down to the ground. Such an action is called "Destructive— *Upaghataka Karma*" which is more effective than Supportive and Counteractive Karma in that it not only obstructs but also destroys the whole force.

There are four classes of *karma* according to the priority of effect.

The first is *Garuka,* which means weighty or serious. This karma, which is either good or bad, produces results in this life, or in the next for certain. If good, it is purely mental as in the case of Jhanas -*Ecstacies.* Otherwise it is verbal or bodily.

The five kinds of Weighty Karma are:

1. matricide;
2. patricide;
3. the Murder of an Arahant;
4. the Wounding of a Buddha; and
5. the Creation of a Schism in the Sangha.

Permanent Scepticism—*Niyata Micchaditthi* is also termed one of the Weighty Karmas.

In the absence of a Weighty Karma to condition the next birth, a death-proximate *karma – Asanna* might operate. This is the *karma* one does immediately before the dying moment.

Habitual – *Acinna Karma* is the next in priority of effect. it is the Karma that one habitually performs and recollects and for which one has a great liking.

The fourth is the "Cumulative – *Katatta Karma*" which embraces all that cannot be included in the above three. This is as it were the reserve fund of a particular being.

The last classification is according to the place in which the *karma* effects transpire, namely:

1. Evil Karma – *Akusala,* which may ripen in the Sentient Plane –

Kamaloka.

2. Good Karma – *Kusala,* which may ripen in the Sentient Plane.

3. Good Karma, which may ripen in the realm of Form – *Rupaloka*

4. Good Karma, which may ripen in the formless realms – *Arupaloka.*

Is Everything Due to Karma?

Although Buddhism attributes the inequality of mankind as one of the chief effects amongst many, yet it does not assert that everything is due to *karma.*

If everything is due to *karma,* a person would always be bad if it was his or her *karma* to be bad. One would not need to consult a physician to be cured of a disease; for if one's *karma* were such, one would be cured.

Why Some Wicked People Enjoy While Some Good People Suffer

Some people ask, 'If good begets good and bad begets bad why should many good people suffer and some wicked people prosper in this world?' The answer to this question, according to the Buddhist point of view, is that although some are good by nature, they have not accumulated enough good merits in their previous birth to compensate for the bad effects of unwholesome *karma* in this present life; somewhere in their past there must have been some defect. On the other hand, some are wicked by nature and yet are able to enjoy this life for a short period due to some strong good *karma* that they accumulated in their previous birth.

For example, there are certain people who by nature have inherited a strong constitution and as a result enjoy perfect health. Their physical power of resistance is strong and hence they are not prone to illnesses. Although they do not take special precautions to lead a hygienic life, they are able to remain strong and healthy. On the other hand, there are others who take various tonics and vitamins—enriched foods to fortify themselves, but in spite of their efforts to become strong and healthy, their health does not show any improvement.

Generally speaking, whatever good and bad deeds people commit within this life-time, they will definitely experience the reaction within this life or hereafter. it is impossible to escape from their results simply by praying, but only by cultivating the mind and leading a noble life.

This is not to say that everything that we suffer or enjoy today is completely controlled by our past actions, which we call *Karma.* The Buddha says that if this was so, then there would be no purpose in living a moral life, as we would then be simply victims of the past. Buddhists assert that while our lives were conditioned in the past, it is entirely within ourselves to change that condition and to create our future and present well being. Buddhists do not subscribe to predestination or fatalism as the only possible explanations for the human condition.

Buddhists are encouraged to do good deeds not for the sake of gaining a place in heaven. They are expected to do good in order to eradicate their selfishness and to experience peace and happiness at each present moment. When each present moment is carefully controlled the future well being is assured.

'He for whom there is neither this shore nor the other shore, nor yet both, He who is free of cares and is unfettered. Him do I call a holyman.

Buddhists regard the doctrine of rebirth not as a mere theory but as a verifiable fact. The acceptance of the truth about rebirth forms a fundamental tenet of Buddhism. However, the belief in rebirth is not confined to Buddhists; it is also found in other countries, in other religions, and even among free thinkers. Pythagoras could remember his previous birth. Plato could remember a number of his previous lives. According to Plato, human beings can be reborn only up to ten times. Plato also believed in the possibility of rebirth in the animal kingdom. Among the ancient people in Egypt and China, a common belief was that only well-known personalities like emperors and kings have rebirths. A Christian authority named Origen, who lived in 185-254 C.E., believed in rebirth. According to him, there is no eternal suffering in hell. Gorana Bruno, who lived in the sixteenth century, believed that the soul of every man and animal transmigrates from one being to another. In 1788, the philosopher Kant criticized the teaching on eternal punishment. Kant also believed in the possibility of rebirth in other celestial bodies. Schopenhauer (1788-1860), another great philosopher, said that where the will to live existed there must be continuity of life. The will to live manifests itself successively in ever new forms. The Buddha explained this 'will to exist' as the craving for existence. And of course the ancient sages of India taught about the transmigration of a soul from the earliest times.

it is possible but not very easy for us to actually verify our past lives. The nature of mind is such that it does not allow most people the recollection of their previous lives. Our minds are overpowered by the five hindrances: sensual desire, ill-will, sloth, restlessness and doubt. Because of these hindrances, our vision is earth-bound and hence we cannot visualise rebirths. Just as a mirror does not reflect an image when it is covered with dirt, so the mind does not allow most people the recollection of previous lives. We cannot see the stars during daytime, not because they are not there in the sky, but because they are outshone by the sunlight. Similarly, we cannot remember our past lives because our mind at present is always over-burdened with many thoughts in the present day-to-day events and mundane circumstances.

A consideration of the shortness of our life span on earth will help us to reflect on rebirth. if we consider life and its ultimate meaning and goal, and all the varied experience possible for a human being, we must conclude that in a single life there is not enough time for a person to carry out all that he or she can do or desires to do. The scale of experience and desire is infinite. There is a vast range of powers latent in human beings which we see and can even develop if the opportunity is presented to us. This is especially true today if special investigation is made. We find ourselves with high aspirations but with no time to attain them. Meanwhile, the great troop of passions and desires, selfish motives and ambitions, make war within us and with others. These forces pursue each other to the time of our death. All these forces must be tried, conquered, subdued and used. One life is just not enough for all this. To say that we must have but one life here with such possibilities put before us and impossible to develop is to make the universe and life a huge and cruel joke.

The Buddhist doctrine of rebirth should be differentiated from the teachings of transmigration and reincarnation of other religions. Buddhism unlike Hinduism does not subscribe to the existence of a permanent, god-created soul or an unchanging entity that transmigrates from one life to another.

Just as relative identity is made possible by causal continuity without a Self or Soul, so death can issue in rebirth without a transmigrating Soul. In a single life, each thought-moment flashes in and out of being, giving rise to its successor with its perishing. Strictly speaking, this momentary rise and fall of every thought is a birth and a death. Thus even in a single life we undergo countless births and deaths every second. But because the mental process continues with the support of a single physical body, we regard the mind-body continuum as constituting a single life.

What we ordinarily mean by death is the cessation of the body's vital functions. "When the physical body loses its vitality it can no longer support the current of consciousness, the mental side of the process. But as long as there is a clinging to life, a desire to go on existing, the current of consciousness does not come to a stop with the body's loss of life. Rather, when death takes place, when the body dies away, the mental current, driven by the thirst for more existence, will spring up again with the support of a new physical body, one which comes into being through the meeting of sperm and egg. Thus, conception takes place immediately after death without a break. The stream of memory may be interrupted and the sense of identity transferred to the new situation, but the entire accumulation of experience and disposition has been transmitted to the new being, and the cycle of becoming begins to revolve for still another term.

For Buddhism, therefore, death does not spell either the entrance to eternal life or complete annihilation. it is, rather, the portal to a new rebirth which will be followed by more growth, decay, and then another death.

While there is a mental continuum, however, at the last moment, no renewed *physical* functioning occurs in a dying person's mind. This is just like a motorist releasing the accelerator before stopping, so that no more pulling power is given to the engine. Similarly, no more material qualities of Karma arise.

Buddhists do not maintain that the present life is the only life between two eternities of misery and happiness; nor do they believe angels will carry them to heaven and leave them there for all eternity. They believe that this present life is only one of the indefinite numbers of states of being and that this earthly life is but one episode among many others. They believe that all beings will be reborn somewhere in some form for a limited period of time as long as their good and bad Karma remains in the subconscious mind as mental energy. Although many eminent psychologists, like Carl Jung for example, have recognised the Buddha's teaching on the subject, the interpretation of the subconscious mind in the Buddhist context should not be confused with that given by modern psychologists, since the concepts are not exactly synonymous.

What is the cause of rebirth? The Buddha taught that ignorance of the real nature of existence produces desires. unsatisfied desire is the cause of rebirth. "When all unsatisfied desire is extinguished, then rebirth ceases. To stop rebirth is to extinguish all desires. To extinguish desire, it is necessary to destroy ignorance. "When ignorance is destroyed, the worthlessness of every such rebirth is perceived, as well as the paramount need to adopt a course of life by which the desire for such repeated births can be abolished.

ignorance also begets the illusory and illogical idea that there is only one existence for human beings, and the other illusion that this one life is followed by permanent states of eternal pleasure or torment.

The Buddha taught that ignorance can be dispelled and sorrow removed by realisation of the Four Noble Truths, and not through any other source. To eradicate all ignorance, one must persevere diligently in the practice of an all-embracing altruism in conduct, intelligence and wisdom. One must also destroy all desire for the lower, personal pleasures and selfish craving.

How Does Rebirth Take Place?

When this physical body is no more capable of functioning, energies do not die with it, but continue to take some other shape or form, which we call another life. The karmic force manifesting itself in the form of a human being can also manifest itself in the form of an animal. This can happen if a person has no chance to develop his or her positive karmic forces. This force, called craving, desire, volition, thirst to live, does not end with the non-functioning of the body but continues to manifest itself in another form, producing re-existence. This is called rebirth or re-becoming. Buddhists do not call it "reincarnation" because no permanent entity or soul moves from one life to the next.

Today, there are people in various countries who have spontaneously developed the memory of their past births. The experiences of these people have been well-documented in newspapers and periodicals. Some of these people never accepted that there was such a thing as rebirth until memory fragments of their previous lives came to them. Much of the information they revealed about their past lives has been investigated and found to be valid.

Through hypnotism, some people have managed to reveal information of previous lives. Certain hypnotic states that penetrate into the subconscious mind make the recalling of past lives possible.

Rebirth or becoming again and again is a natural occurrence not created by any particular religion or god. Belief in rebirth or disbelief does not make any difference to the process of rebirth or avoiding rebirth. Rebirth takes place as long as craving for existence and craving for sensual pleasures or attachment exist in the mind. Those strong mental forces prevail in each and every living being in this universe. Those who hope and pray that they be not born again must understand that their wishes will not materialise until they make earnest efforts to eradicate their craving and attachment from their minds. Having seen and experienced the uncertainty and unsatisfactoriness of life under worldly conditions, wise people try to rid themselves of these repeated births and deaths by following the correct path of mental purification. Those who cannot reduce their craving and attachment must be prepared to face all unsatisfactory and uncertain situations associated with rebirth and becoming again and again.

Is Rebirth Simultaneous?

Another difficult thing to understand about rebirth is whether rebirth occurs immediately upon the ending of the present life. This has been a controversial issue even amongst prominent Buddhist scholars. According to Abhidharma, rebirth (conception) takes place imme-diately after the death of a being without any intermediate state. At the same time, some others believe that a person, after death, would evolve into a spirit form for a certain number of days before rebirth takes place. Another interpretation regarding the same belief is that it is not the spirit, but the deceased person's consciousness or mental energy remaining in space, supported by its own mental energies of craving and attachment waiting until sooner or later rebirth takes place. The spirits *(petas)*, who are beings born in spirit forms, are unfortunate living beings and their lives in the spirit form is not permanent. it is also a form of rebirth which is temporary.

Another concept which many people cannot understand is that in the process of rebirth a person can be reborn as an animal and an animal can be reborn as a human. The animal nature of a person's mind and the animal way of life adopted by him or her can condition that person to be born as an animal. The condition and behaviour of the mind is responsible for the next existence. On the other hand, a person who is born in animal form, owing to certain mental abuses during a previous birth, could be reborn as a human being, depending on the force of karma accumulated in a previous existence. it is a well-known fact that some animals are very intelligent and understanding, showing very human characteristics. A person who is born as an animal can again be born as a human being when the bad *karma* which conditioned his or her birth as an animal is expended and the dormant good *karma* which was stored in the consciousness has an opportunity to take effect.

Dying Moment

There are three types of consciousness *(Vinnana)* functioning at the moment of death in a person: rebirth-linking consciousness *(patisandhi-citta)*, the current of passive consciousness or the current of life-continuum *(bhavanga)* and consciousness disconnecting the present life *(cuti-citta)*. At the last moment of a person's present life the *patisandhi-citta* or rebirth-linking consciousness arises, having the three signs as its objects. The *patisandhi-citta* remains in the course of cognition for five faint thought-moments or *Javana* and then sinks down into *bhavanga*. At the end of *bhavanga* the *cuti-citta* arises, disconnecting the present life and sinks down into *bhavanga*. At this very moment comes the end of the present life. At the end of that *bhavanga* another *patisandhi-citta* rises up in the next life and from this very moment the new life begins. This is the process of death and rebirth according to Buddhism, and only in Buddhism is the process of these natural phenomena found explained in minute and exact detail.

A Buddhist faces death not as a crisis in life but as a normal event, for he or she knows that whoever is born must suffer, 'decay', and ultimately die. Or, as someone so aptly puts it, 'Everyone is born with the certificate of death at birth.' if we could all look at death in such an intelligent and rational way, we would not cling to life so tenaciously.

After He was released from Samsara at the moment of Enligh-tenment, the Buddha declared:

Nirvana

Nirvana is the highest bliss, a supra-mundane state of eternal happiness. The happiness of Nirvana cannot be experienced by indulging the senses but by calming them.

NIRVANA is the final goal of Buddhism. "What is *Nirvana* then? It is not easy to know what *Nirvana* really is; it is easier to know what *Nirvana* is not. *Nirvana* is not nothingness or extinction. Would the Buddha have left His family and kingdom and preached for 45 years—all for nothingness?

Nirvana is not a paradise. Several centuries after the Buddha, some of the Buddhist sects began to describe *Nirvana* as a paradise. Their purpose of equating *Nirvana* with a heavenly world was to convince the 'less-intellectually-gifted' and to attract them to the teachings of the sect. Striving for *Nirvana* came to mean looking for a nice place where everything is beautiful and where everyone is eternally happy. This might be a very comfortable folktale, but it is not the *Nirvana* that the Buddha experienced and described. During His time the Buddha did not deny the idea of paradise or heaven as it was presented in the early indian religions. But the Buddha knew that this paradise was within Samsara and the final liberation was beyond it. The Buddha could see that the Path to *Nirvana* led beyond the heavens.

If *Nirvana* is not a place, where is *Nirvana* then? Strictly speaking we cannot ask where *Nirvana* is. *Nirvana* exists just as fire exists. There is no storage place for fire or for *Nirvana.* But when you rub pieces of wood together, then the friction and heat are the proper conditions for fire to arise. Likewise, when the nature of a person's mind is such that he or she is free from all defilements, then Nirvanic bliss will arise.

Anyone can experience *Nirvana* but until one experiences the supreme state of Nirvanic bliss, one can only speculate as to what it really is, although we can get glimpses of it in everyday life. For those who insist on the theory, the texts offer some help. The texts suggest that *Nirvana* is a supra-mundane state of unalloyed happiness.

By itself, *Nirvana* is quite unexplainable and quite undefinable. As darkness can be explained only by its opposite, light, and as calm can only be explained by its opposite, motion, so likewise *Nirvana,* as a state equated to the extinction of all suffering can be explained by its opposite—the suffering that is being endured in *Samsara.*

As darkness prevails wherever there is no light, as calm prevails wherever there is no motion, so likewise *Nirvana* is everywhere where suffering and change and impurity do not prevail.

A sufferer who scratches his sores can experience a temporary relief. But this temporary relief will only aggravate the wounds and cause the disease to worsen. The joy of the final cure can hardly be compared to the fleeting relief obtained from the scratching. Likewise, satisfying the craving for sense-desires brings only temporary gratification or happiness which prolongs the journey in *Samsara.* The cure for the samsaric disease is *Nirvana. Nirvana* is an end of the cravings which cause all the sufferings of birth, old age, disease, death, grief, lamentation and despair. The joy of Nirvanic cure can hardly be compared to the temporary Samsaric pleasure gained through fulfilling the sense desires.

It is not advisable to speculate on what *Nirvana* is; it is better to know how to prepare the conditions necessary for *Nirvana,* how to attain the inner peace and clarity of vision that leads to *Nirvana.* Follow the Buddha's advice: put His Teachings into practice. Get rid of all defilements which are rooted in greed, hatred, and delusion. Purify yourself of all desires and realise absolute selflessness. Lead a life of right moral conduct and constantly practise meditation. By active exertion, free yourself from all selfishness and illusion. Then, *Nirvana* is gained and experienced.

Nirvana and Samsara

A great Mahayana Buddhist scholar, Nagarjuna, says that *Samsara* and *Nirvana* are one. This interpretation can easily be misunderstood by others. However to state that the concept of *Samsara* and *Nirvana* are the same is to say that there is no difference in voidness of component things and the unconditioned state of *Nirvana.* in accordance with the Pali Tipitaka, *Samsara* is described as the unbroken continuation of the five aggregates, four elements and twelve bases or sources of mental processes whereas *Nirvana* is described as the extinction of those relative physical and mental sources.

Those who gain Nirvanic bliss, can experience it during the remainder of their lives as human beings. After their death, however, the link with those elements will be eliminated, for the simple reason that *Nirvana* is unconditioned, not relative or interdependent. If there is to be anything at all after *Nirvana,* it would have to be 'Absolute Truth'.

Nirvana is attainable in this present life. Buddhism does not state that its ultimate goal could be reached only in the life beyond. "When *Nirvana* is realised in this life with the body remaining it is called *Sopadisesa Nirvana.* When an Arahant attains *Pari Nirvana,* after the dissolution of the body, without any remainder of physical existence, it is called *Anupadisesa Pari Nirvana.*

One must learn to be detached from all worldly things. If there is any attachment to anyone or to anything or if there is any aversion to anyone or anything, one will never attain *Nirvana,* for *Nirvana* is beyond all opposites of attachment and aversion, likes and dislikes.

When that ultimate state is attained, one will fully understand this worldly life for which one now craves. This world will cease to be an object of desire. One will realise the sorrow and impermanence and impersonality of all that lives and that does not live. By depending on teachers or holy books without using one's own effort in the right manner, it is difficult to gain realisation of *Nirvana.* Dreams will vanish. No castles will be built in the air. The tempest will be ended.

Struggles to avoid problems will be over. Nature's

processes will have ceased. All worries, miseries, responsibilities, disturbances, burdens, physical and mental ailments and emotions will vanish after attaining this most blissful state of *Nirvana.*

To say that *Nirvana* is nothingness simply because one cannot perceive it with the five senses, is as illogical as to say that light does not exist simply because the blind do not see it.

Law of Dependent Origination

' No God, no Brahma can be found No matter of this wheel of life Just bare phenomena roll Depending on conditions all.'

The Law of Dependent Origination is one of the most important teachings of the Buddha, and it is also very profound. The Buddha has often expressed His experience of Enlightenment in one of two ways, either in terms of having understood the Four Noble Truths, or in terms of having understood the nature of Dependent Origination. However, more people have heard about the Four Noble Truths and can discuss it than the Law of Dependent Origination, which is just as important.

Although the actual insight into dependent origination arises with spiritual maturity, it is still possible for us to understand the principle involved. The basis of Dependent Origination is that life or the world is built on a set of relations, in which the arising and cessation of factors depend on some other factors which condition them. This principle can be given in a short formula of four lines:

When this is, that is This arising, that arises When this is not, that is not This ceasing, that ceases.

On this principle of interdependence and relativity rests the arising, continuity and cessation of existence. This principle is known as the Law of Dependent Origination or in Pali, *Paticca-samuppada.* This law emphasises an important principle that all phenomena in this universe are relative, conditioned states which cannot arise independently of supportive conditions. A phenomenon arises because of a combination of conditions which are present to support its arising. And the phenomenon will cease when the conditions and components supporting its arising change and no longer sustain it. The presence of these supportive conditions, in turn, depend on other factors for their arising, sustenance and disappearance.

The Law of Dependent Origination is a realistic way of understanding the universe and is the Buddhist equivalent of Einstein's Theory of Relativity. The fact that everything is nothing more than a set of relations is consistent with the modern scientific view of the material world. Since everything is conditioned, relative, and interdependent, there is nothing in this world which could be regarded as a permanent or unique entity, variously regarded as an ego or an eternal soul, which many people believe in.

The phenomenal world is built on a set of relations, but is this the way we normally understand the world to be? We create fictions of its permanency in our minds because of our desires. it is natural for human beings to cling to what they consider as beautiful or desirable, and to reject what is ugly or undesirable. Being subjected to the forces of greed and hatred, they are misled by delusion, clouded by the illusion of the permanency of the object they cling to or reject. Therefore, it is hard for us to realise that the world is like a bubble or mirage, and is not the kind of reality we believe it to be. We do not realise that it is unreal in actuality. It is like a ball of fire, which when whirled around rapidly, can for a time, create the illusion of a circle.

The fundamental principle at work in Dependent Origination is that of cause and effect. in Dependent Origination, what actually takes place in the causal process is described in detail. To illustrate the nature of Dependent Origination of the things around us, let us consider an oil lamp. The flame in an oil lamp burns dependent upon the oil and the wick. "When the oil and the wick are present, the flame in an oil lamp burns. if either of these is absent, the flame will cease to burn. This example illustrates the principle of Dependent Origination with respect to a flame in an oil lamp. Or in an example of a plant, it is dependent upon the seed, earth, moisture, air and sunlight for the plant to grow. All these phenomena themselves arise dependent upon a number of other causal factors, and not independently. Therefore it is impossible to conceive of a first cause. This is the principle of Dependent Origination. in the Dharma, we are interested to know how the principle of Dependent Origination is applied to the problem of suffering and rebirth. The issue is how Dependent Origination can explain why we are still going round in Samsara, or explain the problem of suffering and how we can be free from suffering. it is not meant to be a description of the origin or evolution of the universe. Therefore, one must not be mistaken into assuming that ignorance, the first factor mentioned in the Dependent Origination, is the first cause. Since everything arises because of some preceeding causes, there can be no first cause.

According to the Law of Dependent Origination, there are twelve factors which account for the continuity of existence birth after birth. They are:

1. Through ignorance are conditioned volitional actions or karma-formations.

2. Through volitional actions is conditioned consciousness.

3. Through consciousness are conditioned mental and physical phenomena.

4. Through mental and physical phenomena are conditioned the six faculties (i.e., five physical sense-organs and mind).

5. Through the six faculties is conditioned (sensorial and mental) contact.

6. Through (sensorial and mental) contact is conditioned sensation.

7. Through sensation is conditioned desire, 'thirst'.

8. Through desire ('thirst') is conditioned clinging.

9. Through clinging is conditioned the process of becoming.

10. Through the process of becoming is conditioned birth.

11. Through birth are conditioned decay, death, sorrow, lamentation, pain, grief and despair.

This is how life arises, exists and continues, and how suffering arises. These factors may be understood as sequentially spanning a period of three lifetimes: the past life, the present life, and the future life. in the Dependent Origination, ignorance and mental formation belong to the past life, and represent the conditions that are responsible for the occurrence of this life. The following factors, namely, consciousness, mental and physical phenomena, the six senses, contact, sensation, desire, clinging and becoming, are factors involved in the present life. The last two factors, birth and decay and death, belong to the future life.

in this law, the first factor of ignorance gives rise to volitional Activities (or karma). Ignorance means not knowing or understanding the true nature of our existence.

Through ignorance, good or evil deeds are performed which will lead a person to be reborn. Rebirth can occur in various planes of existence: the human world, the celestial or higher planes, or even suffering planes depending of the quality of a person's karma. "When a person dies, his or her Volitional Activities will condition the arising of Consciousness, in this case to mean the re-linking Consciousness which arises as the first spark of a new life in the process of re-becoming.

Once the re-linking Consciousness has taken place, life starts once again. Dependent on the Consciousness, there arise Mind and Matter, that is, a new 'being' is born. Because there are Mind and Matter, there arise the six Sense-organs (the sixth sense is the mind itself). With the arising of the Sense-organs, there arises Contact. Contact with what? Contact with sights, sounds, smells, tastes, tactile objects, and mental objects.

These sights, sounds, smells, tastes, tactile objects, and mental objects can be beautiful, pleasing and enticing. On the other hand, they can be ugly and distasteful. Therefore, dependent on Contact arises Sensations: feelings that are pleasant, unpleasant or neutral. Because of these feelings, the laws of attraction (greed) and repulsion (aversion) are now set in motion. Beings are naturally attracted to pleasant objects and repelled by unpleasant objects. As a result of Sensation, Desire arises. A person desires and thirsts for forms that are beautiful and enticing; sounds that are beautiful and enticing; tastes, smells, touch, and objects which the mind regards as beautiful and enticing. From these Desires, he or she develops very strong Clinging to the desirable object (or strongly rejects the repulsive object). Now because of this Clinging and attachment, the next life is conditioned and there arises Becoming. in other words, the processes of Becoming are set in motion by Clinging.

The next link in this chain of Dependent Origination is

that Becoming conditions the arising of Birth. And finally, dependent on Birth arise Decay and Death, followed by Sorrow, Lamentation, Pain, Grief and Despair.

The process can be ceased if the formula is taken in the reverse order: Through the complete cessation of ignorance (through the cultivation of Insight and seeing the true nature of all phenomena), volitional activities or karma-formations cease; through the cessation of volitional activities, consciousness ceases;... through the cessation of birth, the other factors of decay, death, sorrow, etc., cease. Therefore, one can be free from the rounds of rebirth through the eradication of ignorance.

To re-iterate what was mentioned earlier, this doctrine of Dependent Origination merely explains the processes of Birth and Death, and is not a theory of the evolution of the world. it deals with the Cause of Re-birth and Suffering, but in no way attempts to show the absolute Origin of Life. Ignorance in Dependent Origination is the ignorance of the Four Noble Truths. it is very important for us to understand the Four Noble Truths because it is the ignorance of these Truths that has trapped us all in the endless cycle of birth and death.

According to the Buddha, while He was speaking to Ananda: "It is by their not being able to comprehend the Dependent Origination, that people are entangled like a ball of cotton, and not being able to see the Truth, are always afflicted by Sorrow,—born often into conditions that are dismal and dreary, where confusion and prolonged suffering prevail. And, they do not know how to disentangle themselves to get out.

Eternalism and Nihilism

The Buddha rejected both extremes of eternalism and nihilism.

The first view is eternalism. This doctrine or belief is concerned with eternal life or with eternal things. Before the Buddha's time, it was thought that there is an abiding entity which could exist forever, and that human beings can live the eternal life by preserving the eternal soul in order to be in union with a Supreme Being. In Bud-dhism, this teaching is called *sassata ditthi*—the erroneous view of eternalists. Such views still exist even in the modern world owing to human beings' craving for eternal life.

Why did the Buddha refute the teaching of eternalism? Because when we understand the things of this world as they truly are, we cannot find anything which is permanent or which exists forever. Things change and continue to do so according to the changing conditions on which they depend. "When we analyse things into their elements or into reality, we cannot find any abiding entity, any everlasting thing. This is why the eternalist view is considered wrong or false.

The second false view is nihilism or the view held by the nihilists who claim that there is no life after death. This view belongs to a materialistic philosophy which refuses to accept knowledge of mental conditionality. To subscribe to a philosophy of materialism is to understand life only partially. Nihilism ignores the side of life which is concerned with mental conditionality. if one claims that after the passing away or ceasing of a life, it does not come to be again, the continuity of mental conditions is denied. To understand life, we must consider all conditions, both mental and material. "When we understand mental and material conditions, we cannot say that there is no life after death and that there is no further becoming after passing away. This nihilist view of existence is considered false because it is based on incomplete understanding of reality. That is why nihilism was also rejected by the Buddha. The teaching of *karma* proves that the Buddha did not teach annihilation after death; Buddhism accepts 'survival ' not in the sense of an eternal soul, but in the sense of a renewed becoming or mental continuum.

Throughout the Buddha's long period of teaching the Dharma to His followers, He actively discouraged speculative arguments. During the 5th century B.C. India was a veritable hive of intellectual activity where scholars, yogis, philosophers, kings and even ordinary householders were constantly engaged in the philosophical arguments pertaining to human existence. Some of these were either ridiculously trivial or totally irrelevant. Some people wasted valuable time arguing at great length about all manner of subjects. They were far more concerned about proving their powers in mental gymnastics than seeking genuine solutions to the problems that beset humanity. (In the 18th century Jonathan Swift satirized a similar pastime in England when he showed the Lilliputians in *'Gulliver's Travels'* waging a war to decide whether an egg should be broken on its sharp end or its broad end).

The Buddha also refused to get involved in speculations regarding the universe. He stated very clearly that the problem facing human beings is not in their past or future but in the immediate present. Knowledge about Eternalism or Nihilism can in no way help them to break the present fetters which bind them to existence and which are the source of all their feelings of discontent which arise from their inability to completely satisfy their cravings. The Buddha stated that before one can begin to tread the path which leads to Nirvana one must have Right view. Only when one knows clearly what one is seeking will one be able to attain it.

Can the First Cause be Known?

It is rather difficult for us to understand how the world came into existence without a first cause. But it is very much more difficult to understand how that first cause came into existence at the beginning.

ACCORDING to the Buddha, it is inconceivable to find a first cause for life or anything else. For in common experience, the cause becomes the effect and the effect becomes the cause. in the circle of cause and effect, a first cause is incomprehensible. With regard to the origin of life, the Buddha declares, *'Without cognizable end is this recurrent wandering in Samsara (cycle of birth and death). Beings are obstructed by ignorance and fettered by craving. A first beginning of these beings is not to be perceived'* (Anamatagga Samyutta in Samyutta Nikaya). This life-stream flows on *ad infinitum,* as long as it is fed by the muddy waters of ignorance and craving. "When these two are cut off, only then does the life-stream cease to flow, only then does rebirth come to an end.

it is difficult to conceive an end of space. it is difficult to conceive an eternal duration of what we call time. But it is more difficult to conceive time when there is no time. Likewise it is rather difficult for us to understand how this world came into existence with a first cause. And it is more difficult to understand how that first cause came into existence at the beginning. For if the first cause can exist though uncreated, there is no reason why the other phenomena of the universe must not exist without having also been created.

As to the question how all beings came into existence without a first cause, the Buddhist's reply is that there is no answer* because the question itself is merely a product of human beings' limited compre-hension. if we can understand the nature of time and relativity; we must see that there could not have been any first beginning. it can only be pointed out that all the usual answers to the question are fundamentally defective. if it is assumed that for a thing to exist, it must have had a creator who existed before it, it follows logically that the creator himself must have had a creator, and so on back to infinity. On the other hand, if the creator could exist without a prior cause in the form of another creator, the whole argument falls to the ground. The theory of a creator does not solve any problems, it only complicates the existing ones.

Thus Buddhism does not pay much attention to theories and beliefs about the origin of the world. "Whether the world was created by a god or it came into existence by itself makes little difference to Buddhists. "Whether the world is finite or infinite also makes little difference. instead of following this line of theoretical speculations, the Buddha advises people to grasp the fact that their present existence is suffering and to work hard to find their own salvation.

Scientists have discovered many causes which are responsible for the existence of life, plants, planets, elements and other energies. But it is impossible for human beings to find out any particular first cause for their existence. if they go on searching for the first cause of any existing life or thing, they point certain causes as the main cause but that never becomes the first cause. in the process of searching for the first cause one after the other, they will come back to the place where they were. This is because, cause becomes the effect and the next moment that effect becomes the cause to produce another effect. That is why the Buddha says, 'a first cause is incomprehensible and the universe is beginningless'.

Is there an Eternal Soul?

The first teacher teaches the existence of an eternal ego-entity that outlasts death: He is the eternalist.

The second teacher teaches a temporary ego-entity which becomes annihilated at death: He is the materialist.

The third teacher teaches neither an eternal nor a temporary ego-entity: He is the Buddha.

The Buddha teaches that what we call ego, self, soul, personality, etc., are merely conventional terms that do not refer to any real, independent entity. According to Buddhism there is no reason to believe that there is an eternal soul that comes from heaven or is created by itself or that it will transmigrate or proceed straight away either to heaven or hell after death. Buddhists cannot accept that there is anything either in this world or any other world that is eternal or unchangeable. We only cling to ourselves and hope to find something immortal. W are like children who wish to grasp a rainbow. To children, a rainbow is something vivid and real; but grown-ups know that it is merely an illusion caused by certain rays of light and drops of water. The colours are only a series of waves or undulations that have no more reality than the rainbow itself.

We have done well without discovering the soul. We show no signs of fatigue or degeneration for not having encountered any soul. No one has produced anything to promote the human race by postulating a soul and its imaginary working. Searching for a soul in man is like searching for something in a dark empty room. But the poor person will never realise that what is being sought for is not in that room. it is very difficult to make such a person understand the futility of the search.

Those who believe in the existence of a soul are not in a position to explain what and where it is. The Buddha's advice is not to waste our time over this unnecessary speculation and devote our time to understand reality. "When we have attained perfection then we will be able to realise whether there is a soul or not. A wandering ascetic named vacchagotta asked the Buddha whether there was an *Atman* (self/soul) or not. The story is as follows:

vacchagotta comes to the Buddha and asks:

'Venerable Gotama, is there an *AtmanT*

The Buddha is silent.

"Then Venerable Gotama, is there no *AtmanT* Again the Buddha is silent. vacchagotta gets up and goes away.

After the ascetic has left, Ananda asks the Buddha why He did not answer vacchagotta's question. The Buddha explains His position:

'Ananda, when asked by Vacchagotta, the Wanderer: "Is there a Self?", if I had answered: "There is a Self", then, Ananda, that would be siding with those recluses and brahmanas who hold the eternalist theory *(sassata-vada).'*

'And Ananda, when asked by the Wanderer: "Is there no Self?", if I had answered: "There is no Self", then that would be siding with those recluses and brahmanas who hold the annihilationist theory *(uccedavada).'*

'Again, Ananda, when asked by Vacchagotta: "Is there a Self?", if I had answered: "There is a Self", would that be in accordance with my knowledge that all Dharmas are without Self?'

'Surely not, Sir.'

'And again, Ananda, when asked by the Wanderer: "Is there no Self?", if I had answered: "There is no Self", then that would have created a greater confusion in the already confused vacchagotta. For he would have thought: Formerly indeed I had an *Atman* (Self), but now I haven't got one' (SAMYUTTA NIKAYA)

The Buddha regarded soul-speculation as illusory. He once said, 'Only through ignorance and delusion do human beings indulge in the dream that their souls are separate and self-existing entities. Their heart still clings to Self. They are anxious about heaven and they seek the pleasure of Self in heaven. Thus they cannot see the bliss of righteousness and the immortality of truth.' Selfish ideas appear in human beings' minds due to their conception of Self and craving for existence.

Anatta: The Teaching of No-Soul

The Buddha countered all soul-theory and soul-speculation with His *Anatta* doctrine. *Anatta* is translated under various labels: No-Soul, No-Self, No-Ego.

To understand the *Anatta* doctrine, one must understand that the eternal soul theory—'I have a soul'—and the material theory—'I have no soul'—are both obstacles to self-realisation or salvation. They arise from the misconception 'I AM'. Hence, to understand the *Anatta* doctrine, one must not cling to any opinion or views on soul-theory; rather, one must try to see things objectively as they are and without any mental projections. One must learn to see the so-called 'I' or Soul or Self for what it really is: merely a combination of changing forces. This requires some analytical explanation.

The Buddha taught that what we conceive as something eternal within us, is merely a combination of physical and mental aggregates or forces *(pancakkhandha)*, made up of body or matter *(rupakkhandha)*, sensation *(vedanakkhandha)*, perception *(sannakkhandha)*, mental formations *(samkharakkhandha)* and consciousness *(vinnanak-khandha)*. These forces are working together in a flux of momentary change; they are never the same for two consecutive moments. They are the component forces of the psycho-physical life. "When the Buddha analyzed the psycho-physical life, He found only these five aggregates or forces. He did not find any eternal soul. However, many people still have the misconception that the soul is the consciousness. The Buddha declared in unequivocal terms that consciousness arises dependent on matter, sensation, perception and mental formations and that it cannot exist independently of them.

The Buddha said, 'The body, O monks, is not the Self. Sensation is not the Self. Perception is not the Self. The mental constructions are not the Self. And neither is consciousness the Self. Perceiving this, O monks, the disciple sets no value on the body, or on sensation, or on perception, or on mental constructions, or on consciousness. Setting no value on them, he becomes free of passions and he is liberated. The knowledge of liberation arises there within him. And then he knows that he has done what has to be done, that he has lived the holy life, that he is no longer becoming this or that, that his rebirth is destroyed.' (Anatta-Lakkhana Sutra)

The *Anatta* doctrine of the Buddha is over 2500 years old. Today the thought current of the modern scientific world is flowing towards the Buddha's Teaching of *Anatta* or No-Soul. In the eyes of modern scientists, a human being is merely a bundle of ever-changing sensations. Modern physicists say that the apparently solid universe is not, in reality, composed of solid substance at all, but is actually a flux of energy. The modern physicist sees the whole universe as a process of transformation of various forces which include the processes which constitute a human being. The Buddha was the first to realize this.

W.S. Wily, an author, once said, 'The existence of the immortal in human beings is becoming increasingly discredited under the influence of the dominant schools of modern thought.' The belief in the immortality of the soul is a dogma that is contradicted by the most clear, empirical investigation.

The mere belief in an immortal soul, or the conviction that something in us survives death, does not make us immortal unless we know what it is that survives and that we are capable of identifying ourselves with it. Most human beings choose death instead of immortality by identifying themselves with that which is perishable and impermanent by clinging stubbornly to the body or the momentary elements of the present personality, which they mistake for the soul or the essential form of life.

In reference to those researches of modern scientists who are now more inclined to assert that the so-called 'Soul' is no more than a bundle of sensations, emotions, sentiments, all relating to the physical experiences, Prof. William James says that the term 'Soul' is a mere figure of speech to which no reality corresponds.

It is the same *Anatta* doctrine of the Buddha that was introduced in the *Mahayana* school of Buddhism as *Sunyata* or voidness. Although this concept was elaborated by a great *Mahayana* scholar, Nagarjuna, by giving various interpretations, there is no extraordinary concept in

Sunyata that is far different from the Buddha's original doctrine of *Anatta.*

The belief in Soul or Self and the Creator God, is so strongly rooted in the minds of many people that they cannot imagine why the Buddha did not accept these two concepts which are indispensable to many religions. In fact some people get a shock or become nervous and emotional when they hear that the Buddha rejected these two concepts. That is the main reason why to many unbiased scholars and psychologists Buddhism stands unique when compared to all the other religions. At the same time, some other scholars who appreciate the various other aspects of Buddhism are convinced that Buddhism would be enriched by deliberately re-interpreting the Buddha word *'Atta'* in order to introduce the concept of Soul and Self into Buddhism. The Buddha was aware of this unsatisfactoriness of humanity and the conceptual upheaval regarding this belief.

All conditioned things are impermanent, All conditioned things are Dukkha-Suffering, All conditioned or unconditioned things (Dharma) are soulless or selfless.

There is a parable in our Buddhist texts with regard to the belief in an eternal soul. A man, who mistook a moving rope for a snake, became terrified by that fear in his mind. upon discovery that it was only a piece of rope, his fear subsided and his mind became peaceful. The belief in an eternal soul is equated to the rope—man's imagination.

6

Is Buddhism Similar to Other Contemporary Teachings in India?

IN His first sermon, the Dharmacakka Sutra, the Buddha said that the Dharma which He preached was unheard of before. Knowledge of the Dharma which arose was clear to His vision, to His knowledge, to His wisdom, to His penetration, and to His Enlightenment.

Some people claim that the Buddha did not preach a new doctrine but merely reformed the old teaching which was existing

in India. However, the Buddha was no mere reformer of Hinduism as some protagonists of this ancient creed make Him out to be. The Buddha's way of life and doctrine were substantially different from the way of life and the religious beliefs that the people in India had. The Buddha lived, taught and died as a non-Vedic and non-Brahmanic religious Teacher. Nowhere did the Buddha acknowledge His indebtedness to the existing religious beliefs and practices. The Buddha considered Himself as initiating a rational spiritual method, as opening a new path.

That was the main reason why many other religious groups could not agree with Him. He was condemned, criticised and insulted by the most noted teachers and sects of the Vedic Brahmanic tradition. It was with the intention of destroying or absorbing the Buddha and His Teaching, that the Brahmans of the pre-Christian era went so far as to accept the Buddha as an Avatara or incarnation of their God. Yet some others despised Him as a *vasalaka*, a *mundaka*, a *samanaka*, a *nastika* and *sudra*. (These words were used in India during the Buddha's time to insult a religious man who was not a Brahman).

There is no doubt that the Buddha reformed certain customs, religious duties, rites and ethics and ways of living prevalent at the time. The greatness of His character was like a pin-point that pricked the balloon of false beliefs and practices so that they could burst and reveal their emptiness.

But as far as the fundamental, philosophical and psychological teachings are concerned, it is groundless to say that the Buddha had copied ideas from any existing religion at that time. For instance, the idea of the Four Noble Truths, the Eightfold Path, Dependent Origination and Nirvana, were not known before His coming. Although the belief in karma and rebirth was very common, the Buddha gave quite logical and reasonable explanations to this belief and introduced it as natural law of cause and effect. Although the Buddha used these terms because they were familiar to His listeners, He gave them very original interpretations, quite different from the way the Brahmans understood them. Despite all these the Buddha did not ridicule any sincere existing religious belief or practice. He appreciated the value of Truth wherever He found it and He even gave a better explanation of their beliefs. That is why He once said that the Truth must be respected wherever it is found. On the other hand, however, He was never afraid to speak out against mythology and false claims.

Is Buddhism a Theory or a Philosophy?

DURING the time of the Buddha there were many

learned men in India who pursued knowledge simply for its own sake. These people were interested only in theoretical knowledge. Indeed, some of them went from city to city challenging anyone to a debate and their greatest thrill was to defeat an opponent in such verbal combats. But the Buddha said that such people were no nearer to the realization of the truth because in spite of their cleverness, knowledge and verbal skills they did not have true wisdom and insight to overcome greed, hatred and delusion. In fact, these people were often proud and arrogant. Their egoistic concepts disturbed the religious atmosphere, and they loved arguing simply for the sake of arguing.

According to the Buddha, one must first seek to understand one's own mind. This was to be done through concentration which gives one a profound inner wisdom or realization. Insight is to be gained not by philosophical argument or worldly knowledge but by the silent realization of the illusion of the self.

Buddhism is a righteous way of life for the peace and happiness of every living being. It is a method to get rid of miseries and to find liberation. The Teaching of the Buddha is not limited to one nation or race. It is neither a creed nor mere faith. It is a Teaching for the entire universe. It is a Teaching for all time. Its objectives are selfless service, goodwill, peace, salvation and deliverance from suffering.

Salvation in Buddhism is an individual affair. You have to save yourself just as you have to eat, drink and sleep by yourself. The advice rendered by the Buddha points the Way to liberation; but His advice was never intended to be taken as a theory or philosophy. When He was questioned as to what theory He propounded, the Buddha replied that He preached no theories and whatever He did preach was the result of His own experience. Thus His Teaching does not offer any theory. Theory cannot bring one nearer to spiritual perfection. Theories are the very fetters that bind the mind and impede spiritual progress. Indian and Chinese philosophies originated in religious beliefs, while some other religions are not based on philosophy but dogma. The Buddha however, taught us to see things as they are, observing phenomena and not relying on anything which cannot be experienced by each individual.

Theories are products of the intellect and the Buddha understood the limitations of the human intellect. He taught that enlightenment is not a product of mere intellect. One cannot achieve emancipation by taking an intellectual course. This statement may seem irrational but it is true. Intellectuals tend to spend too much of their valuable time on study, critical analysis and debate. This is unbalanced because they usually have little or no time for practice.

A great thinker (philosopher, scientist, metaphysician, etc.) can also turn out to be an intelligent fool. He may be an intellectual giant endowed with the power to conceive ideas quickly and to express thoughts clearly. But if he pays no attention to his actions and their consequences, and if he is only bent on fulfilling his own longings and inclinations at any cost, then, according to the Buddha, he is an intellectual fool, a man of inferior wisdom though rich in factual knowledge. Such a person will indeed hinder his own spiritual progress.

The Buddha's Teaching contains practical wisdom that cannot be limited to theory or to philosophy because philosophy deals mainly with knowledge but is not concerned with translating knowledge into day-to-day practices.

Buddhism lays special emphasis on practice and realization. The philosopher sees the miseries and disappointments of life but, unlike the Buddha, offers no practical solution to overcome our frustrations which are part of the unsatisfactory nature of life. The philosopher merely pushes his thoughts to dead ends. Philosophy is useful because it has enriched our intellectual imagination and diminished dogmatic assurance which closes the mind to further progress. To that extent, Buddhism values philosophy, but philoso-phy fails to quench one's spiritual thirst. Philosophy is to know but Buddhism is to practice.

Remember that the chief aim of a Buddhist is to attain purity and enlightenment. Enlightenment vanquishes ignorance which is the root of birth and death. However, this vanquishing of ignorance cannot be achieved except by the exercise of one's confidence. All other attempts—especially mere intellectual attempts are not very effective. This is why the Buddha concluded: 'These [metaphysical] questions are not calculated to profit; they are not concerned with the Dharma; they do not lead to right conduct, or to detachment, or to purification from lusts, or to quietude, or to a calm heart, or to real knowledge, or to higher insight, or to Nirvana'. (Malunkyaputta Sutta—Majjhima Nikaya). In place of metaphysical speculation, the Buddha was more concerned with teaching a practical understanding of the Four Noble Truths that He discovered: what Suffering is; what the origin of Suffering is; what the cessation of Suffering is; how to overcome Suffering and realize final Salvation. These Truths are all practical matters to be fully understood and realized by anyone who really experiences emancipation.

Enlightenment is the dispelling of ignorance; it is the ideal of the Buddhist life. We can now clearly see that enlightenment is not an act of the intellect. Mere speculation does not help a person to come into contact with life so intimately. This is why the Buddha placed great emphasis on personal experience. Meditation is a practical scientific system to verify the Truth that comes through personal experience and insight. Through meditation, the will tries to transcend the condition it has put on itself, and this is the awakening of consciousness. Metaphysics merely ties us down in a tangled and matted mass of thoughts and words.

Is Buddhism Pessimistic?

SOME critics argue that Buddhism is morbid, cynical, hovering on the dark and shadowy side of life, an enemy of harmless pleasures, and an unfeeling trampler on the innocent joys of life. They claim that Buddhism is pessimistic, fostering an attitude of hopelessness towards life, encouraging a vague, general feeling that pain and evil predominate in human affairs. Even the current Pope in Rome has stated that Buddhism teaches a negative attitude to life. These critics base their views on the First Noble Truth that all conditioned things are in a state of suffering. They do not see that not only had the Buddha taught the cause of Suffering, but He also taught the way to end Suffering. In any case, is there any religious teacher who praised this worldly life and advised us to cling to it? Every religion talks about salvation, which means liberation from uncertainty and unsatisfactoriness in this world.

If the founder of this religion, the Buddha, was such a pessimist, one would expect His personality to be portrayed on more severe lines than has been done. The Buddha image is the personification of Peace, Serenity, Hope and Goodwill. The magnetic and radiant smile of the Buddha is the epitome of His doctrine. To the worried and the frustrated, His smile of Enlightenment and hope is an unfailing tonic and soothing balm.

The Buddha radiated His love and compassion in all directions. Such a person can hardly be a pessimist. And when the sword-happy kings and princes listened to Him, they realised that the only true conquest is the conquest of the Self and the best way to win the hearts of the people was to teach them to appreciate the Dharma—Truth.

The Buddha cultivated His sense of humour to such a high degree that His bitter opponents were disarmed with the greatest ease. Often they could not help laughing at themselves. The Buddha had a wonderful tonic; He cleansed their systems of dangerous toxins and they became enthusiastic thereafter to follow in His footsteps. In His sermons, dialogues and discussions, He maintained that poise and dignity which won for Him the respect and affection of the people. How can such a person be a pessimist?

The Buddha never expected His followers to be constantly brooding over the suffering of life and leading a miserable and unhappy existence. He taught the fact of suffering only so that He could show people how to overcome this suffering and move in the direction of happiness. To become an Enlightened person, one must have joy, one of the factors that the Buddha recommended to us to cultivate. joy is hardly pessimistic.

There are two Buddhist texts called the Theragatha and Therigatha which are full of the joyful utterances of the Buddha's disciples, both male and female, who found peace and happiness in life through His Teaching. The king of Kosala once told the Buddha that unlike many a disciple of other religious systems who looked haggard, coarse, pale, emaciated and unprepossessing, His disciples were 'joyful and elated, jubilant and exultant, enjoying the spiritual life, serene, peaceful and living with a gazelle's mind, light-hearted.' The king added that he believed that this healthy disposition was due to the fact that 'these Venerable Ones had certainly realized the great and full significance of the Blessed One's Teachings' (Majjhima Nikaya).

When asked why His disciples, who lived a simple and quiet life with only one meal a day, were so radiant, the Buddha replied: 'They do not repent the past, nor do they brood over the future. They live in the present with contentment. Therefore they are radiant. By brooding over the future and repenting the past, fools dry up like green reeds cut down [in the sun]' (Samyutta Nikaya).

As a religion, Buddhism teaches about the unsatisfactory nature of everything in this world. Yet one cannot simply categorize Buddhism as a pessimistic religion, because it also teaches us how to overcome this unsatisfactoriness. According to the Buddha, even the worst sinner, after paying for what he has done, can attain salvation. Buddhism offers every human being the hope of attaining his or her salvation one day. Other religions, however, take it for granted that some people will be bad forever and have an eternal hell waiting for them. In that respect, such religions are more pessimistic. Buddhists deny such a belief.

Buddhism is neither optimistic nor pessimistic. It does not encourage human beings to look at the world through their changing feelings of optimism and pessimism. Rather, Buddhism encourages us to be realistic: we must learn to see things as they truly are.

Is Buddhism Atheistic?

THE Buddha has condemned godlessness by which He meant the denial of worship and renunciation, the denial of moral, spiritual and social obligations, and the denial of a religious life. He recognized most emphatically the existence of moral and spiritual values. He acclaimed the supremacy of the moral law. Only in one sense can Buddhism be described as atheistic, namely, in so far as it denies the existence of an eternal omnipotent God or Godhead who is the creator and ordainer of the world and who can miraculously save others. The word 'atheism', however, frequently carries a number of disparaging overtones or implications which are in no way applicable to the Buddha's Teaching. Those who use the word 'atheism', often associate it with a materialistic doctrine that knows nothing beyond this world of the senses and the slight happiness it can bestow. Buddhism advocates nothing of that sort.

There is no justification for branding Buddhists as atheists, nihilists, pagans, heathens or communists just because they do not depend on a Creator God. The Buddhist concept of God is different from that of other religions. Differences in belief do not justify name-calling and slanderous words.

Buddhism agrees with other religions that true and lasting happiness cannot be found in this material world. The Buddha adds that true and lasting happiness cannot be found on the higher or supra-mundane plane of existence to which the name of heavenly or divine world is given. While the spiritual values advocated by Buddhism are orientated to a state transcending the world with the attainment of Nirvana, they do not make a separation between the 'beyond' and the 'here and now'. They have firm roots in the world itself, for they aim at the highest realization in this present existence.

7
What is the Purpose of Life?

To know the purpose of life, you will first have to observe it through your experience and insight. Then, you will discover for yourself its true meaning. Guidelines can be given, but you must create the necessary conditions for the arising of realisation yourself.

There are several prerequisites to the discovery of the purpose of life. First, you must understand the nature of human life. Next, you keep your mind calm and peaceful by adopting religious practices. When these conditions are met, the answer you seek will come like the gentle rain from the sky.

Understanding the Nature of Human Beings

Human beings may be clever enough to land on the moon and discover wondrous things in the universe, but they have yet to delve into the inner workings of their own minds. They have yet to learn how their minds can be developed to the fullest potential so that its true nature can be realised.

As yet, human beings are still wrapped in ignorance. They do not know who they really are or what is expected of them. As a result, they misinterpret everything and act according to their imagination. Is it not conceivable that our entire civilisation is built on this misinterpretation? The failure to understand existence leads us to assume a false identity of a bloated, self-seeking egoist, and to pretend to be what we are not or are unable to be.

People must make an effort to overcome ignorance to arrive at realisation and Enlightenment. All great people are born as human beings from the womb, but they work their way up to greatness. Realisation and Enlightenment cannot be poured into the human heart like water into a tank. Even the Buddha had to cultivate His mind to realise the real nature of human life.

Human beings can be enlightened—become a Buddha—if they wake up from the 'dream' that is created by their own ignorance, and become fully awakened. They must realise that what they are today is the result of an infinite number of repetitions of thoughts and actions. They are not ready-made: they are continually in the process of becoming, always changing. And it is in this charac-teristic of change that their future lies, because it means that it is possible for them to mould their character and destiny through the control of their actions, speech and thoughts. Indeed, they become the thoughts and actions that they choose to perform. They are the highest fruit on the tree of evolution. It is for them to realise their position in existence and to understand the true meaning of life.

Understanding the Nature of Life

Most people dislike facing the facts of life and prefer to lull themselves into a false sense of security by dreaming and imagining. They mistake the shadow for the substance. They fail to realise that life is uncertain, but that death is certain. One way of understanding life is to face and understand death which is nothing more than a temporary end to a temporary existence. Many people do not even like to hear of the word 'death'. They forget that death will come, whether they like it or not. Recollections on death with the right mental attitude can give a person courage and calmness as well as an insight into the nature of existence.

Besides understanding death, we need a better understanding of our life. We are living a life that does not always proceed as smoothly as we would like it to. Very often, we face problems and difficulties. We should not be afraid of them because the penetration into the very nature of these problems and difficulties can provide us with a deeper insight into life. The worldly happiness provided by wealth, luxury, respectable positions in life which most people seek is an illusion because it is impermanent. The fact that the sale of sleeping pills and tranquilizers, admissions to mental hospitals and suicide rates have increased in proportion to modern material progress is enough testimony that we have to go beyond worldly, material pleasure to seek for real happiness. This does not mean of course that Buddhism is a negative religion which condemns the acquisition of wealth. Far from it. The Buddha has expressly encouraged hard work to gain wealth because He said that wealth can give a person the opportunity to lead a decent life and to do meritorious action. What He discouraged was attachment to that wealth and the belief that wealth alone can bring ultimate happiness.

The Need for a Religion

Ounderstand the real purpose of life, it is advisable for a person to choose and follow an ethical-moral system that discourages evil deeds, encourages good, and enables the purification of the mind. For simplicity, we shall call this system 'a religion'.

Religion is an expression of the striving of human beings: it is their greatest source of power, leading them onwards to self-realisation. It has the power to transform a person with negative characteristics into someone with positive qualities. It makes the ignoble, noble; the selfish, unselfish; the proud, humble; the haughty, forbearing; the greedy, benevolent; the cruel, kind; the subjective, objective. Every religion represents, however imperfectly, a reaching upwards to a higher level of being. From the earliest times, religion has been the source of humanity's artistic and cultural inspiration. Although many forms of religion had come into being in the course of history, only to pass away and be forgotten, each one in its time had contributed something towards the sum total of human progress. Christianity helped to civilise the West, and the weakening of its influence has marked a downward trend of the Occidental spirit. Buddhism, which civilised the greater part of the East long before, is still a vital force, and in this age of scientific knowledge is likely to extend and to strengthen its influence. It does not, at any point, come into conflict with modern knowledge, but embraces and transcends all of it in a way that no other system of thought has ever done before or is ever likely to do. Westerners seek to conquer the universe for material ends. Buddhism and Eastern philosophy strive to attain harmony with nature and enhance spiritual satisfaction.

Religion teaches a person how to calm down the senses and make the heart and mind peaceful. The secret of calming down the senses is to eliminate desire which is the root of our disturbances. It is very important for us to have contentment. The more people crave for their property, the more they have to suffer. Property does not give happiness. A great many rich people in the world today are suffering from numerous physical and mental problems. With all the money they have, they cannot buy a solution to their problems. Yet, the poorest people who have learnt to have contentment may enjoy their lives far more than the richest people do. As one rhyme goes:

'Some have too much and yet do crave
I have little and seek no more;
They are but poor though much more they have
And I am rich with little store.
They poor, I rich; they beg, I give;
They lack, I have; they pine, I live.'

Searching for a Purpose in Life

The aim in life varies among individuals. An artist may aim to paint masterpieces that will live long after he is gone. A scientist may want to discover a new phenomenon, formulate a new theory, or invent a new machine. A politician may wish to become a prime minister or a president. A young executive may aim to be a managing director of a multinational company. However, when you ask the artist, scientist, politician and the young executive why they aim thus, they will reply that these achievements will give them a purpose in life and make them happy. But will these achievements bring lasting happiness? Everyone aims for happiness in life, yet they suffer more in the process. 'The value of life lies not in the length of the days, but in the use we make of them. People may live long without doing any service to anybody and thus, live very little'.

Realisation

Once we realise the nature of life (characterised by unsatis-factoriness, change, and egolessness) as well as the nature of greed and the means of getting them satisfied, we can understand the reason why the happiness so desperately sought by many people is so elusive like catching a moonbeam in their hands. They try to gain happiness through accumulation. When they are not successful in accumulating wealth, gaining position, power and honour, and deriving pleasure from sense gratification, they pine and suffer, envying others who are successful in doing so. However, even if they are 'successful' in getting these things, they suffer as well because they then fear losing what they have gained, or their desires have now increased for more wealth, higher position, more power, and greater pleasure. Their desires can never seem to be completely satiated. This is why an understanding of life is important so that we do not waste too much time doing the impossible.

It is here that the adoption of a religion becomes important, since it encourages contentment and urges a person to look beyond the demands of his or her flesh and ego. In a religion like Buddhism, people are reminded that they are the heirs of their karma and the master of their destinies. In order to gain greater happiness, they must be prepared to forego short-term pleasures. If people do not believe in life after death, even then it is enough for them to lead a good, noble life on earth, enjoying a life of peace and happiness here and now, as well as performing actions which are for the benefit and happiness of others. Leading such a positive and wholesome life on earth and creating happiness for oneself and others is much better than a selfish life of trying to satisfy one's ego and greed. If we do not know how to live up to the expectations of others, how can we expect others to live according to our expectations?

If, however, people believe in life after death, then according to the Law of Karma, rebirth will take place according to the quality of their deeds. People who have done many good deeds may be born in favourable conditions where they enjoy wealth and success, beauty and strength, good health, and meet good spiritual friends and teachers. Wholesome deeds can also lead to rebirth in the heavens and other sublime states, while unwholesome deeds lead to rebirth in suffering states. "When people understand the Law of Karma, they will then make the effort to refrain from performing bad actions, and to try to cultivate the good. By so acting, they gain benefits not only in this life, but in many other lives to come.

When they understand the nature of human life, then some important realisations arise. They realise that unlike a rock or stone, a human being possesses the innate potential to grow in wisdom, compassion, and awareness—and be transformed by this self-development and growth. They also understand that it is not easy to be born as a human being, especially one who has the chance to listen to the Dharma. In addition, they are fully aware that life is impermanent, and they should, therefore, strive to practise the Dharma while they are still in a position to do so. They realise that the practice of Dharma is a life-long educative process which enables them to release their true potentials trapped within their mind by ignorance and greed. To experience worldly pleasure there must be external objects or partners but to gain mental happiness it is not necessary to have an external object.

Based on these realisations and understanding,they will then try to be more aware of what and how they think, speak and act. They will consider if their thoughts, speech and actions are beneficial, done out of compassion and have good effects for themselves as well as others. They will realise the true value of walking the road that leads to complete self transformation, which is known to Buddhists as the Noble Eightfold Path. This Path can help people to develop their moral strength *(sila)* through the restraint of negative actions and the cultivation of positive qualities conducive to personal, mental and spiritual growth. In addition, it contains many techniques which they can apply to purify their thoughts, expand the possibilities of the mind, and bring about a complete change towards a wholesome personality. This practice of mental culture *(bhavana)* can widen and deepen the mind to gain a better understanding of the nature and characteristics of phenomena, life and the universe. In short, this leads to the cultivation of wisdom *(pannaa)*. As wisdom grows, so will love, compassion, kindness, and joy. They will have greater awareness of all forms of life and better understanding of their own thoughts, feelings, and motivations.

In the process of self-transformation, people will no longer aspire for a divine birth as their ultimate goal in life. They will then set their goal much higher, and model themselves after the Buddha who has reached the summit of human perfection and attained the ineffable state we call Enlightenment or Nirvana. It is here that we develop a deep confidence in the Triple Gem and adopt the Buddha as our spiritual ideal. We will strive to eradicate greed, develop wisdom and compassion, and to be completely liberated from the bonds of samsara.

Buddhism for Human Beings in Society

There are some who believe that Buddhism is so lofty and sublime a system that it cannot be practised by ordinary men and women in the workaday world. They think that one has to retire to a monastery or to some quiet place if one desires to be a true Buddhist.

This is a sad misconception that comes from a lack of understanding of the Buddhist way of life. People jump to such conclusions after casually reading or hearing something about Buddhism. Some people form their impression of Buddhism after reading articles or books that give only a partial or lopsided view of Buddhism. The authors of such articles and books have only a limited understanding of the Buddha's Teaching. His Teaching is not meant only for monks in monasteries. The Teaching is also for ordinary men and women living at home with their families. The Noble Eightfold Path is the Buddhist way of life that is intended for all people. This way of life is offered to all mankind without any distinction. When four aspects of life i.e., Family life, Business life, Social life and Spiritual life are satisfactorily harmonized, lasting happiness is gained.

The vast majority of people in the world cannot become monks or retire into caves or forests. However noble and pure Buddhism may be, it would be useless to the masses if they could not follow it in their daily life in the modern world. But if you understand the spirit of Buddhism correctly, you can surely follow and practise it while living the life of an ordinary person.

There may be some who find it easier and more convenient to practise Buddhism by living in a remote place; in other words, by cutting themselves off from the society of others. Yet, other people may find that this kind of retirement dulls and depresses their whole being both physically and mentally, and that it may therefore not be conducive to the development of their spiritual and intellectual life.

True renunciation does not mean running away physically from the world. Sariputta, the chief disciple of the Buddha, said that one man might live in a forest devoting himself to ascetic practices, but might be full of impure thoughts and 'defilements'. Another might live in a village or a town, practising no ascetic discipline, but his mind might be pure, and free from 'defilements'. 'Of these two', said Sariputta, 'the one who lives a pure life in the village or town is definitely far superior to, and greater than, the one who lives in the forest.' (Majjhima Nikaya)

The common belief that to follow the Buddha's Teaching one has to retire from a normal family life is a misconception. It is really an unconscious defence against practising it. There are numerous references in Buddhist literature to men and women living ordinary, normal family lives who successfully practised what the Buddha taught and realized Nirvana. vacchagotta the Wanderer, once asked the Buddha directly whether there were laymen and women leading the family life who followed His Teaching successfully and attained the high spiritual states. The Buddha categorically stated that there were many laymen and women leading the family life who had followed His Teaching successfully and attained the high spiritual states.

It may be agreeable for certain people to live a retired life in a quiet place away from noise and disturbances. But it is certainly more praiseworthy and courageous to practise Buddhism living among fellow beings, helping them and offering service to them. It may perhaps be useful in some cases for a person to live in retirement for a time in order to improve the mind and character, as a preli-minary to moral, spiritual and intellectual training, to be strong enough to come out later and help others. But if a person lives all his or her life in solitude, thinking only of personal happiness and salvation, without caring for his or her fellowmen, this surely is not completely in keeping with the Buddha's Teaching which is based on love, compassion and service to others.

One might now ask, 'If a person can follow Buddhism while living the life of an ordinary person, why was the Sangha, the Order of monks, established by the Buddha?' The Order provides an opportunity for those who are willing to devote their lives not only to their own spiritual and intellectual development, but also to the service of others. An ordinary layperson with a family cannot be expected to devote a life to the service of others, whereas a monk or nun, who has no family responsibilities or any other worldly ties, is in a position to devote his or her life 'for the good of the many'. (Dr. Walpola Rahula)

And what is this 'good' that many can benefit from? Monks and nuns cannot give material comfort to a layperson, but they can provide spiritual guidance to those who are troubled by worldly, family, emotional problems and so on. Monks and nuns devote their lives to the pursuit of knowledge of the Dharma as taught by the Buddha. They explain the Teaching in simplified form to the untutored layperson. And if the layperson is well educated, they are there to discuss the deeper aspects of the teaching so that both parties can gain intellectually from the discussion.

In Buddhist countries, the Sangha are largely responsible for the education of the young. As a result of their contribution, Buddhist countries have populations which are literate and well-versed in spiritual values. The Sangha also comfort those who are bereaved and emotionally upset by explaining how all humanity is subject to similar disturbances.

In turn, the layperson is expected to look after the material well being of the Sangha who do not earn income to provide themselves with food, shelter, medicine and clothing. In common Buddhist practice, it is considered meritorious for laypeople to contribute to the well being of the Sangha because by so doing they make it possible for the Sangha to continue to minister to the spiritual needs of the people and to develop their own mental purity.

The Buddhist Way of Life for Householders

The Buddha considered economic welfare as a requisite for human comfort, but moral and spiritual development for a happy, peaceful and contented life.

*Aman** named Dighajanu once visited the Buddha and said, 'venerable Sir, we are ordinary laymen, leading a family life with wife and children. Would the Blessed One teach us some doctrines which will be conducive to our happiness in this world and hereafter?'

The Buddha told him that there are four things which are conducive to a human's happiness in this world. (1) he should be skilled, efficient, earnest, and energetic in whatever profession he is engaged, and he should know it well *{utthana-sampadaa)* (2) he should protect his income, which he has thus earned righteously, with the sweat of his brow *(arakkha-sampadaa);* (3) he should have good friends *(kalyana-mittata)* who are faithful, learned, virtuous, liberal and intelligent, who will help him along the right path away from evil; (4) he should spend reasonably, in proportion to his income, neither too much nor too little, i.e., he should not hoard wealth avariciously nor should he be extravagant—in other words he should live within his means *(sama jivikata).*

Then the Buddha expounds the four virtues conducive to a layman's happiness hereafter: (1) *Saddha:* he should have faith and confidence in moral, spiritual and intellectual values; (2) *Sila:* he should abstain from destroying and harming life, from stealing and cheating, from adultery, from falsehood, and from intoxicating drinks; (3) *Caga:* he should practise charity, generosity, without attachment and craving for his wealth; (4) *Panna:* he should develop wisdom which leads to the complete destruction of suffering, to the realisation of Nirvana.

Sometimes the Buddha even went into details about saving money and spending it, as, for instance, when he told the young man Sigala that he should spend one fourth of his income on his daily expenses, invest half in his business and other activities and put aside one fourth for any emergency.

Once the Buddha told Anathapindika, the great banker, one of His most devoted lay disciples who founded for Him the celebrated jetavana monastery at Savatthi, that a layman who leads an ordinary family life has four kinds of happiness. The first happiness is to enjoy economic security or sufficient wealth acquired by just and righteous means *(atthi-sukha)*; the second is spending that wealth liberally on himself, his family, his friends and relatives, and on meritorious deeds *(bhoga-sukha)*; the third to be free from debts *(anana-sukha)*; the fourth happiness is to live a faultless, and a pure life without committing evil in thought, word or deed *(anavajja-sukha)*.

It must be noted here that first three are economic and material happiness which is not as noble as the spiritual happiness arising out of a faultless and good life.

From the few examples given above, one can see that the Buddha considered economic welfare as a requisite for human happiness, but that He did not recognize progress as real and true if it was only material, devoid of a spiritual and moral foundation. While encouraging material progress, Buddhism always lays great stress on the development of moral and spiritual character for a happy, peaceful and contented society.

Many people think that to be a good Buddhist one must have absolutely nothing to do with the materialistic life. This is not correct. What the Buddha teaches is that while we can enjoy material comforts without going to extremes, we must also conscientiously develop the spiritual aspects of our lives. "While we can enjoy sensual pleasures as laypeople, we should never be unduly attached to them to the extent that they hinder our spiritual progress. Buddhism emphasizes the need for a person to follow the Middle Path. The Buddha's teaching is not based on the obliteration of the world but on the obliteration of ignorance and selfish craving.

8

BUDDHIST MORALITY AND PRACTICE

The world today is in a state of turmoil; valuable ethics are being upturned. The forces of materialistic scepticism have turned their dissecting blades on the traditional concepts of what are considered humane qualities. Yet, any person who cares about culture and civilization should be concerned with practical, ethical issues. For ethics has to do with human conduct. It is concerned about our relationship with ourselves and with our fellow human beings.

The need for ethics arises from the fact that human beings are not perfect by nature: they have to train themselves to be good. Thus morality becomes the most important aspect of living.

Buddhist ethics are not arbitrary standards invented by people for their own utilitarian purpose. Nor are they arbitrarily imposed from without. Laws and social customs do not form the basis of Buddhist ethics. For example, the styles of dress that are suitable for one climate, period or civilisation may be considered indecent in another; but this is entirely a matter of social custom and does not in any way involve ethical considerations. Yet the artificialities of social conventions are continually confused with ethical principles that are valid and unchanging.

Buddhist ethics finds its foundation not on changing social customs but rather on the unchanging laws of nature. Buddhist ethical values are intrinsically a part of nature, and the unchanging law of cause and effect *(karma)*. The simple fact that Buddhist ethics are rooted in natural law makes its principles both useful and acceptable to the modern world. The fact that the Buddhist ethical code was formulated over 2,500 years ago does not detract from its timeless character.

Morality in Buddhism serves the practical purpose of leading people to the final goal of ultimate happiness. On the Buddhist path to Emancipation, each individual is considered responsible for his or her own fortunes and misfortunes. Each individual is expected to work out deliverance through understanding and effort. Buddhist salvation is the result of one's own moral development and can neither be imposed nor granted to one by some external agent. The Buddha's mission was to enlighten beings on the nature of existence and to advise them how best to act for their own happiness and for the benefit of others. Consequently, Buddhist ethics are not commandments which people are compelled to follow. The Buddha had given advice on the conditions which were most wholesome and conducive to long term benefit for self and others. Rather than addressing sinners with such words as 'shameful', 'wicked', 'wretched', 'unworthy', and 'blasphemous' He would merely say, 'You are foolish in acting in such a way since this will bring sorrow upon yourselves and others'.

The theory of Buddhist ethics finds its practical expression in the various precepts. These precepts or disciplines are nothing but general guides to show the direction which we should turn to on our way to final salvation. Although many of these precepts are expressed in a negative form, we must not think that Buddhist morality consists of abstaining from evil without the complement of doing good.

The morality found in all the precepts can be summarized in three simple principles—'To avoid evil; to do good, to purify the mind.' This is the advice given by all the Buddhas. (Dhammapada, 183)

In Buddhism, the distinction between what is good and what is bad is very simple: all actions that have their roots in greed, hatred, and delusion that spring from selfishness foster the harmful delusion of selfhood. These actions are demeritorious or unskilful or bad. They are called Akusala Karma. All those actions which are rooted in the virtues of generosity, love and wisdom, are meritorious—

Kusala Karma. The criteria of good and bad apply whether the actions are of thought, word or deed.

Buddhist Morals are Based on Intention or Volition

'Karma is volition,' says the Buddha. Actions themselves are con-sidered as neither good nor bad but 'only the intention and thought makes them so'. Yet Buddhist ethics does not maintain that a person may commit actions that are conventionally regarded as 'sins' provided that he or she does so with the best of intentions. Had this been its position, Buddhism would have confined itself to questions of psychology and left the uninteresting task of drawing up lists of ethical rules and framing codes of conduct to less emancipated teachings. The connection between thoughts and deeds, between mental and material action is an extension of thought. It is not possible to commit murder with a good heart because taking of life is simply the outward expression of a state of mind dominated by aversion anger, hate or greed. Deeds are condensations of thoughts just as rain is a condensation of vapour. Deeds proclaim from the rooftops of action only what has already been committed in the silent and secret chambers of the heart.

A person who commits an immoral act thereby declares that he or she is not free from unwholesome states of mind. Also, a person who has a purified and radiant mind, who has a mind empty of all defiled thoughts and feelings, is incapable of committing immoral actions.

Buddhist ethics also recognizes the objectivity of moral values.

In other words, the karmic consequences of actions occur in accordance with natural karmic law, regardless of the attitude of the individual or regardless of social attitudes toward the act. For example, drunkenness has karmic consequences; it is a negative action since it promotes one's own unhappiness as well as the unhappiness of others. The karmic effects of drunkenness exist despite what the drunkard or society may think about the habit of drinking. The prevailing opinions and attitudes do not in the least detract from the fact that drunkenness is objectively negative. The consequences – psychological, social, and karmic – make actions moral or immoral – regardless of the mental attitudes of those judging the act. Thus while ethical relativism is recognized, it is not considered as undermining the objectivity of values.

What is Vinaya?

Vinaya is the disciplinary code for self-training laid down by the Buddha for monks and nuns to observe. Vinaya plays a pivotal role to ensure their pure religious way of life.

The Buddha did not formulate the code of discipline in a single exercise. However, He instituted certain rules as and when the need arose. vinaya pitaka and its commentary contain many significant stories about how and why certain rules were laid down by the Buddha. According to the Buddha the best form of vinaya was to discipline the mind, words and action through insight and understanding. The early disciples of the Buddha were highly developed spiritually and they had little need for a set of rules to be imposed upon them. However, as the monastic order (the Sangha) grew in numbers, it attracted many others, some of whom were not so developed spiritually. There arose some problems regarding their conduct and way of life such as taking part in lay activities for their livelihood and yielding to temptations of sense pleasure. Owing to this situation, the Buddha had to lay down guidelines for the monks and nuns to follow so that they could distinguish the difference between the life of monks and laymen. The holy order of the monks and the nuns was comparably very highly organised in relation to other existing ascetic communities at that time.

The Buddha prescribed all the necessary guidance to maintain the holy order in every aspect of living. When the Buddha passed away, these rules were collated so that the Order could be organised around them. The code of conduct prescribed by the Buddha can be divided into two broad areas. These are universal Moral Codes, Lokavajja, most of which are applicable to all members of the Order and lay people alike for leading a religious life. Certain other disciplinary codes or rules which can be instituted to meet the existing cultural and social constraints of the country at any one time are called *Pannatti Vajja.* In the first category are the Universal Laws which restricted all immoral and harmful evil deeds. The second category of rules applied almost directly to the monks and nuns in the observance of manners, traditions, duties, customs and etiquette. Breaking of moral codes pertaining to the Lokavajja creates bad reputation, whereas violation of disciplinary codes based on social conditions do not necessarily create bad karma. However, they are subject to criticism as violation in any form pollute the purity and dignity of the holy Order. These rules were largely based on the socio-cultural situation or way of life prevailing in India 25 centuries ago.

According to the Maha Parinirvana Sutra, the Buddha had proclaimed that some 'minor' rules could be altered or amended to accommodate changes due to time and environment, provided they do not encourage immoral or harmful behaviour. In fact, during the Buddha's time itself, certain minor rules were amended by the monks with His permission. The Buddha also advocated that sick monks and nuns be exempted from certain Vinaya rules. However, once the rules had been enumerated by the disciples in the First Council, convened three months after the passing away of the Buddha, it was decided that all the rules should be maintained without any amendment because no one was certain as to which of the rules should be altered. Finally, the disciples decided to uphold all the precepts prescribed by the Buddha.

Another reason why the early disciples did not agree to change any of the precepts was that there was no reason or occasion for them to do so within such a short period of time after the passing away of the Buddha. This was because, at that time, most of those who had renounced their worldly life had done so with sincerity and conviction. However, when the social conditions started to change and when Buddhism spread to many other parts of India and other countries, the decision made by the disciples not to change any precepts in the First Council became a very big problem because some of the rules could not be adapted to meet the varying way of life and economic circumstances.

As time went on, the rules became fossilized and some orthodox disciples insisted that the rules should be followed strictly to the letter rather than in the spirit. It was precisely to prevent rigid adherence to mere rules of this kind that the Buddha did not appoint a successor to take over after Him. He had said that the understanding of the Dharma and upholding of the Dharma as the master should be enough to help one lead a holy life.

Development of Sangha Community

The Sangha community, in the course of time, evolved themselves into several sects, many of whom, while adhering to some major precepts as laid down by the Buddha, had, however, tended to ignore some of the minor rules. The Theravada sect appeared to be more orthodox, while the Mahayana and some other sects tended to be more liberal in their outlook and religious observances. The Theravada sect tried to observe the Vinaya to the very letter despite of changing circumstances and environment. Minor changes to the precepts had, however, taken place from time to time, but were not officially recognised even amongst the members of the Theravada sect. For instance, the Theravada sect observe strictly the rule of not taking food after the stipulated time of the day. The Theravada sect has not openly acknowledged the fact that certain variations could be allowed under special circumstances. Whilst members of other schools adapt themselves to the wearing of robes with appropriate colour and pattern, the Theravada sect has continued to adhere to the use of the original robes that were traditionally prescribed despite the changed social and climatic conditions. As a result many of the practices of the monkhood are clearly understood only by those who are born into traditional Buddhist cultures. This of course creates many problems when Buddhism is spread to other parts of the world, such as western countries.

Then, there are some monks who insist on observing the very letter of the vinaya code rather than in its spirit, even though such action would embarrass the people around them. For example, more and more Buddhist monks are being invited to western countries where the culture of the people and the climatic conditions are so vastly different from that in Asia. If monks insist on behaving exactly as they did in their homelands their behaviour would appear strange and ridiculous. Rather than earning respect, they would be subject to ridicule and suspicion. Here again the monk must apply his common sense and try not to make a mockery of himself in the eyes of people who belong to a culture different than his own. The important rule to be observed is that no immoral, cruel, harmful and indecent acts are committed and that the sensitivities of others are respected. If the monks can lead their lives as honest, kind, harmless and understanding human beings by maintaining their human dignity and discipline, then such qualities will be appreciated in any part of the world. Maintaining the so-called traditions and customs of their respective countries of origin have little to do with the essence of the Dharma as taught by the Buddha.

Then, there is another problem. Many people, especially those in the West who have accepted the Buddhist way of life, having read the vinaya rules in the texts, think that the monks must follow all the rules without amending them in any part of the world, in exactly the same manner as they were recorded in the texts. We must remember that some of these rules which were practiced in Indian society 25 centuries ago are irrelevant even in Asia today. It must be clearly borne in mind that the Buddha instituted the rules only for the members of the Sangha community who lived in India, the region where He lived. Those monks never had any experience of the way of life in another country. Their main concern was with their spiritual development with the minimum of disruption and annoyance to the society where they lived. Today, monks may experience many other new problems, if they strictly observe all the rules in a country where people cannot appreciate or understand them.

The disciplinary code for lay devotees shows how a

layman can lead a virtuous and noble life without renouncing the worldly life. The Buddha's advice to lay people is contained in such discourses as the Mangala, Parabhava, Sigalovada, Vasala and Vygghapajja and many others.

Many Vinaya rules apply only to those who have renounced the worldly life. Of course a lay person may follow some of the rules if they help to develop greater spirituality.

Changing Society

When society changes, monks cannot remain as traditionalists without adapting to the changes, although they have renounced the worldly life. Sometimes conservative people who cannot understand this need for change criticise monks who adapt to the demands made by social reform. This does not mean of course that monks may change the rules to suit their own whims and fancies. When the monks want to amend even certain minor precepts, they would have to obtain the sanction of a recognised Sangha Council. Individual monks are not at liberty to change any Vinaya rules. Such a Council of Sangha members can also impose certain sanc-tions against monks who have committed serious violations of the disciplinary code and whose behaviour discredits the Sangha. The Buddha instituted the Council to help monks to prevent evil deeds and avoid temptation in a worldly life. The rules were guidelines rather than inviolable laws handed down by some divine authority.

In Asian countries particularly, monks are accorded great respect and reverence. Lay people respect them as Dharma masters and as religious people who have sacrificed the worldly life in order to lead a holy life. Monks are expected to devote themselves to the study and practice of the Dharma and not earn a living. Laypeople, therefore, see to their material well being while they in turn look to the monks for their spiritual needs.

As such, monks need to conduct themselves in such a way that will earn them the respect and reverence of the public. If, for example, a monk is seen in a disreputable place, he will be criticized even if he is not involved in any immoral action. Therefore, it is the duty of the monks to avoid certain uncongenial surroundings so as to maintain the dignity of the holy Order.

If the monks do not uphold their disciplinary code, lay people lose their confidence to attend to them. There are many instances recorded in the Buddhist Texts when even during the Buddha's time, lay devotees had refused to look after arrogant, quarrelsome or irresponsible monks. Monks can be criticized for carrying out certain worldly activities which only lay people are at liberty to do.

Dharma and Vinaya

Many people have not yet realised that the Dharma, the Truth expounded by the Buddha, is not changeable under any circum-stances. Certain Vinaya rules are also included in this same category and they are not subject to change. But some other Vinaya rules are subject to change so as to avoid certain unnecessary inconveniences. Dharma and Vinaya are not the same. Certain monks try to observe certain traditions rigidly as if they are important religious principles although others cannot find any religious significance or implication in their practices. At the same time some selfish and cunning persons may even try to maintain certain outward manifestations of purity, in order to mislead innocent devotees to regard them as pious and sincere monks. Many so called Buddhist practices in Asian countries that monks and others follow are not necessarily religious precepts but traditional customs upheld by the people at that time. On the other hand, certain manners introduced for monks to observe as disciplines truly help to maintain the dignity and serenity of the holy Order. Although religious traditions and customs can create a congenial atmosphere for spiritual development, some Vinaya rules need to be amended according to changing social conditions. If this is not done, monks will have to face numerous problems in their association with the public in the modern society and their way of life because it is a mockery in the eyes of the public.

Some lay people criticize monks for handling money. It is difficult to carry out their religious activities and to be active in modern society without dealing with money. What a monk must do is to be unattached to the money or property as personal belongings. That is what the Buddha meant. Of course, there may be some who deliberately misinterpret the rules to suit their material gain. They will have to bear the consequences of facing difficulties in gaining spiritual development.

Of course, those who choose to confine themselves to an isolated area for meditation to gain peace of mind, should be able to carry out their religious duties without hindrance from worldly concerns which can become burdensome. But they must first ensure that they have enough supporters to attend to their basic needs like food, shelter and medicine. While there can be such monks who wish to retire completely from society there must be enough monks in society to attend to the numerous religious needs of the general public. Otherwise, people may conclude that Buddhism cannot contribute very much in their day to day lives and for their well-being.

Characteristics of a Monk

Among the salient characteristics of a monk are purity, voluntary poverty, humility, simplicity, selfless service, self-control, patience, compassion and harmlessness. He is expected to observe the four kinds of Higher Morality—namely:

Patimokkha Sila: The Fundamental Moral Code (major offences related to immoral, cruel, harmful and selfish activities).

Indriyasamvara Sila: Morality pertaining to sense-restraint.

Ajivaparisuddhi Sila: Morality pertaining to purity of livelihood.

Paccayasannissita Sila: Morality pertaining to the use of requisites pertaining to life.

These four kinds of morality are collectively called *Sila-Visuddhi* (Purity of Virtue).

When a person enters the Order and receives his ordination he is called a *Samanera*—Novice Monk. He is bound to observe Ten Samanera Precepts with certain disciplinary codes for leading a monastic life until he receives his higher ordination— *Upasampada* and becomes a Bhikkhu or full fledged monk. A novice nun is called a samaneri, and a full fledged one is called a bhikkhuni.

A bhikkhu or monk is bound to observe the above-mentioned four kinds of higher morality which comprise 227 Precepts apart from several other minor ones. The four major ones which deal with celibacy and abstinence from stealing, murder, and false claims to higher spirituality must strictly be observed. If he violates any one of these, a monk is regarded as a "defeated" person in the Sangha community. He will be deprived of certain religious rights by the Sangha community. In the case of other rules which he violates, he has to face many other consequences and make amends according to the gravity of the offence.

There are no vows or laws for a bhikkhu. He becomes

a bhikkhu of his own accord in order to lead a Holy Life for as long as he likes.

There is therefore no need for him to feel trapped by a vow he made earlier and to be hypocritical because he alone can decide whether or not he wishes to obey the rules. He is at liberty to leave the Order at any time and can lead a lay Buddhist way of life when he feels it is inconvenient. He can also return to the monastic life at any time he desires. The same general rules apply for bhikkhunis as well.

Ten Meritorious and Ten Evil Actions

The performance of good actions gives rise to merit *(punnaa)*, a quality which cleanses the mind. If the mind is unchecked, it has the tendency to be ruled by evil tendencies, leading one to perform bad deeds and get into trouble. Merit purifies the mind of the evil tendencies of greed, hatred and delusion. The greedy mind encourages a person to desire, accumulate and hoard; the hating mind drags him or her to dislike and anger; and the deluded mind makes one become entangled in greed and hatred, thinking that these evil roots are right and worthy. Demeritorious deeds give rise to more suffering and reduce the opportunities for a person to know and practise the Dharma.

Merit is important to help us along our journey through life. It is connected with what are good and beneficial to oneself and others, and can improve the quality of the mind. While the material wealth a person gathers can be lost by theft, flood, fire, confiscation, etc., the benefit of merits follow from life to life and cannot be lost, although it can be exhausted if no attempts are made to perform more merits. A person will experience happiness here and now as well as hereafter through the performance of merit.

Merit is a great facilitator: It opens the doors of opportunity everywhere. A meritorious person will succeed in whatever venture he or she puts effort into. If one wishes to do business, one will meet with the right contacts and friends. If one wishes to be a scholar, one will be awarded with scholarships and supported by academic mentors. If one wishes to progress in meditation, one will meet with a skillful meditation teacher who guides one through one's spiritual development. Dreams will be realised through the grace of the treasury of merit. It is merit which enables a person to be reborn in the heavens, and provides him or her with the right conditions and support for the attainment of Nirvana.

There are several rich fields of merit (recipients of the deed) which give rise to bountiful results to the performer of the good deed. Just as some soil can yield a better harvest (say black fertile soil compared to stony soil), a good deed performed to benefit some persons can give rise to more merits than if it is given to others. The rich fields of merits include the Sangha or holy people, mother, father and the needy. Good deeds performed to these persons will manifest in many ways and be the fountainhead of many wondrous results.

The Buddha taught ten meritorious deeds for us to perform in order to gain a happy and peaceful life as well as to develop knowledge and understanding. The ten meritorious deeds are:

1. Generosity *Dana*
2. Morality *Sila*
3. Mental culture *Bhavana*
4. Reverence or respect *Apachayana*
5. service in helping others *Veyyavaccha*
6. Transference of merits to others *Pattidana*

7. Rejoicing in the merits of others *Pattanumodana*
8. Preaching and teaching the Dharma *Dharma desana*
9. Listening to the Dharma *Dharma savana*
10. Straightening one's views *Ditthijju*

The performance of these ten meritorious deeds will not only benefit oneself, but others as well, besides giving benefits to the recipients. Moral conduct benefits all beings with whom one comes into contact. Mental culture brings peace to others and inspires them to practise the Dharma. Reverence gives rise to harmony in society, while service improves the lives of others. sharing merits with others shows that one is concerned about others' welfare, while rejoicing in others' merits encourages others to perform more merits. Teaching and listening to the Dharma are important factors for happiness for both the teacher and listener, while encouraging both to live in line with Dharma. straightening one's views enables a person to show to others the beauty of Dharma. In the Dharma-pada, the Buddha taught:

'Should a person perform good,
He should do it again and again;
He should find pleasure therein;
For blissful is the accumulation of good.'

'Think not lightly of good, saying,
'It will not come near to me—
Even by the falling of drops a water-jar is filled.
Likewise the wise man, gathering little by little,
Fills himself with good.'

Ten Evil Deeds

There are ten demeritorious deeds from which people are advised to keep away. These deeds are rooted in greed, hatred and delusion, and will bring suffering to others but especially to oneself in this life and later lives. When a person understands the Law of Karma and realises that bad deeds bring bad results, he or she will then practise Right understanding and avoid performing these actions.

There are three bodily actions which are karmically unwhole-some. They are: (1) Killing of living beings, (2) Stealing, and (3) Illicit sexual behaviour. These bodily deeds correspond to the first three of the Five Precepts for people to follow.

The effects of killing to the performer of the deed are short life span, ill health, constant grief due to the separation from the loved ones, and living in constant fear. The bad consequences of stealing are poverty, misery, disappointment, and a dependent livelihood. The bad consequences of sexual misconduct are having many enemies, always being hated, and union with undesirable wives and husbands.

The Four verbal actions which are karmically unwholesome are: (1) Lying, (2) slander and tale-bearing, (3) Harsh speech, and (4) Frivolous and meaningless talk. Except for lying, the other unwholesome deeds performed by speech may be viewed as extensions of the Fourth Precept.

The bad consequences of lying to the one who performs the deed are being subject to abusive speech and vilification, untrustworthiness, and physical unpleasantness. The bad effect of slandering is losing one's friends without any sufficient cause. The results of harsh speech are being detested by others and having a harsh voice. The inevitable effects of frivolous talk are defective bodily organs and speech to which no one pays attention.

The three other demeritorious deeds are performed by the mind, and they are as follows: (1) Covetousness, or eager desires especially of things belonging to others, (2) Ill-will, and (3) Wrong views. These three deeds correspond to the three evil roots of greed, hatred and delusion. The non-observance of the Fifth Precept of abstention from intoxicants can not only lead to the performance of these three demeritorious mental actions after the mind is intoxicated, but also the other demeritorious deeds performed by body and speech.

The undesirable result of covetousness is the non-fulfilment of one's wishes. The consequences of ill will are ugliness, manifold diseases, and having a detestable nature. Finally, the consequences of false view are having gross desires, lack of wisdom, being of dull wit, having chronic diseases and blameworthy ideas.

A person should always perform good actions and restrain him or herself from doing evil actions. if, however, a person has performed an evil action, it is necessary to realise where wrong has been done and make an effort not to repeat the mistake. This is the true meaning of repentence, and in this way only will a person progress along the noble path to emancipation.

Praying for forgiveness is meaningless if, after the prayer is made, a person repeats the evil action again and again. Who is there to 'wash away a person's sins' except oneself? This has to begin with realisation, the wonderful cleansing agent. First, one realises the nature of the deed and the extent of the harm incurred. Next, one realises that this deed is unwholesome, learns from it, and makes the resolution not to repeat it. Then, one performs many good deeds to benefit the affected party as well as others, as much as possible. in this way, the effect of a bad deed is overcome with a shower of good deeds.

No wrong doer, according to Buddhism, is beyond redemption or rehabilitation, especially with realisation and Right Effort. To be seduced into believing that a person can 'wash away' his or her bad deeds through some other 'miraculous' way is not only a mere superstition, but worse, it is also not useful particularly to the spiritual development of the person. it will only cause one to continue to remain ignorant and morally complacent. This misplaced belief can, in fact, do a person much more harm than the effects of the wrong deed which is feared so much.

Precepts

By observing precepts, not only do you cultivate your moral strength, but you also perform the highest service to your fellow beings to live in peace.

EVERY country or society has its code of what is considered to be moral within its own social context. These codes are often linked to the society's interest and its legal system. An action is considered right so long as it does not break the law and transgress public or individual sensitivities. These social codes are flexible and amended from time to time to suit changing circumstances. important as they are to society, these standards cannot serve as a reliable guide to some absolute principles of morality which can be applied universally and for all time.

By contrast, the Buddhist code of morality is not the invention of human minds. They are not based on tribal ethics which were eventually replaced by humanistic codes which are commonly practiced today. Buddhist morality is based on the universal law of cause and effect (Karma), and considers a 'good' or 'bad' action in terms of the manner it affects oneself and others. An action, even if it brings benefit to oneself, cannot be considered a good action if it causes physical and mental pain to another being.

Buddhist morality addresses a very common, yet crucial question: How can we judge if an action is good or bad? The answer, according to Buddhism, is a simple one. The quality of an action hinges on the intention or motivation *(cetana)* from which it originates. if a person performs an action out of greed, hatred, and delusion, his action is considered to be unwholesome. On the other hand, if he performs an action out of love, charity, and wisdom, his action is a wholesome one. Greed, Hatred and Delusion are known as the 'Three Evil Roots', while love, charity and wisdom as 'the three beneficial roots'. The word 'root' refers to the intention from which an action originates. Therefore, no matter how a person tries to disguise the nature of an action, the truth can be found by examining thoughts which gave rise to that action because the mind is the source of all speech and action.

In Buddhism, a person's first duty is to cleanse him or her self of the mental defilements of greed, hatred and ignorance. The reason for doing this is not because of fear or desire to please some divine beings, because if it were so, a person would be considered to be still lacking in wisdom. He or she would be only acting out of fear like the little child who behaves well because he or she is afraid of being punished for being naughty. Buddhists should act out of understanding and wisdom. They perform wholesome deeds because they realise that by so doing they develop their moral strength which provides the foundation for spiritual growth, leading to Liberation. in addition, they realise that their happiness and suffering are self-created through the operation of the Law of Karma. To minimise the occurrence of troubles and problems in their lives, they make the effort to refrain from doing evil. They perform good actions because they know that these will bring them peace and happiness. since everyone seeks happiness in life, and since it is possible for each individual to provide the condition for happiness, then there is every reason to do good and avoid evil. Furthermore, the uprooting of mental defilements, the source of all anti-social acts, will bring great benefits to others in society. Therefore in helping oneself spiritually, one helps others to live peacefully.

Five Precepts

Lay Buddhist morality is embodied in the Five Precepts, which may be considered at two levels. First, it enables people to live together in civilized communities with mutual trust and respect. Second, it is the starting point for the spiritual journey towards Liberation. unlike commandments, which are supposedly divine laws imposed on people, precepts are accepted voluntarily by the people, especially when they realise the usefulness of adopting some training rules for disciplining the body, speech and mind. understanding, rather than fear of punishment, is the reason for following the precepts. Good Buddhists should remind themselves to follow the Five Precepts daily. They are:

i take the training precept to refrain from:

1. killing living creatures
2. taking what is not given
3. sexual misconduct
4. false speech
5. taking intoxicating drugs and liquor

Besides understanding the Five Precepts merely as a set of rules of abstention, Buddhists should remind themselves that through the precepts they practice the Five Ennoblers as well. While the Five Precepts tell them what not to do, the Five Ennoblers tell them which qualities to cultivate, namely, loving kindness, renunciation, contentment, truthfulness, and mindfulness. When people observe the First Precept of not killing, they control their hatred and cultivate loving kindness. in the second Precept, they control their greed and cultivate their renunciation or nonattachment. They control sensual lust and cultivate their contentment in the Third Precept. in the Fourth Precept, they abstain from false speech and cultivate truthfulness, while they abstain from unwholesome mental excitement and develop mindfulness through the Fifth Precept. Therefore, when they understand the ennoblers, they will realise that the observance of the Five Precepts does not cause them to be withdrawn, self-critical and negative, but to be positive personalities filled with love and care as well as other qualities accruing to one who leads a moral life.

The precepts form the basis of practice in Buddhism. The purpose is to eliminate crude passions that are expressed through thought, word and deed. The precepts are also an indispensable basis for people who wish to cultivate their minds. Without some basic moral code, the power of meditation can often be applied for some wrong and selfish ends.

Eight Precepts

In many Buddhist countries, it is customary among the devotees to observe the Eight Precepts on certain days of the month, such as the full moon and new moon days. These devotees will come to the temple early in the morning and spend twenty-four hours there, observing the precepts. By observing the Eight Precepts, they cut themselves off from their daily life which is beset with material and sensual demands. The purpose of observing the Eight Precepts is to develop relaxation and tranquility, to train the mind, and to develop oneself spiritually.

During this period of observing the precepts, devotees spend their time reading religious books, listening to the Teachings of the Buddha, meditating, and also helping with the religious activities of the temple. The following morning, they revert from the Eight Precepts to the Five Precepts intended for daily observance, and return home to resume their normal life.

The Eight Precepts are to abstain from:

1. Killing;

2. Stealing;

3. Sexual acts;

4. Lying;

5. Taking intoxicants;

6. Taking food after noonday;

7. Dancing, singing, music, unseemly shows, the use of garlands, perfumes, and things that tend to beautify, and adorn the person.Some people find it hard to understand the significance of a few of these precepts. They think that Buddhists are against dancing, singing, music, the cinema, perfume, ornaments and luxurious things. There is no rule in Buddhism which states that lay Buddhists must abstain from these things. The people who choose to abstain from these entertainments are devout Buddhists who observe the precepts only for a short period as a way of self-discipline. The reason for keeping away from these entertainments and ornamen-tations is to calm down the senses even for a few hours and to train the mind so as not to be enslaved to sensual pleasures. it helps one to realise that these adornments only increase one's belief in a permanent self or ego. They increase the passions of the mind and arouse emotions which hinder spiritual development. By occasionally restraining themselves, people

will make progress towards overcoming their weaknesses and exercise greater control over themselves. However, Buddhists do not condemn these entertainments as wrong things. it is important for us to appreciate that the practice of these precepts are taken, not out of fear of transgression, but out of the understanding that they are beneficial for us to be humble and to lead a simple lives.

Observance of precepts (both the Five and Eight Precepts) when performed with an earnest and willing mind is certainly a meritorious act. it brings great benefits to this life and the lives hereafter especially in developing the wisdom to see things as they really are. Therefore, people should try their best to observe the precepts with under-standing and as often as they can.

Loving-Kindness

In the world today, there is sufficient material wealth and intellectual development. Although we must admit that it is unevenly distributed, we certainly have an adequate supply of advanced intellectuals, brilliant writers, talented speakers, philosophers, psychologists, scientists, religious advisors, wonderful poets and powerful world leaders. in spite of these intellectuals, there is no real peace and security in the world today. something must be lacking. What is lacking is spirituality and loving-kindness or goodwill amongst mankind.

Material gain in itself can never bring lasting happiness and peace. Peace must first be established in our own hearts before we can bring peace to others and to the world at large. The real way to achieve peace is to follow the advice given by the Buddha. In order to practise loving-kindness, one must first practise the noble principle of non-violence and must always be ready to overcome selfishness and to show the correct path to others. The struggle is not to be done by torturing the physical body, because wickedness is not in our body but in the mind. Non-violence is a more effective weapon to fight against evil than retaliation. The very nature of retaliation is to increase wickedness.

in order to practise loving-kindness, one must also be free from selfishness. Much of the love in this world is self centred, which means only a love of one's own self or seeking to benefit one's own self.

'Not out of love is the husband loved; but the husband is loved for love of self. Children are loved by the parents, not out of love for the children, but for love of self. The gods are loved, not out of love for the gods, but for love for self. Not out of love is anybody loved, but for love of self are they loved.'

The Buddha teaches another kind of love. According to the Buddha we should learn how to practise selfless love to maintain real peace while at the same time working for our own salvation. This is called altruistic love: where a self that does the loving is not identified. Just as suicide kills physically, selfishness kills spiritual progress. Loving-kindness in Buddhism is neither emotional or selfish. it is loving-kindness that radiates through the purified mind after eradicating hatred, jealousy, cruelty, enmity and grudges. According to the Buddha, Metta—Loving-kindness is the most effective method to maintain purity of mind and to purify the mentally polluted atmosphere. This is the kind of love a Bodhisatva practises. The love of a Buddha or an Arahant is pure because it cannot differentiate between that which is loved and that which loves.

The word 'love' is used to cover a very wide range of emotions human beings experience. Buddhists differentiate between "Prema" selfish love and "Karuna" or "Metta" which is pure altruistic love. Emphasis on the base animal lust of one sex for another or between beings of the same sex has much debased the concept of a feeling of amity towards another being. According to Buddhism, there are many types of emotions, all of which come under the general term 'love'. First of all, there is selfish love and there is selfless love. One has selfish love when one is concerned only with the satisfaction to be derived for oneself without any consideration for the partner's needs or feelings. Jealousy is usually a symptom of selfish love. selfless love, on the other hand, is felt when one person surrenders his or her whole being for the good of another – parents feel such love for their children. usually human beings feel a mixture of both selfless and selfish love in their relationships with each other. For example, while parents make enormous sacrifices for their children, they usually expect something in return, so that there is both selfishness and selflessness.

Another kind of love, but closely related to the above, is fraternal love or the love between friends, what we call "Maitri" or Mitra. in a sense, this kind of love can also be considered selfish because the love is limited to particular people and does not encompass others. in another category we have sexual love, where partners are drawn towards each other through physical attraction. it is the kind that is most exploited by modern entertainment and it can cover anything from uncomplicated teenage infatuations to the most complex of relationships between adults.

On a scale far higher than these, is universal love, also called Metta. This all-embracing love for all sentient beings is the great virtue expressed by the Buddha. Lord Buddha, for example, renounced His kingdom, family and pleasures so that He could strive to find a way to release mankind from an existence of suffering.

In order to gain His Enlightenment, He had to struggle for many countless lives. A lesser being would have been disheartened, but not the Buddha-elect. It is for this He is called 'The Compassionate One'. The Buddha's boundless love extended not only to human beings but all living creatures. it was not emotional or selfish, but a love without frontiers, without discrimination. unlike the other kinds of love, universal love can never end in disappointment or frustration because it expects no reward and does not even identify the one who loves. it creates more happiness and satisfaction. Those who cultivate universal love will also cultivate sympathetic joy and equanimity and they will then have attained to the sublime state.

In his book, The Buddha's Ancient Path, Ven. Piyadassi says: 'Love is an active force. Every act of the loving one is done with the stainless mind to help, to succour, to cheer, to make the paths of others easier, smoother and more adapted to the conquest of sorrow, the winning of the highest bliss.'

'The way to develop love is through thinking out the evils of hate, and the advantages of non-hate; through thinking out according to actuality, according to karma, that really there is none to hate, that hate is a foolish way of feeling which breeds more and more darkness, that obstructs right understanding. Hate restricts; love releases. Hatred strangles; love enfranchises. Hatred brings remorse; love brings peace. Hatred agitates; love quietens, stills, calms. Hatred divides; love unites. Hatred hardens; love softens. Hatred hinders; love helps. And thus through a correct study and appreciation of the effects of hatred and the benefits of love, should one develop love.'

In the Metta Sutra, the Buddha has expounded the nature of love in Buddhism. 'Just as a mother would protect her only child even at the risk of her own life, even so, let one cultivate a boundless heart towards all beings. Let his thoughts of boundless love pervade the whole world, above, below and across without any obstruction, without any hatred, without any enmity.'

if our enemies point out our mistakes and weaknesses, we must be grateful to them.

The essence of true charity is to give something without expecting anything in return for the gift. If a person expects some material benefit to arise from the gift, he or she is only performing an act of bartering and not charity. A charitable person should not make other people feel indebted or use charity as a way of exercising control over them. One should not even expect others to be grateful, for most people are forgetful and not necessarily ungrateful. The act of true charity is wholesome, has no strings attached, and leaves both the giver and the recipient free from obligation.

The meritorious deed of charity is highly praised in every religion. Those who have enough to maintain themselves should think of others and extend their generosity to deserving cases. Among people who practise charity, there are some who give as a means of attracting others into their religion or politics. such an act of giving which is performed with the ulterior motive of conversion cannot really be said to be true charity.

Those who are on their way to spiritual growth must try to reduce their own selfishness and strong desire for acquiring more and more. They should reduce their strong attachment to possessions which, if they are not mindful, can enslave them to greed. What they own or have should instead be used for the benefit and happiness of others: their loved ones as well as those who need help.

When giving, they should not perform charity as an act of their body alone, but with their heart and mind as well. There must be joy in every act of giving. A distinction can be made between giving as a normal act of generosity and dana. In the normal act of generosity we must give out of compassion and kindness when we realise that someone else is in need of help, and we are in the position to offer that help. When we perform dana, we give as a means of cultivating charity as a virtue and of reducing selfishness and craving. More importantly, dana is given with understanding, meaning that one gives to reduce and eradicate the idea of self which is the cause of greed, acquisitiveness and suffering. One exercises wisdom when one recalls that dana is a very important quality to be practised by every Buddhist, and is the first perfection (paramita) practised by the Buddha in many of His previous births before His Enlightenment. A person also performs dana in appreciation of the great qualities and virtues of the Triple Gem.

There are many things which we can give. We can give material things: food for the hungry, and money and clothes to the poor. We can also give our knowledge, skill, time, energy or effort to projects that can benefit others. We can provide a sympathetic ear and good counsel to a friend in trouble. We can restrain ourselves from killing other beings, and by so doing perform a gift of life to the helpless beings which would have otherwise been killed. We can also give a part of our body for the sake of others, such as donating blood, eyes, kidney, heart, etc. some who seek to practise this virtue or are moved by great compassion or concern for others may also be prepared to sacrifice their own lives. In His previous births, the Bodhisatva had many a time given away parts of His body for the sake of others. He also sacrificed His life for the sake of others and to restore the other's lives, so great was His generosity and compassion.

But the greatest testimony to the Buddha's great compassion is His priceless gift to humanity—the Dharma which can liberate all beings from suffering. To the Buddhist, the highest gift of all is the gift of Dharma. This gift has great powers to change a life. When people receive the Dharma with a pure mind and practise the Truth with earnestness, they cannot fail to change. They will experience greater happiness, peace and joy in their heart and mind. if they were once cruel, they become compassionate. if they were once revengeful, they become forgiving. Through Dharma, the hateful becomes more compassionate, the greedy more generous, and the restless more serene. When a person has tasted Dharma, not only will happiness be experience here and now, but also in the lives hereafter.

Buddhist Attitude towards Human Organ Donations

From the Buddhist point of view, the donation of organs after one's death for the purpose of restoring the life of another human being clearly constitutes an act of charity – which forms the basis or foundation of a spiritual or religious way of life.

Dana is the Pali term in Buddhism for charity or generosity. The perfection of this virtue consists of its practice in three ways, namely:

1. the giving or sharing of material things or worldly possessions;

2. the offering of one's own bodily organs; and

3. the offering of one's services for a worthy cause to save the life even at the risk of sacrificing one's own life for the well being and happiness of others in need.

It is through such acts of charity that one is able to reduce one's own selfish motives from the mind and begin to develop and cultivate the great virtues of loving kindness, compassion and wisdom.

The teaching of the Buddha is for the purpose of reducing suffering here and now, and to pave the way for the complete cessation of all forms of suffering.

The fear to participate in a noble act such as that of

organ donation lies primarily in a lack of understanding of the real nature of existence.

There are some people who believe that when any part of their body or organ is removed, they will have to go without that organ in their next life or that they will not be eligible to enter the kingdom of heaven. There is no rational basis to such ideas.

From the Buddhist point of view, death takes place when one's consciousness leaves the disintegrating material body. And, it is that relinking of consciousness, which determines one's next life. Some religionists may call this relinking consciousness a "soul", while others may call it "spirit" or "mental energy". "Whatever term is use, it is clear that it has nothing to do with material components of the body which subject are subject to—and which return to their respective sources of energy. The earth element returns to the soil; the water element returns to the streams, and the heat and elements return to the atmosphere. No matter how well the body is preserved, whether in a metal or wooden coffin, decomposition of the body is inevitable. it is only the consciousness, which goes on to the new rebirth.

Instead of allowing the organ to rot away and go to waste, today's technology and surgical methods have enabled their component structures such as the heart and other organs to be used or transplant to restore life.

With the ever-increasing number of organ failure occurring in the country, the time has come for our more understanding members of the public to come forward and volunteer to donate their organs after their death for a worthy cause.

it is the duty of all understanding people to join in this noble cause to help to alleviate suffering humanity. some time ago there was a car sticker which said, "Leave your organs behind, God known we need them here".

The Buddhist Attitude to Animal Life

If we believe that animals were created by someone for the benefit of men, it would follow that men were also created for animals since some animals do eat human flesh as part of their nature.

ANIMALS are said to be conscious only of the present. They live with no concern for the past or future. it is like little children who seem to have no notion of the future. They also live in the present until their faculties of memory and imagination are developed. self-consciousness is a faculty which comes with maturity.

Human beings possess the faculty of reasoning. The gap between human being and animal widens only to the extent that we develop our reasoning faculty and act accordingly. Buddhists accept that animals not only possess instinctive power but also, to a lesser degree, thinking power. But they can use their instinct from birth only to find their food, shelter, protection and sensual pleasure.

In some respects, animals are superior to human beings. Dogs have a keener sense of hearing and smelling; insects have a keener sense of smell; hawks are speedier; eagles can see a greater distance. undoubtedly, we are wiser; but we have so much to learn from the ants and bees. Much of the animal is still in us. But we also have much more: we have the potential for spiritual development.

Buddhism cannot accept that animals were created by someone to benefit human beings; if animals were created for them then it could follow that human beings were also created for animals since there are some animals which eat human flesh because it is in their nature to eat the flesh of living beings.

Buddhists are encouraged to love all living beings and not to restrict their concern only for the welfare of human beings. They should practise loving kindness towards every living being. The Buddha's advice is that it is not right for us to take away the life of any living being since every living being has a right to exist. Animals also have fear and pain as do human beings. it is wrong to take away their lives or hurt them or instill fear in them. We should not misuse our intelligence and strength to destroy animals even though they may sometimes be perceived as a nuisance to us. Animals need our sympathy. Destroying them is not the only way to get rid of them. Every living being is contributing something to maintain this world. it is unfair for us to deprive their living rights.

'We can hardly speak of morals in relation to creatures we systematically devour, mostly singed but sometimes raw. There are men and women who practise horse love, dog love, cat love, bird love. But these very same people would take a deer or a calf by its neck, slit its throat, drink the blood straight away or in a pudding, and bite off the flesh. And who is to say that a horse they cherish is nobler than a deer they feed on? Indeed, there are people who eat cats, dogs and horses but would use a cow only as a work animal and the dogs to protect them and their properties.'

Some cry over a little bird or goldfish that expired; others travel long distances to catch fish on a nasty hook for food or mere pleasure or to shoot birds for fun. some go into deep jungle and to other countries for hunting animals as game while others spend a lot to keep the same animals at home as their pets. Some keep frogs to foretell the weather; others cut off their legs and fry them. some tenderly tend birds in gilded cages; others serve them for breakfast. It is all quite confusing.

Every religion advises us to love our fellow humans.

some even teach us to love them more if they belong to the same religion. But Buddhism is supreme in that it teaches us to show equal care and compassion for each and every creature in the universe. The destruction of any creature represents a disturbance of the Universal order.

The Buddha was very clear in His teachings against any form of cruelty to any living being. One day the Buddha saw a man preparing to make an animal sacrifice. on being asked why he was going to kill innocent animals, the man replied that it was because it would please the gods. The Buddha then offered Himself as the sacrifice, saying that if the life of an animal would please the gods then the life of a human being, more valuable, should please the gods even more. Needless to say, the man was so moved by the Buddha's practical gesture that he gave up the animal sacrifice and accepted the Buddha's Teaching.

Human cruelty towards animals is another expression of our uncontrolled greed. Today we destroy animals and deprive them of their natural rights for our convenience. But we are already beginning to pay the price for this selfish and cruel act. our environment is threatened and if we do not take stern measures for the survival of other creatures, our own existence on this earth may not be guaranteed.

it is true that the existence of certain creatures is a threat to human existence. But we never consider that human beings are the greatest threat to every living being on this earth in the water and in the air whereas the existence of other creatures is a threat only to certain living beings, and even so, they do not pose a threat of extinction, because they take only enough to survive, never for pleasure or uncontrolled greed.

Since every creature contributes something for the maintenance of the planet and atmosphere, destroying them is not the solution to overcome our problems and needs.

We should take other measures to maintain the balance of nature.

The Need for Tolerance Today

'If a person foolishly does me wrong, I will return to him the protection of my boundless love. The more evil that comes from him the more goodwill go from me. I will always give off only the fragrance of goodness.' (Buddha)

PEOPLE today are restless, weary, filled with fear and discontentment. They are intoxicated with the desire to gain fame, wealth and power. They crave for gratification of the senses. People are passing their days in fear, suspicion and insecurity. In this time of turmoil and crisis, it becomes difficult for people to coexist peacefully with their fellow beings. There is therefore, a great need for tolerance and understanding in the world so that peaceful co-existence among the people of the world can be possible.

The world has bled and suffered from the disease of dogmatism and of intolerance. The soil of many countries today is soaked with the blood spilled on the altar of various political struggles, as the skies of earlier millennia were covered with the smoke of burning martyrs of various faiths. Whether in religion or politics people have been conscious of a mission to achieve power and have been aggressive towards other ways of life. Indeed, the intolerance of the crusading spirit has spoiled the records of religions.

Let us look back at the past century of highly publicized 'Progress'—a century of gadgets and inventions. The array of new scientific and technical inventions is dazzling—telephones, electric motors, aeroplanes, radios, television, computers, space ships, satellites and electronic devices. Yet, in the same century the children of the earth who have developed all these inventions as the ultimate in progress, were the same people who butchered millions of others with bayonets or bullets or bombs. Amidst all the great 'progress', where did the spirit of tolerance stand? Where is the love that many religions preach?

Today people are interested in exploring outer space. But they are totally unable to live as neighbours in peace and harmony on the earth. The fear that humans will eventually desecrate the moon and other planets is today very real.

For the sake of material gain, modern people violate nature. Their mental activities are so preoccupied with satisfying their pleasure that they are unable to focus on or even understand the purpose of life. This unnatural behaviour of present human beings is the result of their wrong conception of human life and its ultimate aim. We create more the frustration, fear, insecurity, intolerance and violence.

in fact, today intolerance is still practised in the name of religion. People merely talk of religion and promise to provide short cuts to paradise, they are not interested in practising it. If Christians live by the Sermon on the Mount, if Buddhists follow the Noble Eightfold Path, if Muslims really follow the concept of Brotherhood and if the Hindus shape their life in oneness, definitely there will be peace and harmony in this world. in spite of these invaluable Teachings of the great religious teachers, people have still not realised the value of tolerance. The intolerance that is practised in the name of religion is most disgraceful and deplorable.

The Buddha's advice is 'Let us live happily, not hating those who hate us. Among those who hate us, let us live free from hatred. Let us live happily and free from ailment. Let us live happily and be free from greed; among those who are greedy'.

Buddhist Funeral Rites

AS practised in many Buddhist countries, a Buddhist funeral is a simple, solemn and dignified service. unfortunately, some people have included many unnecessary, extraneous items and superstitious practices into the funeral rites. The extraneous items and practices vary according to the traditions and customs of the people. Rituals were introduced in the past by people who could not understand the nature of life, nature of death, and what life would be after death.

"When such ideas were incorporated as so-called Buddhist practices, critics tended to condemn Buddhism for expensive and meaningless funeral rites. If they approach proper persons who have studied the real Teachings of the Buddha and Buddhist tradition, they could receive advice on how to perform Buddhist funeral rites in the correct manner.

It is most unfortunate that a bad impression has been created that Buddhism encourages people to waste their money and time on unnecessary rites and rituals. It must be clearly understood that Buddhism has nothing to do with such debased practices.

Buddhists are not very particular regarding the burial or cremation of a dead body. In many Buddhist countries, cremation is customary. For hygienic and economic reasons, it is advisable to cremate. Today, the population in the world is increasing and if we continue to have dead bodies occupying valuable land, then one day all remaining available land will be occupied by the dead and the living will have no place to live.

There are still some people who object to the cremation of dead bodies. They say that cremation is against God's law, in the same way they have objected to many other things in the past. it will take some time for such people to understand that cremation is much more appropriate and convenient than burial.

Besides, Buddhists do not believe that one day someone will come and awaken the departed persons' spirits from their graveyards or give life to the ashes from their urns and decide who should go to heaven and who should go to hell.

The consciousness or mental energy of the departed person has no connection with the body left behind or his or her skeleton or ashes. A dead body is simply the rotten old empty house which the departed person's life occupied. The Buddha called it 'a useless log'. Many people believe that if the deceased is not given a proper burial or if a sanctified tombstone is not placed on the grave, then the soul of the deceased will wander to the four corners of the world and weep and wail and sometimes even return to disturb the relatives. Such a belief cannot be found anywhere in Buddhism.

some people believe that if the dead body or the ashes of the departed person is buried or enshrined in a particular place by spending a big amount of money, the departed person will be benefited.

if we really want to honour a departed person, we must do some meritorious deeds such as giving some donations to deserving cases and charitable or religious activities in memory of the departed ones, and not by performing expensive rites and rituals.

Buddhists believe that when a person dies, rebirth will take place somewhere else according to his or her good or bad actions. As long as a person possesses the craving for existence, that person must experience rebirth. Only the Arahants, who have gone beyond all passions will have no more rebirths and so after their death, they will attain their final goal Nirvana.

Why we take Refuge in the Buddha

BUDDHISTS do not take refuge in the Buddha with the belief that He is a God or son of God. The Buddha never claimed any divinity. He was the Enlightened One, the most Compassionate, Wise, and Holy One who ever lived in this world. Therefore, people take refuge in the Buddha as a Teacher or Master who has shown the real path of emancipation. They pay homage to him to show their gratitude and respect, but they do not ask for material favours through Him. Buddhists do not pray to the Buddha thinking that He is a god who will reward them or punish them. They recite verses or some sutras not in the sense of supplication but as a means of recalling His great virtues and good qualities to get more inspiration and guidance for themselves and to develop the confidence to follow His Teachings so that they too could be like Him. There are critics who condemn this attitude of taking refuge in the Buddha. They do not know the true meaning of the concept of taking refuge in and paying homage to a great religious Teacher. They have learned about praying which is the only thing that some people do in the name of religion. When Buddhists seek refuge it means they accept the Buddha, Dharma and the Sangha as the means through which they can eradicate all the causes of their fear and other mental disturbances. Many people, especially those with animistic beliefs, seek protection in certain objects around them which they believe are inhabited by spirits. Buddhist however, know that the only protection they can have is through a complete understanding of their own natures and eradicating their base instincts. To do this they place their confidence in the Buddha's teachings and His Path, because this is the only way to true Emancipation and freedom from suffering.

The Buddha advised about the futility of taking refuge in hills, woods, groves, trees and shrines when people are fear-stricken. No such refuge is safe, no such refuge is supreme. Not by resorting to such a refuge is one freed from all ill. One who has gone for refuge to the Buddha, the Dharma and the Sangha sees with right knowledge the Four Noble Truths—Sorrow, the cause of Sorrow, the transcending of sorrow, and the Noble Eightfold Path which leads to the cessation of Sorrow. This indeed is secure refuge. By seeking such refuge one is released from all Sorrow. (Dhammapada 188-192)

In the Dhajagga Sutra, it is mentioned that by taking refuge in Sakra, the king of gods or any god, the followers would not be free from all their worldly problems and fears. The reason is, such gods are themselves not free from lust, hatred, illusion and fear, but the Buddha, Dharma and the Sangha are free from them. Only those who are free from unsatisfactoriness can show the way to lasting happiness.

Francis Story, a western Buddhist scholar, gives his views on seeking refuge in the Buddha. 'I go for refuge to the Buddha. I seek the presence of the Exalted Teacher by whose compassion I may be guided through the torrents of Samsara, by whose serene countenance i may be uplifted from the mire of worldly thoughts and cravings, seeing there in the very assurance of Nirvanic Peace, which He himself attained. in sorrow and pain i turn to Him and in my happiness i seek His tranquil gaze. I lay before His Image not only flowers and incense, but also the burning fires of my restless heart, that they may be quenched and stilled. i lay down the burden of my pride and my selfhood, the heavy burden of my cares and aspirations, the weary load of this incessant birth and death.'

Sri Rama Chandra Bharati, an Indian poet, gives another meaningful reason for taking refuge in the Buddha.

'I seek not thy refuge for the sake of gain, Not fear of thee, nor for the love of fame, Not as thou hailest from the solar race, Not for the sake of gaining knowledge vast, But drawn by the power of the boundless love, And thy all-embracing peerless ken, The vast Samsara's sea safe to cross, I bend low, O lord, and become thy devotee.'

Some people say that since the Buddha was only a man, there is no meaning in taking refuge in Him. But they do not know that although the Buddha very clearly said that He was a man, He was not an ordinary man like any of us. He was an extraordinary and incomparably holy person who possessed supreme Enlightenment and great compassion toward every living being. He was a man freed from all human weaknesses, defilements and even from ordinary human emotions. Of Him it has been said, 'There is none so godless as the Buddha, and yet none so godlike'. In the Buddha is embodied all the great virtues, sacredness, wisdom and enlightenment.

Another question that people very often raise is this: 'If the Buddha is not a god, if He is not living in this world today, how can He bless people?' According to the Buddha, if people follow His advice by leading a religious life, they would certainly receive blessings. Blessing in a Buddhist sense means the joy we experience when we develop confidence and satisfaction. The Buddha once said, 'If anyone wishes to see me, he should look at My Teachings and practise them.' (Samyutta Nikaya) Those who understand His Teachings easily see the real nature of the Buddha reflected in themselves. The image of the Buddha they maintain in their minds is more real than the image they see on the altar, which is merely a symbolic representation. ' *Those who live in accordance with the Dharma (righteous way of life) will be protected by that very Dharma* (Theragatha). One who knows the real nature of existence and the facts of life through Dharma will not have any fear and will secure a harmonious way of life.

In other religions, people worship their God by asking for favours to be granted to them. Buddhists do not worship the Buddha to ask for worldly favours, but they respect Him for His supreme achievement. "When Buddhists respect the Buddha, they are indirectly elevating their own minds so that one day they also can get the same enlightenment to serve mankind if they aspire to become a Buddha. Since the Buddha has been a human being, His experiences and achievements are the domain of all mortals. The Buddha's Teachings are for all of us, and certainly not beyond our capabilities as ordinary mortals.

Buddhists respect the Buddha as their Master. However, this respect does not imply an attachment to or a dependence on the Teacher. This kind of respect is in accordance with His Teaching which is as follows:

'Monks, even if a monk should take hold of the edge of My outer robe and should walk close behind me, step for step, yet if he should be covetous, strongly attracted by pleasures of the senses, malevolent in thought, of corrupt mind and purpose, of confused recollection, inattentive and not contemplative, scatter-brained, his sense-faculties uncontrolled, then he is far from Me and I am far from him.'

'Monks, if the monk should be staying even a hundred miles away, yet he is not covetous, not strongly attracted by the pleasures of the senses, not malevolent in thought, not of corrupt mind and purpose, his recollection firmly set, attentive, contemplative, his thoughts be one-pointed, restrained in his sense-faculties, then he is near Me and I am near him.' (Samyutta Nikaya)

No Self Surrender

BUDDHISM is a gentle religion where equality, justice and peace reign supreme. To depend on others for salvation is negative, but to depend on oneself is positive. Dependence on others means surrendering one's intelligence and efforts.

Everything which has improved and uplifted humanity has been done by human beings themselves. Their improvement must come from their own knowledge, understanding, effort and experience and not from heaven. They should not be slaves even to the great forces of nature because even though they are crushed by them they remain superior by virtue of their understanding. Buddhism carries the Truth further: it shows that by means of understanding, people can also control their environment and circumstances. They can cease to be crushed and use their power to raise themselves to great heights of spirituality and nobility.

Buddhism gives due credit to human intelligence and effort in their achievements without relying on supernatural beings. True religion should mean faith in the good of humanity rather than faith in unknown forces. In that respect, Buddhism is not merely a religion, but a noble method to gain peace and eternal salvation through living a respectable way of life. From the very outset, Bud-dhism appeals to the cultured and the intellectual minds. Every cultured person in the world today respects the Buddha as a rational Teacher.

The Buddha taught that what we need for our happiness is not a religion with a mass of dogmas and theories but knowledge— knowledge of the cosmic forces and their relationship to the law of cause and effect. Until this principle that life is merely an imperfect manifestation of nature is fully understood, no human can be fully emancipated.

The Buddha has given a new explanation of the universe. It is a new vision of eternal happiness, the achievement of perfection. The winning of the human goal in Buddhism is the permanent state beyond impermanence, the attainment of Nirvana beyond all the worlds of change, and the final deliverance from the miseries of existence.

Buddhists do not regard humans as sinful by nature or 'in rebellion against god'. Every human being is a person of great worth who has within him or herself a vast store of good as well as evil habits. The good in a person is always waiting for a suitable opportunity to flower and to ripen. Remember the saying, 'There is so much that is good in the worst of us and so much that is bad in the best of us.'

Buddhism teaches that everyone is responsible for his or her own good and bad deeds, and that each individual can mould his or her own destiny. Says the Buddha, 'These evil deeds were only done by you, not by your parents, friends, or relatives; and you yourself will reap the painful results.' (Dhammapada 165)

Our sorrow is of our own making and is not handed down as a family curse or an original sin of a mythical primeval ancestor. Buddhists do not accept the belief that this world is merely a place of trial and testing. This world can be made a place where we can attain the highest perfection. And perfection is synonymous with happiness. To the Buddha, human beings are not an experiment in life created by somebody and who can be done away with when unwanted. If a sin could be forgiven, people could take advantage and commit more and more sins. The Buddhist has no reason to believe that the sinner can escape the consequences of his or her actions by the grace of an external power. If we thrust our hand into a furnace, the hand will be burnt, and all the prayer in the world will not remove the scars. The same is with the person who walks into the fires of evil action. This is not to say that every wrong doing will automatically be followed by a predictable reaction. Evil actions are prompted by evil states of mind.

If one purifies the mind, then the effects of previous actions can be reduced or eradicated all together. The Buddha's approach to the problems of suffering is not imaginary, speculative or metaphysical, but essentially empirical and impartial.

According to Buddhism, there is no such thing as "sin" as explained by other religions. In these religions sin is a trangression of a law laid down by a Divine law giver. To the Buddhists, sin is unskilful or unwholesome action—Akusala Karma which creates papa—the downfall of people. The wicked person is an ignorant one who needs instruction more than punishment and condemnation. That person is not regarded as violating god's will or as a person who must beg for divine mercy and forgiveness. What is needed is only guidance for enlightenment.

All that is necessary is for someone to help them to use their reason to realise that they are responsible for their wrong action and that they must pay for the consequences. Therefore the belief in confession is foreign to Buddhism, although Buddhists are encouraged to acknowledge their wrong doings and remind themselves not to repeat their mistakes.

The purpose of the Buddha's appearance in this world is not to wash away the sins committed by human beings nor to punish or to destroy wicked people, but to make them understand how foolish it is to commit evil and to point out the consequences of such evil deeds. Therefore there are no commandments in Buddhism, since no one can control another's spiritual upliftment The Buddha has encouraged us to develop and use our understanding. He has shown us the path for our liberation from suffering. The precepts that we undertake to observe are not commandments: they are observed voluntarily. The Buddha's Teaching is this: 'Pay attention; take this advice and think it over. If you think it is suitable for you to practise My advice, then try to practise it. You can see the results through your own experience.' There is no religious value in blindly observing any commandment without proper conviction and understanding. However, we should not take advantage of the liberty given by the Buddha to do anything we like. It is our duty to behave as cultured, civilised and understanding human beings to lead a religious life. If we can understand this, commandments are not important. As an enlightened teacher, the Buddha advised us how to lead a pure life without imposing commandments and using the fear of punishment. The Five Precepts that a Buddhist takes as part of the daily practice are therefore not commandments. They are by definition training rules which one voluntarily undertakes for spiritual development.

Knowing that no external sources, no faith or rituals can save us, Buddhists understand the need to rely on self effort. We gain confidence through self-reliance. We realise that the whole responsibility of our present life as well as the future life depends completely on ourselves alone. Each must seek salvation for himself or herself. Achieving salvation can be compared to curing a disease: if one is ill, one must go to a doctor. The doctor diagnoses the ailment and prescribes medicine. The medicine must be taken by the persons themselves. They cannot depute someone else to take the medicine for them. No one can be cured by simply admiring the medicine or just praising the doctor for a good prescription.

In order to be cured, the patient must faithfully follow the instructions given by the doctor with regard to the manner and frequency in taking medicine, daily diet and other relevant medical restraints. Likewise, a person must follow the precepts, instructions or advice given by the Buddha (who gives prescriptions for liberation) by controlling or subduing greed, hatred and ignorance. No one can find salvation by simply singing praises of the Buddha or by making offerings to Him. Neither can one find salvation by celebrating certain important occasions in honour of the Buddha. Buddhism is not a religion where people can attain salvation by mere prayers or begging to be saved. They must strive hard by controlling their minds to eradicate their selfish desires and emotions in order to attain perfection.

Human Beings are Responsible for Everything

According to the buddha, human beings themselves are the makers of their own destiny. They have none to blame for their lot since they alone are responsible for their lives. They mould their lives for better or for worse.

The Buddha says: humans create everything. All our grief, perils and misfortunes are of our own creation. We spring from no other source than our own imperfections of heart and mind. We are the results of our good and bad actions committed in the past under the influence of greed and delusion. And since we ourselves brought them into being, it is within our power to overcome bad effects and cultivate good natures.

The human mind, like that of an animal, is sometimes governed by animal instincts. But unlike the animal mind, the human mind can be trained for higher values. If the mind is not properly cultured, that uncultured mind creates a great deal of trouble in this world. sometimes human behaviour is more harmful and more dangerous than animal behaviour. Animals have no religious problems, no language problems, no political problems, no social and ethical problems, no ethnic problems. They fight only for food, shelter and sensual pleasure. But, there are thousands of problems created by human beings. Their behaviour is such that they are not able to solve any of these problems without creating further problems. They are reluctant to admit their weaknesses and are not willing to shoulder their responsibilities. Their attitude is always to blame others for their failures. If we become more responsible in our actions, we can maintain peace and happiness.*

Human Beings are their own Jailors

When we consider human freedom, it is very difficult to see whether we are really free to do anything according to our own wishes. We are bound by many conditions both external and internal: we are asked to obey the laws that are imposed on us by the government; we are bound to follow certain religious principles; we are required to co-operate with the moral and social conditions of the society in which we live; we are compelled to follow certain national and family customs and traditions. In modern society, we are under great pressure; we are expected to conform by adapting ourselves to the modern way of life. We are bound to co-operate with natural laws and cosmic energy, because we are also part of the same energy. We are subjected to the weather and climatic conditions of the region. Not only do we have to pay attention to our lives or to physical elements, but we have also to make up our minds to control our own emotions. In other words, we have no freedom to think freely because we are overwhelmed by new thoughts which may contradict or do away with our previous thoughts and convictions. At the same time, we may believe that we have to obey and work according to the will of god, and not follow our own free will.

Taking into consideration all the above changing conditions to which we are bound, we can ask 'Is there any truth to the claim that we should be given freedom to do things as we like?'

Why do human beings have their hands tied so firmly? The reason is that there are various bad elements within them. These elements are dangerous and harmful to all living creatures. For the past few thousand years, all religions have been trying to tame this unreliable attitude and to teach mankind how to live a noble life. But it is most unfortunate that they are still not ready to be trustworthy, however good they may appear to be. Human beings still continue to harbour all these evil elements within themselves. These evil elements are not introduced or influenced by external sources but are created by themselves. If these evil forces are made by themselves they must work hard to get rid of them after recognising their danger. Unfortunately the majority of people are cruel, cunning, wicked, ungrateful, unreliable, unscrupulous. If they are allowed to live according to their own free will without moderation and restraint, they would most definitely violate the peace and happiness of innocent people. Their behaviour would probably be much worse than that of other dangerous living beings.

Religion is required to train them to lead a respectable life and to gain peace and happiness here and hereafter.

Another obstacle confronting religious life and spiritual progress is racial arrogance. The Buddha advised His followers not to bring forward any racial issue when they come to practise religion. Buddhists are taught to understand that concepts like racial origin and caste or class distinction are all made by deluded minds which cannot see the essential unity of all that exists. People of all religions should not discriminate against any groups of people by glorifying their own ways of life. They should treat everyone equally, especially in the religious field. Unfortunately, followers of different religions encourage discrimination and hostility towards other religious groups.

While working with others, true disciples should not disturb their feelings because of their own traditions and customs. They can follow traditions and customs that are in keeping with the religious principles and moral codes of their religions.

Racial arrogance is a great hindrance to religious and spiritual progress. The Buddha once used the simile of ocean water to illustrate the harmony which can be experienced by people who have learnt to cast aside their racial arrogance: Different rivers have different names. The waters of the individual rivers all flow into the ocean and become ocean water, with one taste, the taste of salt. In a similar manner, all those who have come from different communities and different castes, must forget their differences and think of themselves only as human beings.

You Protect Yourself

ONCE the Blessed One told His monks the following story: 'There was once a pair of jugglers who did their acrobatic feats on a bamboo pole. One day the master said to his apprentice: "Now get on my shoulders and climb up the bamboo pole.' When the apprentice had done so, the master said: 'Now protect me well and I shall protect you. By watching each other in that way, we shall be able to show our skill, we shall make a good profit and you can get down safely from the bamboo pole'. But the apprentice said: "Not so, master. You! O Master, should protect yourself, and I too shall protect myself. Thus self-protected and self-guarded we shall safely do our feats, and protect each other.'

'This is the right way,' said the Blessed One and spoke further as follows:

'It is just as the apprentice said: 'I shall protect myself,' in that way the Foundation of Mindfulness should be practised. 'I shall protect others,' in that way the Foundation of Mindfulness should be practised. Protecting oneself one protects others; protecting others one protects oneself.

'And how does one, in protecting oneself, protect others? By the repeated and frequent practice of meditation'.

'And how does one, by protecting others, protect oneself? By patience and forbearance, by a non-violent and harmless life, by loving kindness and compassion.' (Satipatthana, Samyutta, No. 19).

'Protecting oneself one protects others' 'Protecting others one protects oneself'.

These two sentences complement each other and should not be taken (or quoted) separately.

Nowadays, when social service is so greatly emphasised, people may for instance, be tempted to quote, in support of their ideas, only the second sentence. But any such one-sided quotation would misrepresent the Buddha's statement. It has to be remembered that in our story, the Buddha expressly approved the words of the apprentice, which is that one has first to carefully watch one's own steps if one wishes to protect others from harm. He who is sunk in the mire himself cannot help others out of it. In that sense, self-protection is not selfish protection. It is the cultivation of self-control, and ethical and spiritual self-development.

Protecting oneself one protects others—the truth of this statement begins at a very simple and practical level. At the material level, this truth is so self-evident that we need not say more than a few words about it. It is obvious that the protection of our own health will go far in protecting the health of our closer or wider environment, especially where contagious diseases are concerned. Caution and circumspection in all our doings and movements will protect others from harm that may come to them through our carelessness and negligence. By careful driving, abstention from alcohol, by self-restraint in situations that might lead to violence—in all these and many other ways we shall protect others by protecting ourselves. We can even go as far as to say that by enhancing our own economic position, we are in a better position to help others.

We come now to the ethical level of that truth. Moral self-protection will safeguard others, individual and society, against our own unrestrained passions and selfish impulses. If we permit the Three Roots of everything evil, Greed, Hate and Delusion, to take a firm hold in our minds, then that which grows from those evil roots will spread around like the jungle creeper which suffocates and kills the healthy and noble tree. But if we protect ourselves against these Three Roots of Evil, fellow beings too will be safe from our reckless greed for possession and power, from our unrestrained lust and sensuality, from our envy and jealousy. They will be safe from the disruptive, or even destructive and murderous, consequences of our hate and enmity, from the outbursts of our anger, from our spreading an atmosphere of antagonism and quarrelsomeness which may make life unbearable for those around us. But the harmful effects of our greed and hate on others are not limited to cases when they become the passive objects or victims of our hate, or their possessions the object of our greed. Greed and hate have an infectious power, which can multiply the evil effects. If we ourselves think of nothing else than to crave and grasp, to acquire and possess, to hold and cling, then we may rouse or strengthen these possessive instincts in others too. Our bad example may become the standard of behaviour of our environment for instance among our own children, our colleagues, and so on. Our own conduct may induce others to join us in the common satisfaction of rapacious desires; or we may arouse feelings of resentment and competitiveness in others who wish to beat us in the race. If we are full of sensuality we may kindle the fire of lust in others. Our own hate may cause the hate and vengeance of others. It may also happen that we ally ourselves with others or instigate them to common acts of hate and enmity.

You Have to Save Yourself

NEsELF, indeed, is one's saviour, for what other saviour would there be? With oneself well controlled the problem of looking for an external saviour is solved.

As the Buddha was about to pass away, His disciples came from everywhere to be near Him. "While the other disciples were constantly at His side and in deep sorrow over the impending loss of their Master, a monk named Attadatta went into his cell and practised meditation. The other monks, thinking that he was unconcerned about the welfare of the Buddha, were upset and reported the matter to Him. The monk, however, addressed the Buddha thus, 'Lord as the Blessed One would be passing away soon, I thought the best way to honour the Blessed One would be by attaining Arahantship during the lifetime of the Blessed One itself. The Buddha praised his attitude and his conduct and said that one's spiritual welfare should not be abandoned for the sake of others.

In this story is illustrated one of the most important aspects of Buddhism. A person must constantly be on the alert to seek his or her own deliverance from samsara, and 'salvation' must be brought about by the individual alone. One cannot look to any external force or agency for help to attain Nirvana.

People who do not understand Buddhism criticise this concept and say that Buddhism is a selfish religion which only talks about the concern for one's own freedom from pain and sorrow. This is not true at all. The Buddha states clearly that one should work ceaselessly for the spiritual and material welfare of all beings, while at the same time diligently pursuing one's own goal of attaining Nirvana.

Selfless service is highly commended by the Buddha.

Again, people who do not understand Buddhism may ask, 'It may be alright for the fortunate human beings, in full command of their mental powers, to seek Nirvana by their own efforts. But what about those who are mentally and physically or even materially handicapped? How can they be self-reliant? Do they not need the help of some external force, some god or deva to assist them?'

The answer to this is that Buddhists do not believe that the final release must necessarily take place in one lifetime. The process can take a long time, over the period of many births. One has to apply oneself, to the best of one's ability, and slowly develop the powers of self-reliance. Therefore, even those who are handicapped mentally and spiritually must make an effort, however small, to begin the process of deliverance and the duty of those more able is to help them do this; e.g. monks and nuns help lay people to understand and practise the Dharma.

Once the wheels are set in motion, the individual slowly trains himself or herself to improve that power of self-reliance. The tiny acorn will one day grow into a mighty oak, but not overnight. Patience is an essential ingredient in this difficult process.

For example, we know from experience how many parents do everything in their power to bring up their children according to the parents' hopes and aspirations. And yet when these children grow up, they develop in their own way, not necessarily the way the parents wanted them to be. In Buddhism, we believe that while others can exert an influence on someone's life, the individual will in the end create his or her own karma and be responsible for their own actions. No human being or deva can, in the final analysis, direct or control an individual's attainment of the ultimate salvation. This is the meaning of self-reliance.

This does not mean that Buddhism teaches one to be selfish. In Buddhism, when people seek, by their own effort, to attain Nirvana, they are determined not to kill, steal, tell lies, lust after others, or lose the control of their senses through intoxication. When they control themselves thus they automatically contribute to the happiness of others. so is not this so-called 'selfishness' a good thing for the general welfare of others?

On a more mundane level it has been asked how the lower forms of life can extricate themselves from a mere meaningless round of existence. surely in that helpless state some benevolent external force is necessary to pull the unfortunate being from the quicksand. To answer this question we must refer to our knowledge of the evolution theory. It is clearly stated that life began in very primitive forms—no more than a single cell floating in the water. Over millions of years these basic life forms evolved and became more complex, more intelligent. It is at this more intelligent level that life forms are capable of organization, independent thought, conceptualization and so on.

When Buddhists talk about the ability to save oneself, they are referring to life forms at this higher level of mental development. In the earlier stages of evolution karmic and mental forces remain dormant, but over countless rebirths, a being raises itself to the level of independent thought and becomes capable of rational rather than instinctive behaviour. It is at this stage that the being becomes aware of the meaninglessness of undergoing endless rebirths with its natural concomitants of pain and sorrow.

It is then that the being is capable of making its determination to end rebirth and seek happiness by gaining enlightenment and Nirvana. With this high level of intelligence, the individual is indeed capable of self-improvement and self-development.

We all know human beings are born with many varying levels of intelligence and powers of reasoning. some are born as geniuses, while at the other end of the spectrum, some are born with very low intelligence. Yet every being has some ability to distinguish between choices or options, especially when they concern survival. If we extend this fact of survival even to the animal world we can distinguish between higher and lower animals, with this same ability (in varying degrees of course) to make choices for the sake of survival.

Hence, even a lower form of life has the potential to create a good karma, however limited its scope. With the diligent application of this and the gradual increase of good karma a being can raise itself to higher levels of existence and understanding.

To look at this problem from another angle, we can consider one of the earliest stories that have been told to show how the Buddha-to-be first made the initial decision to strive for Enlightenment. A great many rebirths before the Buddha was born as siddharta, he was born as an ordinary man.

One day while travelling in a boat with his mother, a great storm arose and the boat capsized, throwing the occupants into the angry sea. With no thought for his personal safety, this brave young man carried his mother on his back and struggled to swim to dry land. But so great was the expanse of water ahead of him that he did not know the best route to safety. When he was in this dilemma, not knowing which way to turn, his bravery was noticed by one of the devas. This deva could not physically come to his aid, but he was able to make him to know the best route to take. The young man listened to the deva and both he and his mother were saved. After his mother had been saved, he reflected on how much happiness he had gained from saving a single being. How much greater would that happiness be, if he perfected himself and then saved all sentient beings? There and then he made a firm deter-mination and life after life he went on cultivating his life for gaining Enlightenment.

This story illustrates the fact that Buddhists can and do seek the help of devas in their daily lives. A deva is a being who by virtue of having acquired great merit is born with the power to help other beings. But this power is limited to material and physical things. In our daily existence, we can seek help of the devas (when misfortune strikes, when we need to be comforted, when we are sick or afraid, and so on).

The fact that we seek the aid of these devas means that we are still tied to the material world. We must accept the fact that by being born we are subject to physical desires and needs. And it is not wrong to satisfy these needs on a limited scale. "When the Buddha advocated the Middle Path, He said that we should neither indulge ourselves in luxury nor completely deny ourselves the basic necessities of life.

However, we should not stop at that. "While we accept the con-ditions of our birth, we must also make every effort, by following the Noble Eightfold Path, to reach a level of development where we realize that attachment to the material world creates only pain and sorrow.

As we develop our understanding over countless births, we crave less and less for the pleasures of the senses. It is at this stage that we become truly self-reliant. At this stage, the devas cannot help us anymore, because we are not seeking to satisfy our material needs.

Buddhists who really understand the fleeting nature of the world practise detachment from material goods. As they are not unduly attached to them, they share the goods freely with those who are more unfortunate than they are—

they practise generosity. In this way again Buddhists contribute to the welfare of others.

When the Buddha gained Enlightenment as a result of His own efforts, He did not selfishly keep this knowledge to Himself. In fact, after His supreme Enlightenment, there was nothing He needed for Himself—but His Compassion moved Him to show the Path

He had discovered to others. He spent no less than forty five years imparting His knowledge not only to men and women but even to the devas.

It is often said that the Buddha helped devotees who were in trouble. But He did this, not through the performance of miracles such as restoring the dead to life and so on, but through His acts of wisdom and compassion which helped these people to understand the reality of existence.

In one instance, a woman named Kisa Gotami went to seek the help of the Buddha in restoring her dead child to life. Knowing that He could not reason with her as she was so distressed and overwhelmed with grief, the Buddha told her that she should first obtain a handful of mustard seeds from a person who had never lost a dear one through death.

The distracted woman ran from house to house and while everyone was only too willing to give her the mustard seeds, no one could honestly say that they had not lost a dear one through death. slowly, Kisa Gotami came to the realization that death is a natural occurrence to be experienced by any being that is born. Filled with this realisation she returned to the Buddha and thanked Him for showing her the truth about death.

Now, the point here is that the Buddha was more concerned with the woman's understanding about the nature of life than giving her temporary relief by restoring her child to life—the child would have grown old and still have died. With her greater realisation Kisa Gotami was able not only to come to terms with the phenomenon of death but also to learn about the cause of sorrow through attachment. she was able to realise that attachment causes sorrow, that when attachment is destroyed, then sorrow is also destroyed.

Therefore in Buddhism, a person can seek the help of external agencies (like devas) in the pursuit of temporal happiness, but in the later stages of development when attachment to the worldly conditions ceases, there begins the path towards renunciation and enlightenment at which point one must stand alone. When one seeks to gain liberation, to break away from the endless cycle of birth and death, to gain realisation and enlightenment, one can only do this by one's own effort and own concentrated will power. "No one saves us but ourselves".

* For further clarification on devas, refer to sections entitled *Belief in Deities - Devas, spirit world* and *The Significance of Transference of Merit to the Departed* in this book.

Buddhism gives great credit to human beings. It is the only religion which states that human beings have the power to help and free themselves. In the later stages of their development, they are not at the mercy of any external force or agency which they must constantly please by worshipping or offering sacrifices.*

Faith, Confidence and Devotion

FAITH in the theistic sense is not found in Buddhism because of its emphasis on understanding. Theistic faith is a sedative for the emotional mind and demands belief in things which cannot be explained. Knowledge destroys faith and faith destroys itself when a mysterious belief is examined under the spotlight of reason. Confidence cannot be obtained by faith since it places little or no emphasis on reason.

Referring to the unintelligible and 'blind' nature of faith, Voltaire said, 'Faith is to believe in something which your reason tells you cannot be true; for if your reason approved of it, there could be no question of blind faith.'

Confidence, however, is not the same as faith. For confidence is not a meek acceptance of that which cannot be known. Confidence is an assured expectation, not of an unknown beyond, but of what can be tested as experienced and understood personally. Confidence is like the understanding that a student has in his teacher who explains in the classroom the inverse square law of gravitation as stated by Newton. He should not adopt an unquestioning belief of his teacher and his textbook. He studies the fact, examines the scientific arguments, and makes an assessment of the reliability of the information. If he has doubts, he should reserve his judgement until such time as when he is able to investigate the accuracy of the information for himself. To a Buddhist, confidence is a product of reason, knowledge and experience. When it is developed, confidence can never be blind faith. Confidence becomes a power of the mind to understand the nature and the meaning of life.

'The question of belief arises when there is no seeing—seeing in every sense of the word. The moment you see, the question of belief disappears. If I tell you that I have a gem hidden in the folded palm of my hand, the question of belief arises because you do not see it yourself. But if I unclench my fist and show you the gem, then you see it for yourself, and the question of belief does not arise. A phrase in the ancient Buddhist texts therefore reads: 'Realising, as one sees a gem (or a myrobalan fruit) in the palm.

The Meaning of Prayer

Nature is impartial; it cannot be flattered by prayers. It does not grant any special favours on request. Humans are not fallen creatures but rising angels. Prayers are answered by the power of their own minds.

ACCORDING to Buddhism, humans are potential masters of themselves. Only because of their deep ignorance do they fail to realise their full potential. Since the Buddha has shown this hidden power, people must cultivate their minds and try to develop it by realising their innate ability.

A story will illustrate this point. An eagle once laid her egg in the nest of a hen. The hen hatched the eagle's egg along with her own. The hatchlings then followed the mother hen about as she taught them to focus on the ground to find their food. The eaglet, thinking it was a chicken did the same. One day however, it saw an eagle flying high up in the sky, and decided to do the same.

The other chickens laughed at him, but he did not care. Everyday he perservered until one day he became strong enough and soared up into the air and became a lord of the skies, while the other chickens continued to eke out a living on the ground. We must think like that eagle.

Buddhism gives full responsibility and dignity to human beings. It makes them their own masters. According to Buddhism, no higher being sits in judgement over a person's affairs and destiny. That is to say, our life, our society, our world, is what you and I want to make out of it, and not what some other unknown being wants it to be.

Remember that nature is impartial; it cannot be flattered by prayers. Nature does not grant any special favours on request. Thus in Buddhism, prayer is meditation which has self-change as its object. Prayer in meditation acts as an aid to recondition one's nature. It is the transforming of one's inner nature accomplished by the purification of the three faculties—thought, word and deed. Through meditation, we can understand that 'we become what we think', in accordance with the discoveries of psychology. "When we pray, we experience some relief in our minds; that is, the psychological effect that we have created through our faith and devotion. After reciting certain verses we also experience the same result. Religious names or symbols are important to the extent that they help to develop devotion and confidence, but must never be considered as ends in themselves.

The Buddha Himself has clearly expressed that neither the recital of holy scriptures, nor self-torture, nor sleeping on the ground, nor the repetition of prayers, penances, hymns, charms, mantras, incantations and invocations can bring the real happiness of Nirvana, only purification of the mind through self effort can do this.

Regarding the use of prayers for attaining the final goal, the Buddha once used an analogy of a man who wants to cross a river. If he sits down and prays, imploring that the far bank of the river will come to him and carry him across, then his prayer will not be answered.

If he really wants to cross the river, he must make some effort; he must find some logs and build a raft, or look for a bridge or construct a boat or perhaps swim. somehow he must work to get across the river. Likewise, if he wants to cross the river of samsara, prayers alone are not enough. He must work hard by living a religious life, by controlling his passions, calming his mind, and by getting rid of all the impurities and defilements in his mind. Only then can he reach the final goal. Prayer alone will never take him to the final goal.

If prayer is necessary, it should be to strengthen and focus the mind and not to beg for gains. The following prayer of a poet teaches us how to pray. Buddhists can regard this as meditation to cultivate the mind:

'Let me not pray to be sheltered from dangers, but to be fearless in facing them. Let me not beg for the stilling of my pain, but for the heart to conquer it. Let me not crave in anxious fear to be saved, but for the patience to win my freedom.'

Meditation

Meditation is the psychological approach to mental culture, training and purification of the mind.

IN place of prayer, Buddhists practise meditation for mental culture and for spiritual development. No one can attain Nirvana or salvation without cultivating the mind through meditation. Any amount of meritorious deeds alone will not lead a person to attain the final goal without the corresponding mental purification. Naturally, the untrained mind is very elusive and persuades people to commit evil and become slaves of the senses.

Imagination and emotions always mislead humans if their minds are not properly trained. One who knows how to practise meditation will be able to control the mind when it is misled by the senses.

Most of the troubles which we are confronting today are due to the untrained and undeveloped mind. It is already established that meditation is the remedy for many physical and mental sicknesses. Medical authorities and great psychologists all over the world say that mental frustration, worries, miseries, anxieties, tension and fear are the causes of many diseases, stomach ulcers, gastritis, nervous complaints and mental illness. And even latent sickness will be aggravated through such mental conditions.

When the conscious 'I' frets too much, worries too much, or grieves too long and too intensely, then troubles develop in the body. Gastric ulcers, tuberculosis, coronary diseases and a host of functional disorders are the products of mental and emotional imbalance. In the case of children, the decay of the teeth and defective eyesight are frequently related to emotional disorders.

Many of these sicknesses and disorders can be avoided if people could spend a few minutes a day to calm their minds through the practice of meditation. Many people do not believe this or are too lazy to practise meditation owing to a lack of understanding. Some people say that meditation is only a waste of time. We must remember that every spiritual master in this world attained the highest point

of his life through the practice of meditation. They are honoured today by millions of people because they have done tremendous service to humanity with their supreme wisdom which they obtained through the practice of meditation.

Meditation should not be a task to which we force ourselves 'with gritted teeth and clenched fists', it should rather be something that draws us, because it fills us with joy and inspiration. so long as we have to force ourselves, we are not yet ready for meditation. Instead of meditating we are violating our true nature. Instead of relaxing and letting go, we are holding on to our ego. In this way meditation becomes a game of ambition, of personal achievement and aggrandizement. Meditation is like love: a spontaneous experience—not something that can be forced or acquired by strenuous effort.

Therefore Buddhist meditation has no other purpose than to bring the mind back into the present, into the state of fully awakened consciousness, by clearing it from all obstacles that come through the senses and mental objects.

The Buddha obtained His Enlightenment through the

development of His mind. He did not seek divine power to help Him. He gained His wisdom through self-effort by practising meditation. To have a healthy body and mind and to have peace, one must learn how to practise meditation.

Nature of Modern Life

TODAY we are living in a world where people have to work very hard physically and mentally. Without hard work, there is no place for people in modern society. very often keen competition is going on everywhere. One is trying to beat the others in every sphere of life and human beings have no rest at all. Mind is the nucleus of life. "When there is no real peace and rest in the mind, the whole life will collapse. People naturally try to overcome their miseries through pleasing the senses: they drink, gamble, sing and dance—all the time having the illusion that they are enjoying the real happiness of life. sense stimulation is not the real way to have relaxation.

The more we try to please the senses through sensual pleasures, the more will we become slaves to the senses. There will be no end to our craving for satisfaction. The real way to relax is to calm the senses by the control of mind. If we can control the mind, then we will be able to control everything. When the mind is fully controlled and purified, it will be free from mental disturbances. When the mind is free from mental disturbances it can see many things which others cannot see with their naked eyes. ultimately, we will be able to attain our salvation and find peace and happiness.

To practise meditation, one must have strong determination, effort and patience. Immediate results cannot be expected. We must remember that it takes many years for a person to be qualified as a doctor, lawyer, mathematician, philosopher, historian or a scientist. similarly to be a good meditator, it will take some time for the person to control the elusive mind and to calm the senses. Practising meditation is like swimming in a river against the current. Therefore one must not lose patience for not being able to obtain rapid results. At the same time the meditator must also cultivate morality. A congenial place for meditation is another important factor. The meditator must have a suitable object for meditation, for without an object the jumping mind is not easy to trap. The object must not create lust, anger, delusion, and emotion in the meditator's mind.

When we start to meditate, we switch the mind from the old discursive way of thinking, or habitual thought into a new unimpeded or unusual way of thinking. "While meditating when we breathe in mindfully, we absorb cosmic energy. When we breathe out mindfully with Metta—loving kindness, we purify the atmosphere.

We spend most of our time on our body: to feed it, to clothe it, to cleanse it, to wash it, to beautify it, to relax it, but how much time do we spend on our mind for the same purposes?

What is a suitable object to meditate upon? Some people take the Buddha Image as an object and concentrate on it. Some concentrate on inhaling and exhaling the breath. Whatever may be the method, if anyone tries to practise meditation, it is necessary to find relaxation. Meditation will help a person a great deal to have physical and mental health and to control the mind when it is necessary.

We can do the highest service to society by simply abstaining from evil. The cultured mind that is developed through meditation performs a most useful service to others. Meditation is certainly not a waste of valuable time. The advanced mind of a meditator can solve so many human problems and is very useful to enlighten others. Meditation is very useful to help a person live peacefully despite various disturbances that are so prevalent in this modern world. We cannot be expected to retire to a jungle or forest to live in ivory towers—'far from the madding crowd'.

By practising right meditation we can have an abode for tem-porary oblivion. Meditation has the purpose of training a person to face, understand and conquer this very world in which we live. Meditation teaches us to adjust ourselves to bear with the numerous obstacles to life in the modern world.

If you practise meditation, you can learn to behave like a noble person even though you are disturbed by others. Through meditation you can learn how to relax the body and to calm the mind; you can learn to be tranquil and happy within.

Just as an engine gets overheated and damaged when it is run for a prolonged period and requires cooling down to avoid this, so also the mind gets overtaxed when we subject it to a sustained degree of mental effort and it is only through meditation that relax-ation or cooling can be achieved.

Meditation strengthens the mind to control human emotion when it is disturbed by negative thoughts and feelings such as jealousy, anger, pride and envy. Meditation helps us to let go, to get a much needed reprieve from life's daily pressures.

If you practise meditation, you can learn to make the proper decision when you are at a crossroads in life and are at a loss as to which way to turn. These qualities cannot be purchased from anywhere. No amount of money or property can buy these qualities, yet you can attain them through meditation. But we must never lose sight of the fact that the ultimate object of Buddhist meditation is to eradicate all defilements from the mind and to attain the final goal—Nirvana.

Nowadays, however, the practice of meditation has been abused by people. They want immediate and quick results, just as they expect quick returns for everything they do in daily life. Some people practise meditation in order to satisfy their material desires; they want to further their material gains. They want to use meditation to get better jobs. They want to earn more money or to operate their businesses more efficiently. Although this is not exactly a bad thing, perhaps they fail to understand that the aim of meditation is not to increase but to decrease desires. Materialistic motives are hardly suitable for proper meditation, the goal of which lies beyond worldly affairs. One should meditate to try to attain something that even money cannot buy.

In Buddhism, as is the case with other eastern cultures, patience is a most important quality. The mind must be brought under control in slow degrees and one should not try to reach for the higher states without proper training. We have heard of over-enthusiastic young men and women literally going out of their minds because they adopted the wrong attitudes towards meditation.

Meditation is a gentle way of conquering the defilements which pollute the mind. If people want 'success' or 'achievement' to boast to others that they have attained this or that level of meditation, they are abusing the method of mental culture. One must be trained in morality and one must clearly understand that to be successful in the discipline of meditation worldly achievements must not be equated with spiritual development. Ideally, it is good to work under an experienced teacher who will help a student to develop along the right path. But above all one must never be in a hurry to achieve too much too quickly.

The Significance of Paritta Chanting

Paritta chanting is the recital of some of the Sutras uttered by the Buddha in the Pali language for the blessing and protection of the devotees.

PARITTA Chanting or Sutra Chanting is a well known Buddhist practice conducted all over the world, especially in Theravada Buddhist countries where the Pali language is used for recitals. Many of these are important sutras from the basic teachings of the Buddha which were recorded by His disciples. Originally, these sutras were recorded on ola leaves about two thousand years ago. Later, they were compiled into a book known as the 'Paritta Chanting Book'. The names of the original books from which these sutras were selected are the Anguttara Nikaya, Majjhima Nikaya, Digha Nikaya, Samyutta Nikaya and Kuddaka Nikaya in the Sutra Pitaka.

The sutras that Buddhists recite for protection are known as Paritta Chanting. Here 'protection means shielding ourselves from various forms of evil spirits, misfortune, sickness and influence of the planetary systems as well as instilling confidence in the mind'. The vibrant sound of the chanting creates a very pleasing atmosphere in the vicinity. The rhythm of the chanting is also important. One might have noticed that when monks recite these sutras, different intonations are adopted to harmonise with different sutras intended for different quarters. It was found very early during man's spiritual development that certain rhythms of the human voice could produce significant psychological states of peacefulness and serenity in the minds of ardent listeners. Furthermore, intonation at certain levels would appeal to devas, whilst certain rhythms would create a good influence over lower beings like animals, snakes, or even spirits or ghosts. Therefore, a soothing and correct rhythm is an important aspect of Paritta Chanting.

The use of these rhythms is not confined to Buddhism alone. In every religion, when the followers recite their prayers by using the holy books, they follow certain rhythms. We can observe this when we listen to Quran reading by Muslims and the Veda Mantra Chanting by Hindu priests in the sanskrit language, some lovely chanting is also carried out by certain Christian groups, especially the Roman Catholic and Greek Orthodox sects.

When the sutras are chanted, three great and powerful forces are activated. These are the forces of the Buddha, Dharma and the Sangha. Buddhism is the combination of these 'Three Jewels' and when invoked together they can bring great blessings to mankind.

(1) The Buddha. He had cultivated all the great virtues, wisdom and enlightenment, and spiritual development before He gave us His noble Teachings. Even though the physical presence of the Teacher is no more with us, His Teachings have remained for the benefit of mankind. similarly, the man who discovered electricity is no more with us, yet by using his knowledge, the effect of his wisdom still remains. The illumination that we enjoy today is the result of his wisdom. The scientists who discovered atomic energy are no longer living, but the knowledge to use it remains with us. Likewise the Noble Teachings given us through the Buddha's wisdom and enlightenment, are a most effective power for people to draw inspiration from. When you remember Him and respect Him, you develop confidence in Him. When you recite or listen to the words uttered by Him, you invoke the power of His blessings.

(2) Dharma. It is the power of truth, justice and peace discovered by the Buddha which provides spiritual solace for devotees to maintain peace and happiness. "When you develop your compassion, devotion and understanding, this power of the Dharma protects you and helps you to

develop more confidence and strength in your mind. Then your mind itself becomes a very powerful force for your own protection. "When it is known that you uphold the Dharma, people and other beings will respect you. The power of the Dharma protects you from various kinds of bad influence and evil fórces. Those who cannot understand the power of the Dharma and how to live in accordance with the Dharma, invariably surrender themselves to all forms of superstitious beliefs and subject themselves to the influence of many kinds of gods, spirits and mystical powers which require them to perform pointless rites and rituals. By so doing, they only develop more fear and suspicion born out of ignorance. Large sums of money are spent on such practices and this could be easily avoided if people were to develop their confidence in the Dharma. Dharma is also described as 'nature' or 'natural phenomena', 'cosmic law' or 'gravity' or a 'magnet'. Those who have learnt the nature of these forces can protect themselves through the Dharma by harmonising with them. "When the mind is calmed through perfect knowledge disturbances cannot create fear.

(3) The Sangha. This word refers to the holy order of monks who have renounced their worldly life for their spiritual development. They are considered as disciples of the Buddha, who have cultivated great virtues to attain sainthood or Arahantahood. We pay respect to the Sangha community as the custodians of the Buddha Sasana or those who had protected and introduced the Dharma to the world over the last 2,500 years. The services rendered by the sangha community has guided mankind to lead a righteous and noble life. They are the living link with the Enlightened One who bring His message to us through the recital of the words uttered by Him.

The chanting of sutras for blessing was started during the Buddha's time. Later, in certain Buddhist countries such as Sri Lanka, Thailand and Myanmar, this practice was developed further by organising prolonged chanting for one whole night or for several days. With great devotion, devotees today participate in the chanting sessions by listening attentively and intelligently. There were some occasions when the Buddha and His disciples chanted sutras to bring spiritual solace to people suffering from epidemics, famines, sickness and other natural disasters. On one occasion, when a child was reported to be affected by some evil influence, the Buddha instructed His monks to recite sutras to give protection to the child.

The blessing service, by way of chanting, was effective. Of course, there were instances when the sutra chanting could not be effective if the victims had committed some strong bad karma. Nevertheless, certain minor bad karmic effects can be overcome by the vibrant power combined with the great virtues and compassion of those holy people who chant these sutras. However the effect of strong bad karma can be temporarily delayed, but it cannot be eradicated altogether.

Devotees who were tired or fatigued have experienced relief and calmness after listening to the chanting of sutras. Such an experience is different from that provided by music because music can create excitement in our mind and pander to our emotions but does not create spiritual devotion and confidence.

For the last 2,500 years, Buddhist devotees have experienced the good effects of sutra chanting. We should try to understand how and why the words uttered by the Buddha for blessing purposes could be so effective even after His passing away. It is mentioned in the Buddha's teaching that ever since He had the aspiration to become a Buddha during His previous births, He had strongly upheld one particular principle, namely, 'to abstain from telling lies'. Without abusing or misusing His words, He spoke gently without hurting the feelings of others. The power of Truth has become a source of strength in the words uttered by the Buddha with great compassion. However, the power of the Buddha's word alone is not enough to secure blessing without the devotion and understanding of the devotees.

The supernatural effect experienced by many people in ridding themselves of their sickness and many other mental disturbances through the medium of the Buddhist sutras and meditation are proof that they can be extremely efficacious if used with devotion and confidence.

Are Buddhists Idol Worshippers?

Buddhists are not idol worshippers but ideal worshippers.

ALTHOUGH it is customary amongst Buddhists to keep Buddha images and to pay their respects to the Buddha, Buddhists are not idol worshippers. Idolatry generally means erecting images of unknown gods and goddesses in various shapes and sizes and to pray directly to these images as if the images themselves are the gods. The prayers are a request to the gods for guidance and protection. The gods and goddesses are asked to bestow health, wealth, prosperity and to provide for various needs; they are also asked to forgive transgressions.

The 'worshipping' at the Buddha image is quite a different matter. Buddhists revere the image of the Buddha as a gesture of respect to the greatest, wisest, most benevolent, compassionate and holy man who has ever lived in this world. It is a historical fact that this great religious teacher actually lived in this world and has done a great service to humanity. The worship of the Buddha really means paying homage, veneration and devotion to Him and what He represents, and not to the stone or metal figure.

The image is a visual aid that helps one to recall the Buddha in the mind and to remember His great qualities which inspired millions of people from generation to generation throughout the civilized world. Buddhists use the statue as a symbol and as an object of concentration to gain peace of mind. "When Buddhists look upon the image of the Buddha, they put aside thoughts of strife and think only of peace, serenity, calmness and tranquility. The statue enables the mind to recall this great man and inspires devotees to follow His example and instructions. In their minds, devout Buddhists feel the living presence of the Master. This feeling makes their acts of worship vivid and significant. The serenity of the Buddha image influences and inspires them to observe the right path of conduct and thought.

Understanding Buddhists never ask for worldly favours from the image nor do they request forgiveness for evil deeds committed. They try control their mind, to follow the Buddha's advice, to get rid of worldly miseries and to find their salvation. Those who criticize Buddhists for practising idol worship are really misinterpreting what Buddhists do. If people can keep the photographs of their parents and grandparents to cherish in their memory, if people can keep the photographs of kings, queens, prime ministers, great heroes, philosophers, and poets, there is certainly no reason why Buddhists cannot keep their beloved Master's picture or image to remember and respect Him.

What harm is there if people recite some verses praising the great qualities of their Master? If people can lay wreaths on the graves of beloved ones to express their gratitude, what harm is there if Buddhists too offer some flowers, joss-sticks, incense, etc., to honour their beloved Teacher who devoted His life to help suffering humanity? People make statues of certain conquering heroes who were in fact murderers and who were responsible for the deaths of millions of innocent people. For the sake of power, these conquerors committed murder with hatred, cruelty and greed. They invaded poor countries and created untold suffering by taking away the lands and properties of others, and caused much destruction. Many of these conquerors are regarded as national heroes; memorial services are conducted in honour of them and flowers are offered on their graves and tombs. "What is wrong then, if Buddhists pay their respects to their world honoured Teacher who renounced all worldly pleasures for the sake of Enlightenment and showed others the Path of Liberation?

Images are the language of the subconscious. Therefore, the image of the Enlightened One is often created within one's mind as the embodiment of perfection. The image will deeply penetrate into the subconscious mind and (if it is sufficiently strong) can act as an automatic brake against impulses. The recollection of the Buddha produces joy, invigorates the mind and elevates man from states of restlessness, worry, tension and frustration. Thus the worship of the Buddha is not a prayer in its usual sense but a meditation. Therefore, it is not idol worship, but 'ideal' worship. Thus Buddhists can find fresh strength to build a shrine of their lives. They cleanse their hearts until they feel worthy to bear the image in this innermost shrine. Buddhists pay respects to the great person who is represented by the image. They try to gain inspiration from His Noble perso-nality and emulate Him. Buddhists do not see the Buddha image as a dead idol of wood or metal or clay. The image represents something vibrant to those who understand and are purified in thought, word and deed.

The Buddha images are nothing more than symbolic representations of His great qualities. It is not unnatural that the deep respect for the Buddha should be expressed in some of the finest and most beautiful forms of art and sculpture the world has ever known. It is difficult to understand why some people look down on those who respect images which represent holy religious teachers.

The calm and serene image of the Buddha has been a common concept of ideal beauty the world over. The Buddha's image is the most precious, common asset of Asian cultures. Without the image of the Buddha, where can we find a serene, radiant and spiritually emancipated personality?

The image of the Buddha is appreciated not only by Asians or Buddhists. Anatole France in his autobiography writes, 'On the first of May, 1890, chance led me to visit the Museum in Paris. There standing in the silence and simplicity of the gods of Asia, my eyes fell on the statue of the Buddha who beckoned to suffering humanity to develop understanding and compassion. If ever a god walked on this earth, I felt here was He. I felt like kneeling down to Him and praying to Him as to a God.'

Once a general sent an image of the Buddha as a legacy to Winston Churchill during the 2nd World War. The general said, 'If ever your mind gets perturbed and perplexed, I want you to see this image and be comforted.' What is it that makes the message of the Buddha so attractive to people who have cultivated their intellect? Perhaps the answer can be seen in the serenity of the image of the Buddha.

Not only in colour and line did people express their faith in the Buddha and the graciousness of His Teaching. Human hands worked in metal and stone to produce the Buddha image that is one of the greatest creations of the human genius. Witness the famous image in the Abhayagiri Vihara in Sri Lanka, or the Buddha image of Sarnath or the celebrated images of Borobudur. The eyes are full of compassion and the hands express fearlessness, or goodwill and blessings, or they unravel some thread of thought or call the earth to witness His great search for Truth. Wherever the Dharma went, the image of the great Teacher went with it, not only as an object of worship but also as an object of meditation and reverence. 'I know of nothing,' says Keyserling, 'more grand in this world than the figure of the Buddha. It is an absolutely perfect embodiment of spirituality in the visible domain.'

A life so beautiful, a heart so pure and kind, a mind so deep and enlightened, a personality so inspiring and selfless—such a perfect life, such a compassionate heart, such a calm mind, such a serene personality is really worthy of respect, worthy of honour and worthy of offering. The Buddha is the highest perfection of humanity.

The Buddha image is the symbol, not of a person, but of Buddhahood—that to which all people can attain though few do. Buddhahood is not for one but for many: 'The Buddhas of the past ages, the Buddhas that are yet to come, the Buddha of the present age; humbly I each day adore.'

However, it is not obligatory for every Buddhist to have a Buddha image to practise Buddhism. Those who can discipline their mind and the senses, can certainly do so without an image as an object. If Buddhists truly wish to behold the Buddha in all the majestic splendour and beauty of His ideal presence, they must translate His Teachings into practice in their daily lives. It is in the practice of His Teachings that they can come closer to Him and feel the wonderful radiance of His undying wisdom and compassion. Simply respecting the images without following His Sublime Teachings is not the way to find salvation. "He who sees the Dhamma sees Me".

We must also endeavour to understand the spirit of the Buddha. His Teaching is the only way to save this troubled world. In spite of the tremendous advantages of science and technology, people in the world today are filled with fear, anxiety and despair. The medicine for our troubled world is found in the Teachings of the Buddha.*

For a more detailed treatment of the subject, read the booklet 'Are Buddhists Idol worshippers?' by the same author What Buddhists Believe - Chapter 10

Religious Significance of Fasting

Many people in the world face untimely death owing to over-eating.

*I*N Buddhism, fasting is recognised as one of the methods for practising self-control. The Buddha advised monks not to take solid food after noon. Lay people who observe the Eight Precepts on full moon days also abstain from taking any solid food after noon.

Critics sometimes regard these practices as religious fads. To understanding people, they are not religious fads but practices based on a moral and psychological insight.

In Buddhism, fasting is an initial stage of self-discipline to acquire self-control. In every religion, there is a system of fasting. By fasting and sacrificing a meal once a day or for any period, we can contribute our food to those who are starving or who do not even have one proper meal each day.

'A man who eats too much', writes Leo Tolstoy, 'cannot strive against laziness, while a gluttonous and idle man will never be able to contend with sexual lust. Therefore, according to all moral teachings, the effort towards self-control commences with a struggle against the lust of gluttony – commences with fasting just as the first condition of a good life is self-control, so the first condition of a life of self-control is fasting.'

sages in various countries who practised self-control

began with a system of regulated fasting and succeeded in attaining unbelievable heights of spirituality. An ascetic was kicked and tortured, and then his hands and feet were severed on the orders of a rakish king. But the ascetic, according to the Buddhist story, endured the torture with equanimity and without the slightest anger or hatred. such religious people have developed their mental energy through restraining sensual indulgence which we crave for.

Vegetarianism

One should not judge the purity or impurity of persons simply by observing what they eat.

' Neither meat, nor fasting, nor nakedness, Nor shaven heads, nor matted hair, nor dirt, Nor rough skins, nor fire-worshipping, Nor all the penances here in this world, Nor hymns, nor oblation, nor sacrifice, Nor feasts of the season, Will purify a man overcome with doubt.'

Taking fish and meat by itself does not make people become impure. They become impure by bigotry, deceit, envy, self-exaltation, disparagement and other evil intentions. Through their evil thoughts and actions, they make themselves impure. There is no strict rule in Buddhism which stipulates that the followers of the Buddha should not take fish and meat. The only advice given by the Buddha is that they should not be involved in killing intentionally or they should not ask others to kill any living being for them.

Though the Buddha did not advocate vegetarianism for the monks, He did advise the monks to avoid taking ten kinds of meat for their self-respect and protection. They are: humans, elephants, horses, dogs, snakes, lions, tigers, leopards, bears, hyenas. some animals attack people when they smell the flesh of their own kind.

When the Buddha was asked to introduce

vegetarianism into the holy Order by Devadatta, one of His disciples, the Buddha refused to do so. As Buddhism is a free religion, His advice was to leave the decision regarding vegetarianism to the individual disciple. It clearly shows that the Buddha had not considered this as a very important religious observance. The Buddha did not mention anything about vegetarianism for the Buddhists in His Teaching.

Jivaka Komarabhacca, the physician, discussed this controversial issue with the Buddha: 'Lord, I have heard that animals are slaugh-tered on purpose for the recluse Gotama, and that the recluse Gotama knowingly eats the meat killed on purpose for him. Lord, do those who say animals are slaughtered on purpose for the recluse Gotama, and the recluse Gotama knowingly eats the meat killed on purpose for him. Do they falsely accuse the Buddha? Or do they speak the truth? Are your declarations and supplementary declarations not thus subject to be ridiculed by others in any manner?'

'Jivaka, those who say: 'Animals are slaughtered on purpose for the recluse Gotama, and the recluse Gotama knowingly eats the meat killed on purpose for him', do not say according to what I have declared, and they falsely accuse me. Jivaka, I have declared that one should not make use of meat if it is seen, heard or suspected to have been killed on purpose for a monk. I allow the monks meat that is quite pure in three respects: if it is not seen, heard or suspected to have been killed on purpose for a monk.'

In certain countries, the followers of the Mahayana school of Buddhism are strict vegetarians. Those who take vegetable food and abstain from animal flesh are praiseworthy. However, while appreciating their observance in the name of religion, we should like to point out that they should not condemn those who are not vegetarians. They must remember that there is no precept in the original Teachings of the Buddha that requires all

Buddhists to be vegetarians. We must realise that Buddhism is known as the Middle Path. It is a liberal religion and the Buddha's advice was that it is not necessary to go to extremes to practise His Teachings.

vegetarianism alone does not help a person to cultivate humane qualities. There are kind, humble, polite and religious people amongst non-vegetarians. Therefore, one should not condone the statement that a pure, religious person must practise vegetarianism.

On the other hand, if anybody thinks that people cannot have a healthy life without taking fish and meat, it does not necessarily follow that they are correct since there are millions of pure vegetarians all over the world who are stronger and healthier than the meat-eaters. In fact the Buddha declared that it is not what goes into a person's mouth that pollutes, it is what comes out.

People who criticize Buddhists who eat meat do not understand the Buddhist attitude towards food. A living being needs nourishment. We eat to live. As such human beings should supply their bodies with the food needed to keep them healthy and to give them energy to work. However, as a result of increasing wealth, more and more people, especially in developed countries, eat simply to satisfy their palates. If one craves for any kind of food, or kills to satisfy one's greed for meat, this is wrong. If one eats moderately without greed and without directly being involved in the act of killing but merely to sustain the physical body, he or she is practising self-restraint. The destruction of greed should be the primary aim, not the kind of food that is taken.

The Moon and Religious Observances

The outstanding events in the life of the Buddha took place on full moon days.

MANY people would like to know the religious significance of full moon and new moon days. To Buddhists, there is a special religious significance especially on full moon days because certain important and outstanding events connected with the life of Lord Buddha took place on full moon days. The Buddha was born on a full moon day. His renunciation took place on a full moon day. His Enlightenment, the delivery of His first sermon, His passing away into Nirvana and many other important events associated with His life span of eighty years, occurred on full moon days.

Buddhists all over the world have a high regard for full moon days. They celebrate this day with religious fervour by observing precepts, practising meditation and by keeping away from the sensual worldly life. On this day they direct their attention to spiritual development. Apart from Buddhists, it is understood that other co-religionists in Asia also believe that there is some religious significance related to the various phases of the moon. They also observe certain religious disciplines such as fasting and praying on full moon days.

The Ancients in India believed that the moon is the controller of the water, which, circulating through the universe, sustaining all living creatures, is the counterpart on earth of the liquor of heaven, 'amrta' the drink of the gods. Dew and rain become vegetable sap, sap becomes the milk of the cow, and the milk is then converted into blood—Amrta water, sap, milk and blood, represent but different states of the one elixir. The vessel or cup of this immortal fluid is the moon.

It is believed that the moon, like the other planets, exerts a considerable degree of influence on human beings. It has been observed that people suffering from mental ailments invariably have their passions and emotional feelings affected during full moon days. The word 'lunatic' derived from the word 'lunar' (or moon) is most significant and indicates very clearly our understanding of the influence of the moon on human life. some people, suffering from various forms of illness invariably find their sickness aggravated during such periods. Researchers have found that certain phases of the moon not only affect humans and animals, but also influence plant life and other elements. Low-tides and high-tides are a direct result of the overpowering influence of the moon.

Our human body consists of about seventy percent liquid. It is accepted by physicians that our bodily fluids flow more freely at the time of full moon. People suffering from asthma, bronchitis and even certain skin diseases, find their ailments aggravated under the influence of the moon. More than five thousand years ago, people had recognised the influence of the moon on cultivation. Farmers were very particular about the effect of the moon on their crops. They knew that certain grains and paddy would be affected if flowering took place during a full moon period. Medical science has also ascertained the different reactions of certain medicines under different facets of the moon, because of the influence of the moon on human beings.

In view of the possible influence of the moon, the ancient sages advised people to refrain from various commitments on this particular day and take it easy for the day. People are advised to relax their minds on this particular day and to devote their time to spiritual pursuits. All those who have developed their minds to a certain extent can achieve enlightenment since the brain is in an awakened state. Those who have not trained their minds through religious discipline are liable to be subjected to the strong influence of the moon. The Buddha attained His Enlightenment on a full moon day for He had been developing and attuning it correctly for a long period.

In days gone by, full moon and new moon days were declared public holidays in many Buddhist countries and people were encouraged to devote their time to spiritual development. It was only during the colonial period that holidays were switched over to Sundays. In view of this, some Buddhist countries are now trying to re-introduce the former lunar system of holidays. It is advisable to observe full moon day as a religious day to concentrate on peace and happiness by calming down the senses. Many Buddhists observe the eight precepts on full moon days, to be free from various commitments and to keep away from worldly pleasures in order to have peace of mind for their spiritual development. The effect of the moon on life and earth has been analysed scientifically.

One writer says: 'I have been reading an article in an American science magazine recently where the writer brings together the present research on the subject of the moon to prove how decisively this age old object of the skies influences our lives, particularly at each of the four phases it passes through in its 28-day cycle.'

This research, by the way, was done at the American universities of Yale, Duke and Northwestern and they have 'independently' come up with the astonishing evidence that the moon plays a big part in our daily life and indeed, in the lives of all living things.

We are assured that there is nothing very occult in this pheno-menon but that the phases of the moon do in fact stimulate various bodily actions like modifying metabolism, electrical charges and blood acidity.

One of the key experiments performed to establish this fact was on fiddler crabs, mice and some plants. They were all placed in chambers where weather conditions could not affect them, but were subjected to air pressure, humidity, light and temperature under controlled conditions.

The hundreds of observations made pointed to a remarkable fact, namely that all the animals and plants operated on a 28-day cycle. Metabolism which was found to have dropped at the time of the new moon was twenty percent higher at the time of the phase of the full moon. This difference is described as a striking variation.

Once a nurse in Florida told a doctor that she noticed a lot more bleeding occurred when the moon was full. Like many doctors who are sceptical about such beliefs, he laughed at this statement.

But the nurse produced records of surgical operations which clearly showed that during full moon, more patients had to be returned to the operating theatre than at any other time for treatment for excessive bleeding after operations. To satisfy himself, this doctor started keeping records on his own and he came to a similar conclusion. When we consider all those occurrences, we can understand why our ancestors and religious teachers had advised us to change our daily routine and to relax physically and mentally on full moon and new moon days. The practice of religion is the most appropriate method for people to experience mental peace and physical relaxation. Buddhists are merely observing the wisdom of the past when they devote more time to activities of a spiritual nature on New Moon and Full Moon days.

9

Human Life in Society

THE Buddha advised us not to believe in anything simply because it is our tradition or custom. However, we are not advised to suddenly do away with all traditions. ' You must try to experiment with them and put them thoroughly to test.

If they are reasonable and conducive both to your happiness and to the welfare of others, only then should you accept and practise these traditions and customs. This is certainly one of the most liberal declarations ever made by any religious teacher. This tolerance of others' traditions and customs is not known to some other religionists.

These religionists usually advise their new converts to give up all their traditions, customs and culture without considering whether they are good or bad. While preaching the Dharma, Buddhist missionaries have never advised the people to give up their traditions as long as they are reasonable. But the customs and traditions must be within the framework of religious principles. In other words, one should not violate the universal religious precepts in order to follow one's traditions.

If people are very keen to follow their own traditions which have no religious value at all, they can do so provided that they do not practise these traditions in the name of religion. Even then, such practices must be harmless to oneself and to all other living creatures.

Rites and Rituals

These are included within customs and traditions. The Rites and Rituals are an ornamentation or a decoration to beautify a religion in order to attract the public. They provide psychological help to some people. But one can practise religion without any rites and rituals. Certain rites and rituals that people consider as the most important aspect of their religion for their salvation are not considered as such in Buddhism. According to the Buddha, one should not cling to such practices for one's spiritual development or mental purity.

Festivals

Genuine and sincere Buddhists do not observe Buddhist festivals by enjoying themselves under the influence of liquor and merry-making or holding feasts following the slaughtering of animals. True Buddhists observe festival days in an entirely different manner. On the particular festival day, they devote their time to abstaining from all evil. They practise charity and help others to relieve themselves from their suffering. They entertain friends and relatives in a dignified way.

The festivals that have been incorporated into religion sometimes could pollute the purity of a religion. On the other hand a religion without festivals can become very dull and lifeless to many people. usually children and youths come to appreciate religion through religious festivals. To them the attraction of a religion is based on its festivals. On the other hand, to a meditator or a spiritually mature person, festivals can become a hindrance to true practice.

Of course, some people may not be satisfied with religious observances only during a festival. They prefer year-round merry-making and will settle for any excuse to have a "good time". Rites and rituals, ceremonies, processions and festivals are organised to quench that thirst for emotional satisfaction through religion. No one can say that such practices are wrong, but devotees have to organise those ceremonies in a cultured manner, without causing a nuisance to others. Especially in a multi-religious society, they have to organize festivals in such a way that they do not become a mockery in the eyes of the public.

Status of Women in Buddhism

A female child may even prove to be a better offspring than a male.

WOMEN'S position in Buddhism is unique. The Buddha gave women full freedom to participate in a religious life. The Buddha was the first religious Teacher who gave this religious freedom to women. Before the Buddha, women's duties had been restricted to the kitchen; women were not even allowed to enter any place of worship or to recite any religious scripture. During the Buddha's time in India, women's position in society was very low. The Buddha was criticized by the prevailing establishment when He gave this freedom to women. His move to allow women to enter the Holy Order was extremely radical for the times. Yet the Buddha allowed women to prove themselves and to show that they too had the capacity like men to attain the highest position in the religious way of life by attaining Arahantahood. Every woman in the world must be grateful to the Buddha for showing them the real religious way of living and for giving such freedom to them for the first time in world history.

A good illustration of the prevailing attitude towards women during the Buddha's time is found in these words of Mara: 'No woman, with the two-finger wisdom (narrow) which is hers, could ever hope to reach those heights which are attained only by the sages.' The nun *(bhikkhuni)* to whom Mara addressed these words, gave the following reply: 'When one's mind is well concentrated and wisdom never fails, does the fact of being a woman make any difference?'

The Buddha has confirmed that man is not always the only wise one; woman is also wise. King Kosala was very disappointed when he heard that his Queen had given birth to a baby girl.

He had expected a boy. undoubtedly, the Buddha was vehement in contradicting such attitudes. To console the sad King, the Buddha said:

A *female child, O Lord of men, may prove to be even a better offspring than a male. For she may grow up wise and virtuous, her husband's mother reverencing a true wife. The boy that she may bear may do great deeds, a rule great realms. Yes, such a son of noble wife becomes his country's guide.'*

Nowadays many religionists like to claim that their religions give women equal rights. We only have to look at the world around us today to see the position of women in many societies. It seems that they have no property rights, are discriminated against in various fields and generally suffer abuse in many subtle forms.

*For a deeper discussion on this subject, read the booklet Status of Women in Buddhism by the same author.

Even in western countries, women like the Suffragettes had to fight very hard for their rights.

According to Buddhism, it is not justifiable to regard women as inferior. The Buddha Himself was born as a woman on several occasions during His previous births in Samsara and even as a woman

He developed the noble qualities and wisdom at that time until He gained Enlightenment or Buddhahood.*

Buddhism and Politics

The Buddha had gone beyond all worldly affairs, but still gave advice on good government.

THE Buddha came from the warrior caste and was naturally brought into association with kings, princes and ministers. Despite His origin and association, He never resorted to the influence of political power to introduce His teaching, nor allowed His Teaching to be misused for gaining political power. But today, many politicians try to drag the Buddha's name into politics by introducing Him as a communist, capitalist, or even an imperialist. They have forgotten that the new political philosophy as we know it really developed in the West long after the Buddha's time. Those who try to make use of the good name of the Buddha for their own personal advantage must remember that the Buddha was the Supremely Enlightened One who had gone beyond all worldly concerns.

There is an inherent problem of trying to intermingle religion with politics. The basis of religion is morality, purity, faith and wisdom while that for politics is power. In the course of history, religion has often been used to give legitimacy to those in power and their exercise of that power.

When religion is used to pander to political whims, it has to forego its high moral ideals and become debased by worldly political demands. It is in these circumstances that religion was used to justify wars and conquests, persecutions, atrocities, rebellions, destruction of works of art and culture.

The Buddha Dharma is not directed at the creation of new political institutions and establishing political arrangements. Basically, it seeks to approach the problems of society by reforming the individuals constituting that society and by suggesting some general principles through which the society can be guided towards greater humanism, improved welfare of its members, and more equitable sharing of resources.

There is a limit to the extent to which a political system can safeguard the happiness and prosperity of its people. No political system, regardless of how ideal it may appear to be, can bring about peace and happiness as long as the people in the system are dominated by greed, hatred and delusion. In addition, no matter what political system is adopted, there are certain universal factors which the members of that society will have to experience: the effects of good and bad karma, the lack of real satisfaction or everlasting happiness in the world characterised by *dukkha* (unsatis-factoriness), *anicca* (impermanence), and *anatta* (unsubstantiality/ egolessness).

Although a good and just political system which guarantees basic human rights and which contains checks and balances to the use of power is an important condition for a happy life in society, people should not fritter away their time by endlessly searching for the ultimate political system where men can be completely free, because complete freedom cannot be found in any system but only in minds which are free. To be free, people will have to look within their own minds and work towards freeing themselves from the chains of ignorance and craving. Freedom in the truest sense is only possible when a person uses the Dharma to develop character through good speech and action and to train the mind so as to expand the mental potential and achieve the ultimate aim of enlightenment.

While recognising the usefulness of separating religion from politics and the limitations of political systems in bringing about peace and happiness, there are several aspects of the Buddha's teaching which have close correspondence to the political arrangements of the present day. Firstly, the Buddha spoke about the equality of all human beings long before Abraham Lincoln and taught that classes and castes are artificial barriers erected by society. According to the Agganna Sutra, the only classification of human beings, according to the Buddha, is based on the quality of their moral conduct. Secondly, the Buddha encouraged the spirit of social co-operation and active participation in society. This spirit is actively promoted in the political process of modern societies. Thirdly, since no one was appointed as the Buddha's successor, the members of the Order were to be guided by the Dharma and Vinaya, or the Righteous Rule of Law. Until today every member of the Sangha agrees to abide by the Rule of Law which governs and guides his conduct.

Fourthly, the Buddha encouraged the spirit of consultation and the democratic process. This is shown within the community of the Order in which all members have the right to decide on matters of general concern. When a serious question arose demanding attention, the issues were put before the monks and discussed in a manner similar to the democratic parliamentary system used today.

This self-governing procedure may come as a surprise to many to learn that in the assemblies of Buddhists in India 2,500 years and more ago are to be found the rudiments of the parliamentary practice of the present day. A special officer similar to 'Mr. Speaker' was appointed to preserve the dignity of the assembly. A second officer, who played a role similar to the Parliamentary Chief "Whip, was also appointed to see if the quorum was secured.

Matters were put forward in the form of a motion which was open to discussion. In some cases it was done once, in others three times, thus anticipating the practice of Parliament in requiring that a bill be read a third time before it becomes law. If the discussion showed a difference of opinion, it was to be settled by the vote of the majority through balloting.

The Buddhist approach to political power is the moralization and the responsible use of public power. The Buddha preached non-violence and peace as a universal message. He did not approve of violence or the destruction of life, and declared that there is no such thing as a 'just' war. He taught: 'The victor breeds hatred, the defeated lives in misery. He who renounces both victory and defeat is happy and peaceful.'

Not only did the Buddha teach non-violence and peace, He was perhaps the first and only religious teacher who went to the battlefield personally to prevent the outbreak of a war. He diffused tension between the Sakyas and the Koliyas who were about to wage war over distribution rights of the waters of Rohini. He also dissuaded King Ajatasattu from attacking the Kingdom of the vajjis.

The Buddha discussed the importance and the prerequisites of a good government. He showed how the country could become corrupt, degenerate and unhappy when the head of the government becomes corrupt and unjust. He spoke against corruption and how a government should act based on humanitarian principles. The Buddha once said:

'When the ruler of a country is just and good, the ministers become just and good, when the ministers are just and good, the higher officials become just and good, when the higher officials are just and good, the rank andfile become just and good, when the rank and file become just and good, the people become just and good.

In the Cakkavatti Sihanada Sutta, the Buddha said that im-morality and crime, such as theft, falsehood, violence, hatred, cruelty, could arise from poverty. Kings and governments may try to suppress crime through punishment, but it is futile to eradicate crimes through force.

In the Kutadanta Sutta, the Buddha suggested economic development instead of force to reduce crime. The government should use the country's resources to improve the economic conditions of the country. It could embark on agricultural and rural development, provide financial support to those who undertake an enterprise and business, provide adequate wages for workers to maintain a decent life with human dignity.

In the Jataka stories, the Buddha gave 10 rules for Good Government, known as *Dasa Raja Dharma.* These ten rules can be applied even today by any government which wishes to rule the country peacefully. According to these rules a ruler must:

1. be liberal and avoid selfishness,
2. maintain a high moral character,
3. be prepared to sacrifice his own pleasure for the well being of the subjects,
4. be honest and maintain absolute integrity,
5. be kind and gentle,
6. lead a simple life for the subjects to emulate,
7. be free from hatred of any kind,
8. exercise non violence,
9. practise patience, and
10. respect public opinion to promote peace and harmony.

Regarding the behaviour of rulers, He further advised:

1. A good ruler should act impartially and should not

be biased and discriminate between one particular group of subjects against another.

2. A good ruler should not harbour any form of hatred against any of his subjects.

3. A good ruler should show no fear whatsoever in the enforcement of the law, if it is justifiable.

4. A good ruler must possess a clear understanding of the law to be enforced. it should not be enforced just because the ruler has the authority to enforce the law. it must be done in a reasonable manner and with common sense.

In the Milinda Panha, it is stated: 'If a man, who is unfit, incompetent, immoral, improper, unable and unworthy of kingship, has enthroned himself a king or a ruler with great authority, he is subject to a variety of punishment by the people, because, being unfit and unworthy, he has placed himself unrighteously in the seat of sovereignty. The ruler, like others who violate and transgress moral codes and basic rules of all social laws of mankind, is equally subject to punishment; and moreover, to be censured is the ruler who conducts himself as a robber of the public.' In a Jataka story, it is mentioned that a ruler who punishes innocent people and does not punish the culprit is not suitable to rule a country.

The king always improves himself and carefully examines his own conduct in deeds, words and thoughts, trying to discover and listen to public opinion as to whether or not he had been guilty of any faults and mistakes in ruling the kingdom. if it is found that he rules unrighteously, the public will complain that they are ruined by the wicked ruler with unjust treatment, punishment, taxation, or other oppressions including corruption of any kind, and they will react against him in one way or another. On the contrary, if he rules righteously they will bless him: 'Long live His Majesty.' (Majjhima Nikaya)

We can note in passing why the Buddha's Teaching is called the Eternal Dharma or Truth. From the points mentioned above we can see that the Teachings are universal and can be applied to all human societies no matter how separated they are in time and space.

The Buddha's emphasis on the moral duty of a ruler to use public power to improve the welfare of the people inspired Emperor Asoka in the Third Century B.C. to do likewise. Emperor Asoka, a sparkling example of this principle, resolved to live according to the Dharma and to serve his subjects and all humanity. He declared his non-aggressive intentions to his neighbours, assuring them of his goodwill and sending envoys to distant kings bearing his message of peace and non-aggression. He promoted the energetic practice of the socio-moral virtues of honesty, truthfulness, compassion, benevolence, non-violence, considerate behaviour towards all, non-extravagance, non-acquisitiveness, and non-injury to animals. He encouraged religious freedom and mutual respect for other people's beliefs. He went on periodic tours preaching the Dharma to the rural people. He undertook works of public utility, such as founding of hospitals for men and animals, supplying of medicine, planting of roadside trees and groves, digging of wells, and construction of watering sheds and rest houses. He expressly forbade cruelty to animals.

sometimes the Buddha is described as a social reformer although this was not His primary concern. Among other things, He con-demned the caste system, recognised the equality of people, spoke on the need to improve socio-economic conditions, recognised the importance of a more equitable distribution of wealth among the rich and the poor, raised the status of women, recommended the incorporation of humanism in government and administration, and taught that a society should not be run by greed but with consideration and compassion for the people. Despite all these, His contribution to mankind is much greater because He took off at a point which no other social reformer before or ever since had reached, that is, by going to the deepest roots of human ill which are found in the human mind. it is only in the human mind that true reform can be effected. Reforms imposed by force upon the external world have a very short life because they have no roots. But those reforms which spring as a result of the transformation of man's inner consciousness remain rooted. While their branches spread outwards, they draw their nourishment from an unfailing source—the subconscious imperatives of the life-stream itself. So reforms come about when men's minds have prepared the way for them, and they live as long as men revitalise them out of their own love of truth, justice and their fellow men. The Buddhist attitude is that social reform can be achieved, not by harshness and punishment, but through education and compassion.

The doctrine preached by the Buddha is not one based on 'Political Philosophy'. Nor is it a doctrine that encourages people to incline towards worldly interests. It sets out a way to attain Nirvana. In other words, its ultimate aim is to put an end to craving *(tanha)* that keeps men in bondage to this world. Everything else including social reformation, is of a secondary concern. A stanza from the Dhammapada best summarises this statement: 'The path that leads to worldly gain is one, and the path that leads to Nirvana (by leading a religious life) is another'. However, this does not mean that Buddhists cannot or should not get involved in the political process, which is a social reality. The entire Teaching can be broadly divided into two categories: mundane and supramundane.

The first refers to our material concerns pertaining to this human existence; the second concerns our spiritual aspirations which transcend worldly needs. The Buddha has said that living comfortable, secure and contented lives are a necessary prerequisite to prepare the mind to seek spiritual fulfillment.

The lives of the members of a society are shaped by laws and regulations, economic arrangements allowed within a country and institutional arrangements, which are influenced by the political situation of that society. Nevertheless, if Buddhists wish to be involved in politics, they should not misuse religion to gain political powers, nor is it advisable for those who have renounced the worldly life in order to lead a pure, religious life to be actively involved in politics.

10

MARRIAGE, BIRTH CONTROL AND DEATH

MARRIAGE is a social convention, an institution created by human beings for their well being and happiness to differentiate human society from animal life and to maintain order and harmony in the process of procreation. Even though the Buddhist texts are silent on the subject of monogamy or polygamy, the Buddhist lay person is advised to limit himself or herself to one spouse. The Buddha did not lay rules on married life but gave necessary advice on how to live a happy married life. There

are ample inferences in His sermons that it is wise and advisable to be faithful to one spouse and not to be sensual and to run after other partners. The Buddha taught that one of the main causes of the downfall of man is his involvement with other women. Of course the implication is that a woman who gets involved with many men is also bound to suffer.

A person must realise the difficulties, the trials and tribulations that one has to undergo just to maintain a family life. These would be magnified many times when faced with self induced complications. Knowing the frailties of human nature, the Buddha did, in one of His precepts, advise His followers to refrain from committing adultery or sexual misconduct.

The Buddhist views on marriage are very liberal: in Buddhism, marriage is regarded entirely as a personal and individual concern, and not as a religious duty. There are no religious laws in Buddhism compelling a person to be married, to remain single or to lead a life of total celibacy. it is not laid down anywhere that Buddhists must produce children or regulate the number of children that they produce. Buddhism allows each individual the freedom to decide for him or herself all the issues pertaining to marriage. It might be asked why Buddhist monks do not marry, since there are no laws for or against marriage.

The reason is obviously that to be of service to mankind, the monks have chosen a way of life which includes celibacy. Those who renounce the worldly life keep away from married life voluntarily to avoid various worldly commitments in order to maintain peace of mind.

They wish to dedicate their lives solely to serve others in the attainment of spiritual emancipation. In modern society, although Buddhist monks do not solemnize a marriage ceremony, they can be called upon to perform religious services in order to bless the couples. These remarks are all equally applicable to nuns.

Divorce

Separation or divorce is not prohibited in Buddhism though the necessity would scarcely arise if the Buddha's injunctions were strictly followed. Men and women must have the liberty to separate if they really cannot agree with each other. separation is preferable to living a miserable family life for a long period of time for both partners and innocent children. The Buddha further advises old men not to have young wives as the old and young are unlikely to be compatible, which can create undue problems, disharmony and downfall (Parabhava Sutra).

*Read the book "Happy Married Life" by the same author for more details.

A society grows through a network of relationships which are mutually intertwined and inter-dependent. Every relationship is a wholehearted commitment to support and to protect others in a group or community. Marriage plays a very important part in this strong web of relationships of giving support and protection.

A good marriage should grow and develop gradually from understanding and not impulse, from true loyalty and not just sheer indulgence. The institution of marriage provides a fine basis for the development of culture, a delightful association of two individuals to be nurtured, and to be free from loneliness, depri-vation and fear. in marriage, each partner develops a complementary role, giving strength and moral courage to one another, each manifesting a supportive and appreciative recognition of the other's skills. There must be no thought of either man or woman being superior; each is complementary to the other, in a partnership of equality, exuding gentleness, self-control, respect, generosity, calm and dedication.

Birth Control, Abortion and Suicide

Although a human being has freedom to plan a family according to his or her own convenience, abortion is not justifiable.

THERE is no reason for Buddhists to oppose birth control. They are at liberty to use any of the old or modern measures to prevent conception. Those who object to birth control by saying that it is against God's law to practise it, must realise that their concept regarding this issue is not reasonable. in birth control what is done is to prevent the coming into being of an existence. There is no killing involved and there is no akusala karma (unskillful action). However, if people take any action to have an abortion, this action is wrong because it involves taking away or destroying a visible or invisible life. Therefore, abortion is not justifiable.

According to the Teachings of the Buddha, five conditions must be present to constitute the evil act of killing. They are:

1. a living being
2. knowledge or awareness it is a living being
3. intention of killing
4. effort to kill, and
5. consequent death

At conception, there is a being in the womb and this fulfils the first condition. After a couple of months, the mother knows that there is a new life within her and this satisfies the second condition. Then for some reason or other, she wants to do away with this being in her. so she begins to search for an abortionist to do the job and in this way, the third condition is fulfilled. When the abortionist does his job, the fourth condition is provided for and finally, the being is killed because of that action. so all the conditions are present. In this way, there is a violation of the First Precept 'not to kill', and this is tantamount to killing a human being. Conversely, however, by birth control, a life does not come into being, and therefore all the above five conditions cannot operate.

According to Buddhism, there is no ground to say that we have the right to take away a life once it has come into being. under certain circumstances, people feel compelled to do that for their own convenience. But they should not justify this act of abortion as somehow or other they will have to face some sort of bad consequences. in certain countries abortion is legalised, but this is to overcome some social problems. Religious principles should never be surrendered for the pleasure of human beings. They stand for the welfare of the whole of mankind.

Committing Suicide

Taking one's own life under any circumstances is morally and spiritually wrong. Taking one's own life owing to frustration or disappointment only causes greater suffering. suicide is a cowardly way to end one's problems in life. A person cannot commit suicide if his or her mind is pure and tranquil. If one leaves this world with a confused and frustrated mind, it is most unlikely that he or she would be born again in a better condition. Suicide is an unwholesome or unskilful act since it is encouraged by a mind filled with self importance, greed, hatred and most importantly, delusion. Those who commit suicide have not learnt how to face their problems, how to face the facts of life, and how to use their mind in a proper manner. such people have not been able to understand the nature of life and worldly conditions.

some people sacrifice their own lives for what they deem as a good and noble cause. They take their own lives by such methods as self-immolation, bullet-fire, or starvation. such actions may be classified as brave and courageous. However, from the Buddhist point of view, such acts are not to be condoned. The Buddha has clearly pointed out that suicidal states of mind lead to further suffering. This whole attitude again proves how much Buddhism is a positive, life affirming religion.

Why Does the World Population Increase?

The credit or responsibility for the population increase must go to the medical and other facilities available today.

IF Buddhists do not believe in a soul created by god,

how are they going to account for the increase of population in the world today? This is a very common question that is asked by many people. People who ask this question usually assume that there is only one world where living beings exist. One must consider that it is quite natural for the population to increase in such places where good climatic conditions, medical facilities, food and pre-cautions are available to produce and to protect living beings.

One must also consider that there is really no ground to think that this is the only period in which the population in the world has increased. There are no means of comparison with any period of ancient history. vast civilisations existed and have disappeared in Central Asia, the Middle East, Africa and Ancient America. No census figures on these civilisations are even remotely available. Population, as everything else in the universe, is subject to cycles of rise and fall. in cycles of alarming increases of birth rate, one might be consequently tempted to argue against rebirth in this or other worlds. For the last few thousand years, there has been no evidence to prove that there were more people in some parts of the world than there are today. The number of beings existing in the various world systems is truly infinite. if human lives can be compared to only few grains of sand, the number of beings in the universe can be said to be greater than the grains of sand on all the beaches in the world. When conditions are right and when supported by their good karma, a few of these infinite number of beings are reborn as human beings. The advancement of medicine especially in the 19th and 20th centuries has enabled human beings to live longer and healthier lives.

This is a factor that contributes to population increase. Popu-lation can further increase unless sensible people take measures to control it. Hence, the credit or responsibility for increasing the population must be given to medical facilities and other qualified authorities available today. This credit or responsibility cannot be allotted to any particular religion or any external sources.

There is a belief among certain people that all unfortunate occurrences that destroy human lives are created by God in order to reduce the population of the world. instead of giving so much suffering to his own creatures, why cannot he control the population? Why does he create more and more people in thickly populated countries where there is no proper food, clothing and other basic and necessary requirements? Those who believe that God created everything cannot give a satisfactory answer to this question. Poverty, unhappiness, war, hunger, disease, famine are not due to the will of God or to the whim of some devil, but to causes which are not so difficult to discover.

Sex and Religion

Human beings are the only living beings that do not have periods of natural sexual inactivity during which the body can recover its vitality.

THE sex impulse is the most dynamic force in human nature. So far-reaching is the sexual force that some measure of self-control is necessary even in ordinary existence. in the case of the spiritual aspirants, for those who want to bring their mind under complete control, a still greater measure of self-discipline is necessary. such a powerful force in human character can be subdued only if the aspirants control their thoughts and practise con-centration. The conservation of the sexual force helps to develop this strength. For if they control the sexual force, they will have more control over their whole make-up, over their baser emotions. "Control" means we voluntarily exercise restraint by understanding the need to do so. This is very different from "suppressing" which means simply trying to pretend the urge is not there. suppression can have dangerous consequences.

Celibacy is recommended for those who like to develop their spiritual development for perfection. However, it is not compulsory for each and every person to observe complete celibacy in order to practise Buddhism. The Buddha's advice is that observing celibacy is more congenial for a person who wants to cultivate his or her spiritual achievements. For ordinary Buddhist lay persons, the precept is to abstain from sexual misconduct. This means that a householder may indulge in legitimate sex. This is because in such legitimate sexual activity there is no guilt and no sense of exploitation of the other party.

However, there is a need even for Buddhist lay people to exercise some degree of control over their sexual force. The human sexual urge must be controlled properly otherwise people will behave worse than animals when they are intoxicated with lust. Consider the sexual behaviour of what we call the 'lower animal'. Which really is often 'lower'—the animal or the man? Which acts in a normal, regular manner as regards sexual behaviour? And which runs off into all manner of irregularities and perversities? Often it is the animal that is the higher creature and the human that is the lower. And why is this? it is simply because humans who possess the mental capacity which if rightly used, could make them masters over their sex impulses, have actually used their mental powers in such deplorable fashions as to make themselves slaves to those impulses. Thus people can, at times, be considered lower than animals.

Our ancestors played down this sexual impulse; they knew that it was strong enough without giving it any extra encouragement. But today we have blown it up with a thousand forms of incitation, suggestive advertisements, emphasis and display; and we have armed the sexual force with the doctrine that inhibition is dangerous and can even cause mental disorders.

Although inhibition—the restriction which controls the impulse—is the first principle of any civilization, in our modern civilization too, we have polluted the sexual atmosphere that surrounds us—and greatly exaggerated the mind/body urge for sexual gratification through the mass media.

As a result of this sex exploitation by the hidden persuaders of modern society, the youth of today have developed an attitude towards sex that is becoming a public nuisance. in many cases, innocent girls have no freedom to move anywhere without being disturbed.

Human beings are the only animals that do not have periods of natural sexual inactivity during which the body can recover its vitality. unfortunately, commercial exploitation of this erotic nature has caused them to be exposed to a ceaseless barrage of sexual stimulation from every side. Much of the neuroses of present-day life are traceable to this unbalanced state of affairs. Men in modern societies are expected to be monogamous, yet women are exploited in every possible way to 'glamorise' themselves, not for their husbands alone, but to excite in every man passions that society forbids him to indulge in.

sex should be given its due place in normal human life; it should be neither unhealthily repressed nor morbidly exaggerated. And it should always be under the control of the will, as it can be if it is regarded sanely and placed in its proper perspective.

unlike what we are made to believe, sex should not be considered as the most important ingredient for one's happiness in a married life. Those who over-indulge can become slaves to sex which could ultimately ruin love and humane considerations in marriage. As in everything, one must be temperate and rational in one's sexual demands taking into consideration the partner's intimate feelings and temperament.

Marriage is a bond of partnership for life entered into by a man and a woman. Patience, tolerance and understanding are the three principal qualities that should be developed and nurtured by the couple. "Whilst love should be the knot tying the couple together, material necessities for sustaining a happy home should be made available for the couple to share.

The qualification for a good partner-ship in marriage should be 'ours' and not 'yours' or 'mine'. A good couple should 'open' their hearts to one another and refrain from entertaining 'secrets'. Keeping secrets to oneself could lead to suspicion and suspicion is the element that could destroy love in a partnership. Suspicion breeds jealousy, jealousy creates anger, anger develops hatred, hatred turns into enmity and enmity could cause untold sufferings including bloodshed, suicide and even murder.

NATURE, VALUE AND CHOICE OF RELIGIOUS BELIEFS

*H*UMANS developed religion in order to satisfy their desire to understand the life within them and the world outside them. The earliest religions had animistic origins, and they arose out of their fear of the unknown and their desire to placate the forces which they thought inhabited inanimate objects.

Over time these religions underwent changes, being shaped by the geographical, historical, socio-economic, political, and intellectual environment existing at that time.

Many of these religions have become organised and are flourishing to this day, backed by a strong following of devotees.

Many people are drawn to organised religions because of the pomp and ceremony in the rituals, while there are some who prefer to practice their own personal religion, inwardly venerating their religious teachers and applying moral principles in their daily life. Because of the importance of practice, every religion claims to be a way of life, not merely a faith. In view of their various origins and paths of development which religions undergo, it is hardly surprising that the religions of human beings should differ in their approach, the understanding and interpretation of their followers, their goal and how it can be achieved, and their concept of reward and punishment for deeds performed.

In terms of approach, religious practices may be based on faith, fear, rationality or harmlessness: Faith forms the basis of many religious practices which were developed to overcome people's fear and to meet their needs. A religion highlighting miraculous or mystical powers exploits that fear which arises from ignorance and makes promises of material gain based on greed. A religion encouraging devotion is based on emotion and the fear of the supernatural which, it is so believed, can be appeased through rites and rituals. A religion of faith is based on the desire for gaining confidence in the face of the uncertainty of human life and destiny.

Some religious practices grew as a result of the development of human knowledge, experience and wisdom. The rational approach to religion had been adopted in this case, incorporating the principles of human value and natural or universal laws. It is based on humanism and concentrates on the cultivation of humane qualities. A religion of cause and effect or karma is based on the principle of self-help and assumes that the individual alone is responsible for his or her own happiness and suffering as well as salvation. A religion of wisdom is based on the application of reason and seeks to understand life and the reality of worldly conditions through analytical knowledge. Science asks and seeks to explain what the world is while religion asks what mankind and society should become.

The fostering of harmlessness and goodwill are common elements found in religion. A religion of peace is based on the principle of causing no harm to oneself as well as others, and its followers are urged to cultivate a harmonious, liberal and peaceful life. A religion of goodwill or loving-kindness is based on sacrifice and service, for the welfare and happiness of others.

Religions differ according to the understanding capacity of their followers and the interpretations which religious authorities give to religious doctrines and practices. In some religions, authorities have a strong say in enforcing religious laws and moral codes, while in others they only provide advice on the need and the way to follow these codes. Every religion will offer reasons to explain the existing human problems and inequalities and the way to remedy the situation. By way of explanation, some religions claim that they have to face these problems because they are on trial in this world. When such an explanation is given, another may ask, 'For what purpose? How can human be judged on the basis of just one life when human beings generally differ in their experiences of physical, intellectual, social, economic and environmental factors and conditions?'

Every religion has its own concept of what is regarded to be the goal of spiritual life. For some religions, eternal life in heaven or paradise with the Lord is the final goal. For some the ultimate aim in life is the union of universal consciousness, because it is believed that life is a unit of consciousness and it must return to the same original consciousness. For others, even heavenly bliss or union with

Brahman (primal force) is secondary to the uncertainty of existence, no matter what form it takes. And there are even some who believe that the present life itself is more than enough to experience the aim of life.

The medicine which cures one man's sickness can become poison to another man according to the constitution of his body. In the same way one man's concept of what religious way of life is best to follow can become a nuisance to another person depending on his mentality.

To attain the desired goal, every religion offers a method. Some religions ask their followers to surrender to God or depend on God for everything. Others call for stringent asceticism as the means of purging oneself of all evil through self-mortification. Some others recommend the performance of animal sacrifices and many kinds of rites and rituals as well as the recital of mantras for their purification to gain the final goal. There is yet another which upholds diverse methods and devotions, intellectual realisation of truth, and concentration of the mind through meditation.

Each religion has a different concept of punishment for evil deeds. According to some religions, humans are doomed forever by God for their transgressions in this one life. Some others say that action and reaction (cause and effect) operate due to natural laws and the effect of a deed will only be experienced for a certain period. Some religions maintain that this life is only one of so many, and a person will always have a chance to reform in stages until he or she finally evolves to attain the goal of Supreme Bliss.

Given such a wide variety of approaches, interpretations and goals of different religions adopted by mankind, it is useful for people not to hold dogmatic views about their religion but to be open to and tolerant of other religious views.

The Buddha said: 'One must not accept my teachings from reverence, but first try them as gold is tried by fire.'

After emphasising the importance of maintaining an open mind towards religious doctrines, it is useful to remember that a religion should be practised for the welfare, freedom and happiness of all living beings. That is, religious principles should be used positively to improve the quality of life of all beings. Yet today, humankind is corrupted and has gone astray from basic religious principles. Immoral and evil practices have become common among many people, and religious-minded people experience difficulties trying to maintain certain religious principles in modern life. At the same time, the standard of basic religious principles is also lowered to pander to the demands of polluted and selfish minds. Humans should not violate universal moral codes to suit their own greed or indulgence; rather they should try to adjust themselves according to the moral codes taught by religion.

Religious precepts have been introduced by enlightened religious teachers who have realised the noble way of life which leads to peace and happiness. Those who violate these precepts transgress the universal laws, which, according to Buddhism will bring bad effects.

This does not mean, on the other hand, that a person should slavishly follow what is found in his or her religion, regardless of its relevance to modern times. Religious laws and precepts should enable people to lead a meaningful life, and are not to be used to bind them to archaic practices and superstitious rituals and beliefs. A person who upholds the basic religious principles should give credit to human intelligence and live respectably with human dignity. There must be some changes in our religious activities to correspond to our education and the nature of our changing society, without at the same time sacrificing the noble universal principles. But it is recognised that making changes to any religious practices is always difficult because many conservative people are opposed to changes, even if they are for the better. Such conservative views are like a stagnant pool of water, while fresh ideas are like the waterfall where the water is constantly being renewed and is, therefore, usable all the time.

Misconceptions on Religion

Despite the value of religion in moral upliftment, it is also true to say that religion is a fertile soil for the development of superstitions and devotional beliefs, wrapped under the cloak of religiosity. Many people use religion to escape from the realities of life and put on the garb of religion and religious symbols with little or no inner development. They may even pray very often in places of worship, yet they are not sincerely religious minded and do not understand what religion stands for. When a religion has been debased by ignorance, greed for power and selfishness, people quickly point an accusing finger and say that religion is irrational. But 'Religion' (the ritualistic external practice of any teaching) must be distinguished from the teaching itself. Before one criticizes, one must study the original teachings of the founder and see if there is anything intrinsically wrong with it.

Religion advises people to do good and be good, but they are not interested in acting thus. Instead they prefer to cling to the external practices which have few religious values. Had they tried to culture their minds by eradicating jealousy, pride, cruelty and selfishness, at least they would have found the correct way to practise a religion. Unfortunately, they develop jealousy, pride, cruelty and selfishness instead of eradicating them. Many people pretend to be religious, but commit the greatest atrocities in the name of religion. They fight, discriminate and create unrest for the sake of religion, losing sight of its lofty purpose. From the increase in the performance of various so called religious activities, we may get the impression that religion is progressing, but the opposite is really the case since very little mental purity and understanding are actually being practised.

Practising a religion is nothing more than the development of one's inner awareness, goodwill and understanding. Problems would have to be faced squarely by relying on one's spiritual strength. Running away from one's problems in the name of spiritualism is not courageous, much less spiritual. Under today's chaotic condi-tions, men and women are rapidly sliding downhill to their own destruction. The irony is that they imagine they are progressing towards a glorious civilisation that is yet to be realised.

In the midst of this confusion, imaginary and plastic religious concepts are propagated to create more temptation and confusion in the human mind. Religion is being misused for personal gain and political power. Certain immoral practices, such as free sex, have been encouraged by some irresponsible religious groups to introduce their religion among youths. By arousing lustful feelings, these groups hope to seduce boys and girls into following their religion. Today religion has degenerated into a cheap commodity in the religious market giving scant regard to moral values and what they stand for. Some missionaries claim that the practice of morals, ethics and precepts are not important as long as they have faith and pray to God, which is believed to be sufficient to grant their salvation. Having witnessed how some religious authorities have misled and blindfolded their followers in Europe, Karl Marx made a caustic remark: 'Religion is the sigh of the oppressed creature, the feelings of a heartless world, just as it is the soul of soulless conditions. It is the opium of the people.'

We need a religion not for the reason of giving us a dream for our next life or providing us with some dogmatic ideas to follow, in such a way that we surrender our human intelligence and become a nuisance to our fellow beings. A religion should be a reliable and reasonable method for people to live 'here and now' as cultured, understanding beings, while setting a good example for others to follow. Many religions turn our thoughts away from ourselves towards a supreme being, but Buddhism directs our search for peace inwards to the potentialities that lie hidden within ourselves. Buddhism respects and encourages our intelligence. The Buddha pointed out the mind's great potential and how to develop it. Therefore, true religion, which is Dharma, is not something outside us that we acquire, but the cultivation and realisation of wisdom, compassion and purity that we develop within ourselves.

Which is the Proper Religion?

If any religion has the Four Noble Truths and the Eightfold Path, then it can be regarded as a proper religion.

IT is very difficult for people to discover why there are so many different religions, and which religion is the true one. Followers of every religion are trying to show the superiority of their religion. Diversity has given rise to some forms of development, but in matters of religion, people look upon each other with jealousy, hatred and disdain. The most respected religious practices in one religion are deemed ridiculous to others.

To introduce their divine and peaceful messages some people have resorted to weapons and wars. Have they not polluted the good name of religion? It seems that certain religions are responsible for dividing instead of uniting mankind. Today we have more than enough religions which encourage their followers to hate another religion, but not enough religions which encourage respect for another religion. Every religion teaches about love but one religion cannot love another religion.

To find a true and proper religion, we must weigh with an unbiased mind what exactly is a false religion. False religions or philosophies include: materialism which denies survival after death; amoralism which denies good and evil; any religion which asserts that man is miraculously saved or doomed; theistic evolution which holds that everything is preordained and everyone is destined to attain eventual salvation through mere faith.

Buddhism is free from unsatisfactory and uncertain foundations. Buddhism is realistic and verifiable. Its Truths have been verified by the Buddha, verified by His disciples, and always remain open to be verified by anyone who wishes to do so. And today, the Teachings of the Buddha are being verified by the most severe methods of scientific investigation.

The Buddha advises that any form of religion is proper if it contains the Four Noble Truths and the Noble Eightfold Path. This clearly shows that the Buddha did not want to form a particular religion. What He wanted was to reveal the Ultimate Truth of our life and the world. Although the Buddha expounded the Four Noble Truths and the Eightfold Noble Path, this method is not the property of Buddhists alone. This is a universal Truth and is open to anyone who wishes to understand the human condition and attain happiness.

Most people find it necessary to put forth arguments to 'prove' the validity of the religion that they are following. Some claim that their religion is the oldest and therefore contains the truth. Others claim that their religion is the latest or newest and therefore contains the truth. Some claim that their religion has the most followers and therefore contains the truth. Yet none of these arguments are valid to establish the truth of a religion. One can judge the value of a religion by using only common sense and understanding.

Some religious traditions require people to be subservient to a greater power than them, a power that determines and controls their creation, actions and their final deliverance. The Buddha did not accept such powers. Rather, He assigned that very power to themselves by asserting that each person is his or her own creator, responsible for their salvation.

That is why it is said that 'There is none so godless as the Buddha and yet none so godlike'. The religion of the Buddhists gives humanity a great sense of dignity; at the same time it also gives them great responsibility. Buddhists cannot put the blame on an external power when evil befalls them. But they can face misfortune with equanimity because they know that they have the power to extricate themselves from all misery.

One of the reasons why Buddhism appeals to intellectuals and those with a good education, is that the Buddha expressly discouraged His followers from accepting anything they heard without first testing its validity. The teachings of the Buddha have remained and survived precisely because many intellectuals have challenged every aspect of the teachings and have concluded that the Buddha had always spoken the undeniable Truth.

While other religionists are trying to reassess their founders' teachings in the light of modern knowledge about the Universe, the Buddha's teachings are being verified by scientists.

Moral and Spiritual Development

Without a spiritual background humans have no moral

responsibility: humans without moral responsibility pose a danger to society

BUDDHISM has been an admirable lighthouse for guiding many human beings to salvation from the suffering in Samsara. Buddhism is especially needed in the world today which is riddled with racial, economic and ideological misunder-standings. These misunderstandings can never be effectively cleared until the spirit of benevolent tolerance is extended towards others. This spirit can be best cultivated under the guidance of Buddhism which inculcates ethical-moral co-operation for universal good.

We know that it is easy to learn vice without a master, whereas virtue requires a tutor. There is a very great need for the teaching of virtue by precepts and examples.

Without a spiritual background, we have no moral responsibility: human life without moral responsibility poses danger to society.

In the Buddha's Teaching, it is said that the spiritual development of humans is more important than the development of material welfare. History has taught us that it is unreasonable to expect to gain both worldly happiness and everlasting Happiness at the same time. The lives of most people are generally regulated by spiritual values and moral principles which only religion can effectively provide. Governmental interference in the lives of people can be made comparatively unnecessary if men and women can be made to realise the value of self discipline and are able to practise the ideals of truth, justice and service.

virtue is necessary to attain salvation, but virtue alone is not enough. virtue must be combined with wisdom. virtue and wisdom are like the pair of wings of a bird. Wisdom can also be compared to the eyes of a person; virtue, to the feet. virtue can be likened to a vehicle that brings people up to the gate of salvation. But wisdom is the actual key that opens the gate. virtue is a part of the technique of skilful and noble living. Without any ethical discipline, there cannot be a purification of the defilements of sentient existence.

Buddhism is not mere mumbo-jumbo, a myth told to entertain the human mind or to satisfy the human emotion, but a liberal and noble method for those who sincerely want to understand and experience the reality of life.

There are four ways by which humanity tries to realize the aim of life: 1. Material or physical level (wealth). 2. Emotional level-likes or dislikes; or pleasant or unpleasant feelings. 3. Intellectual level—studying or reasoning. 4. Spiritual level—sympathetic understanding based on justice, purity and fair dealing.

The last one is the realistic and lasting method which never creates disappointment.

The God-Idea

The reality or validity of belief in God is based on our understanding capacity and the maturity of the mind.

The Development of the God-idea

TO trace the origin and development of the god-idea, one must go back to the time when civilisation was still in its infancy and modern science was still unknown. Primitive people, out of fear of and admiration for natural phenomena, had believed in different spirits and gods. They used their belief in spirits and gods to form religions peculiar to the area they lived in. According to their respective circumstances and understanding capacity different people worshipped different gods and founded different faiths.

At the beginning of the god-idea, people worshipped many gods-gods of trees, streams, lightning, storm, winds, the sun and all other terrestrial phenomena. These gods were related to various manifestations of nature. Then gradually human beings began to attribute to these gods, sex and form as well as the physical and mental attributes of their own nature: love, hate, jealousy, fear, pride, envy and other emotions found among human beings. From all these gods, there slowly grew a realisation that the phenomena of the universe were not many but One. This understanding gave rise to the monotheistic god of comparatively recent ages.

In the process of development, the god-idea was moulded through a variety of changing social and intellectual climates. It was regarded

by different people in different ways. Some idealised god as the King of Heaven and Earth; they had a conception of god as a person. Others thought of god as an abstract principle. Some raised the ideal of Supreme deity to the highest heaven, while others brought it down to the lowest depths of the earth. Some pictured god in a paradise, while others made an idol and worshipped it. Some went so far as to say that there is no salvation without god—no matter how much good you do, you will not receive the fruits of your actions unless you act out of a faith in that particular god and no other. The Atheists said, 'No' and went on to affirm that god did not really exist at all. The Sceptics or Agnostics said, 'We do not or we cannot know.' 'The Positivists said that the god-idea was a meaningless problem since the idea of the term god 'was not clear'. Thus there grew a variety of ideas and beliefs and names for the god-idea: pantheism, idolatory, belief in a formless god, and belief in many gods and goddesses.

Even the monotheistic God of recent times has gone through a variety of changes as it passed through different nations and people. The Hindu god is quite different from the Christian god. The Christian god is again different from gods of other faiths. Thus numerous religions came into existence; each differed greatly from the other in the end, although each claims that ' God is One'.

The God-idea and Creation

AS each religion came into existence and developed around the god-idea, different religions developed their own particular explanations of creation. Thus the god-idea became associated with various myths. People used the god-idea as a vehicle for their explanations of the existence of humans and the nature of the universe.

Today, intelligent people, who have carefully reviewed all the available facts, have come to the conclusion that, like the god-idea, the creation of myths must be regarded as an evolution of the human imagination which began with the misunderstanding of natural phenomena. These misunderstandings were rooted in the fear and ignorance of primitive people. Even today, some people still retain their primitive interpretations of creation. In the light of recent, scientific thinking, the theological definition of god is vague and hence has no place in the contemporary creation theories.

If humans were created by an external source, then they must belong to that source and not to themselves. According to Buddhism, humans are responsible for everything they do. Thus Buddhists have no reason to believe that beings came into existence in human form through any external sources.

We believe that we are here today because of our own craving, attachment and karmic actions. We are neither punished nor rewarded by anyone but by ourselves according to our own good and bad action. In the process of evolution, the human being came into existence. There are no Buddha-words to support the belief that the world was created by anybody. However, the scientific discovery of gradual development of the world-system conforms with the Buddha's Teachings.

Human Weakness and the Concept of God

BOTH the concept of God and its associated creation myths have been protected and defended by believers who need these ideas to justify their existence and usefulness to human society. All the believers claim to have received their respective scriptures as Revelation; in other words, they all profess to come directly from one God. Each god-religion claims that it stands for Universal Peace and Universal Brotherhood and other such high ideals.

However great the ideals of the religions might be, the history of the world shows that some religions at least up to the present day have also helped in spreading superstitions. Some have stood against science and the advancement of knowledge, leading to ill-feelings, murders and wars. In this respect, the god-religions have failed in their attempt to enlighten mankind.

For example, in certain countries when people pray for mercy, their hands are stained with the blood of the morbid sacrifices of innocent animals and sometimes, even fellow human beings. Poor and helpless creatures are slaughtered at the desecrated altars of imaginary and imperceptible gods. It has taken a long time for people to understand the futility of such cruel practices in the name of religion. The time has come for them to realise that the path of real purification is through love and understanding.

Dr. G. Dharmasiri in his book 'Buddhist critique of the Christian Concept of God' has mentioned, 'I see that though the notion of God contains sublime moral strands, it also has certain implications that are extremely dangerous to humans as well as to the other beings on this planet.'

'One major threat to humanity is the blindfold called "authority" imposed on humans by the concept of God. All theistic religions consider authority as ultimate and sacred. It was this danger that the Buddha was pointing at in the Kalama Sutra.

At the moment, human individuality and freedom are seriously threatened by various forms of authorities. Various "authorities" have been trying to make "you" a follower. On top of all our "traditional" authorities, a new form of authority has emerged in the name of 'science '. And lately, the mushrooming new religions and the menace of the Gurus have become live threats to the individual's human freedom and dignity. The Buddha's eternal plea is for you to become a Buddha, and He showed, in a clearly rational way, that each and every one of us has the perfect potentiality and capacity to attain that ideal.'

God-religions offer no salvation without God. Thus a person might conceivably have climbed to the highest pinnacle of virtue, and he or she might have led a righteous way of life, and might even have climbed to the highest level of holiness, yet that person is to be condemned to eternal hell just because he or she did not believe in the existence of the God of a particular group. On the other hand, a person might have sinned deeply and yet, having made a late repentance, that person can be forgiven and therefore 'saved'. From the Buddhist point of view, there is no justification in this kind of teaching.

Despite the apparent contradictions of the god-religions, however it is not deemed advisable to preach a godless doctrine since the belief in god has also done a tremendous service to mankind, especially among less spiritually developed people to whom the god concept is desirable. This belief in god has helped people to control their animal nature. And much help has been granted to others in the name of god. For the most part, they feel insecure without the belief in god. They find protection and inspiration when that belief is in their mind. The reality or validity of such a belief is based on their understanding capacity and spiritual maturity.

However, religion should also concern our daily life. It is to be used as a guide to regulate our conduct in the world. Religion tells us what to do and what not to. do. If we do not follow a religion sincerely, mere religious labels or belief in god do not serve us in our daily life.

It must be remembered that if the followers of various religions are going to quarrel and to condemn other beliefs and practices— especially to prove or disprove the existence of their god—and if they are going to harbour enmity towards other religions because of their different religious views, then they are creating enormous disharmony amongst the various religious communities. "Whatever religious differences we have, it is our duty to practise tolerance, patience and understanding. It is our duty to respect others' religious beliefs even if we cannot accommodate them. Religious tolerance or understanding of each other's religion is necessary for the sake of harmonious and peaceful living.

However, it does not serve any purpose to introduce this concept of god to those who are not ready to appreciate it. To some people this belief is not important to lead a righteous life. There are many who lead a noble life without such beliefs while amongst believers there are many who violate the peace and happiness of innocent people.

Buddhists can also co-operate with those who hold this concept of god, provided that they use this concept for the peace, happiness and welfare of mankind. But they must part company with those who abuse this concept by threatening people in order to introduce this belief just for their own benefit and with ulterior motives.

For more than 2,500 years, all over the world, Buddhists have practised and introduced Buddhism very peacefully without the necessity of sustaining the concept of a creator God. And they will continue to sustain this religion in the same manner without disturbing the followers of other religions.

Therefore, with due respect to other religionists, it must be mentioned that any attempt to introduce this concept into Buddhism is unnecessary. Let Buddhists maintain their belief since it is harmless to others and, let the basic Teachings of the Buddha remain because they do not try to drag others into Buddhism.

From time immemorial, Buddhists have led a peaceful religious life without incorporating the particular concept of God. They should be capable of sustaining their particular religion without the necessity, at this juncture, of someone trying to force something down their throats against their will. Having full confidence in their Buddha Dharma, Buddhists should be permitted to work and seek their own salvation without any undue interference from other sources. Others can uphold their beliefs and concepts, Buddhists will uphold theirs, without any rancour. We do not challenge others in regard to their religious persuasions, we expect reciprocal treatment in regard to our own beliefs and practices.

Changing a Religious Label before Death

Merely to believe that there is someone to wash away our sins without suppressing our evil state of mind, is not in accordance with the Teachings of the Buddha.

VERY often we come across cases of people who change their religion at the last moment when they are about to die. By embracing another religion, some people are under the mistaken belief that they can 'wash away their sins' and gain an easy passage to heaven. They also hope to ensure themselves a more emotionally charged and aesthetically more attractive burial. For people who have been living a whole life time with a particular religion, to suddenly embrace a religion which is totally new and unfamiliar and to expect an immediate salvation through their new faith is indeed very far-fetched.

This is only a dream. Some people are even known to have been converted into another faith when they are in a state of unconsciousness and in some cases, even posthumously. Those who are over zealous and crazy about converting others into their faith, have misled uneducated people into believing that theirs is the one and only faith with an easy method or short-cut to heaven. If people are led to believe that there is someone sitting somewhere up there who can wash away all the sins committed during a lifetime, then this belief will only encourage others to commit evil without fear.

According to the Teachings of the Buddha there is no such belief that there is someone who can wash away sins. It is only when people sincerely realise that what they are doing is wrong and after having realised this, try to mend their ways and do good that they can suppress or counter the bad reactions that would accrue to them for the evil they had committed.

It has become a common sight in many hospitals to see purveyors of some religions hovering around the patients promising them ' life after death'. This is exploiting the basic ignorance and psychological fear of the patients. If they really want to help, then they must be able to work the 'miracles' they so proudly claim lies in their holy books. If they can work miracles, we will not need hospitals and cemeteries. Buddhists must never become victims to these people. They must learn the basic teachings of their noble religion which tell them that all suffering is the basic lot of mankind. The only way to end suffering is by purifying the mind. The individual creates his or her own suffering and it is that person alone who can end it. One cannot hope to eradicate the consequences of one's evil actions simply by changing one's religious label at the doorstep of death.

A dying person's destiny in the next life depends on the last thoughts which appear according to the good and bad karma accumulated during the current lifetime, irrespective of what type of religious label a person prefers to display at the last moment.

Short-cut to Paradise and End of the World

Paradise is open not only to the followers of a particular religion, but it is open to each and every person who leads a righteous and noble way of life.

THERE is no difficulty at all for Buddhists to go to heaven if they really want to. But there are some people who go from house to house trying to convert other religionists into their faith and promising them the heaven they carry in their bags. They claim that they are the only blessed people who can go to heaven; they also claim that they have the exclusive authority to send others to the same goal. They introduce their religion like a patent medicine and this has become a nuisance to the public today. Many innocent people who lack the knowledge of their own religion, have become victims of these paradise peddlars.

If Buddhists can understand the value of the Noble Teachings of the Buddha, they will not be misled by such people. These paradise sellers are also trying to mislead the people by saying that this world which is created by god, is going to end very soon. Those who want to have a wonderful everlasting life in heaven must accept their particular religion before the end of the world comes, otherwise people would miss this golden opportunity and would have to suffer in eternal hell. We note with a smile how many red faces there were among these people who proclaimed loudly that the world would come to an end on 31st December, 1999, only to wake up very much alive to celebrate the beginning of the year 2000. But they do not give up so easily. Now they will go around saying that they misread their Holy Book and that the world will surely end in the following century.

This threat of the end of the world had been going on for hundreds of years. The wonder of it all is that there are still people today who believe in such a threat which is irrational and imaginary. some people get converted after hearing such preaching; without using their common sense.

In Buddhism, there is no personal judge either to condemn or to reward but only the working of an impersonal moral causation and natural law.

PROMOTER OF TRUE HUMAN CULTURE

BUDDHIST ideas have greatly contributed to the enrichment of both ancient and modern thought. Its teaching of causation and relativism, its doctrine of sense data, its pragmatism, its emphasis on morality, its non-acceptance of a permanent soul, its unconcern about external supernatural forces, its denial of unnecessary rites and religious rituals, its appeal to reasoning and experience and its compatibility with modern scientific discoveries all tend to establish its superior claim to modernity.

Buddhism is able to meet all the requirements of a rational religion which suit the needs of the future world. it is so scientific, so rational, so progressive that it will be a matter of pride for people in the modern world to call themselves Buddhists. In fact, Buddhism is more scientific in approach than science; it is more socialistic than socialism.

Among all the great founders of religions, it was the Buddha alone who encouraged the spirit of investigation among His followers and who advised them not to accept even His own Teaching with blind faith. Therefore, it is no exaggeration to say that Buddhism can be called a modern religion.

Buddhism is a well-elaborated scheme of how to lead a practical life and a carefully thought-out system of self-culture. But more than that, it is a scientific method of education. This religion is best able in any crisis to restore our peace of mind and to help us to face calmly whatever changes the future may have in store. Without sensual pleasure, would life be endurable? Without belief in immortality, can people be moral? Without resorting to divinity, can we advance towards righteousness? YEs, is the answer given by Buddhism. These ends can be attained by knowledge and by the purification of the mind. Knowledge is the key to the higher path. Purification is that which brings calmness and peace to life and renders a person indifferent to and detached from the vagaries of the phenomenal world.

Buddhism is truly a religion suited to the modern, scientific world. The light which comes from nature, from science, from history, from human experience, from every point of the universe, is radiant with the Noble Teachings of the Buddha.

Religion in a Scientific Age

Religion without science is lame, while science without religion is blind.

TODAY we live in a scientific age in which almost every aspect of our lives has been affected by science. Since the scientific revolution during the seventeenth century, science has continued to exert tremendous influence on what we think and do.

The impact of science has been particularly strong on traditional religious beliefs. Many basic religious concepts are crumbling under the pressure of modern science and are no longer acceptable to the intellectual and the well-informed person. No longer is it possible to assert truth derived merely through theological speculations or based on the authority of religious scriptures in isolation from scientific consideration. For example, the findings of modern psychologists indicate that the human mind, like the physical body, works according to natural, causal laws without the presence of an unchanging soul as taught by some religions.

Some religionists choose to disregard scientific discoveries which conflict with their religious dogmas. Such rigid mental habits are indeed a hindrance to human progress. Since modern people refuse to believe anything blindly, even though it had been traditionally accepted, such religionists will only succeed in increasing the ranks of non-believers with their faulty theories.

On the other hand, some religionists have found it necessary to accommodate popularly accepted scientific theories by giving new interpretations to their religious dogmas. A case in point is Darwin's Theory of Evolution. Many religionists maintain that human beings were directly created by God. Darwin, on the other hand, argued that human beings had evolved from the ape, a theory which upset the doctrines of divine creation. Since all enlightened thinkers have accepted Darwin's theory, the theologians today have little choice except to give a new interpretation to their doctrines to suit this theory which they had opposed for so long. In 1998 Pope John Paul II announced that human beings may be the result of gradual evolution and not the immediate creation of God as previously proclaimed. (NEW SUNDAY TiMES—October of 1998). Increasingly the same is becoming true about rebirth, which no intelligent person disputes today. It is a matter of time before some holy books will be re-written on that subject as well.

In the light of modern scientific discoveries, it is not difficult to understand that many of the views held by many religions regarding the universe and life are merely conventional thoughts which have long been superceded.

Buddhism and Science

Until the beginning of the last century, Buddhism was confined to countries untouched by modern science. Nevertheless, from its very beginning, the Teachings of the Buddha were always open to scientific thinking and critical examination.

One reason why the Teaching can easily be embraced by the scientific spirit is that the Buddha never encouraged rigid, dogmatic belief. He did not claim to base His Teachings on faith, belief, or divine revelation, but allowed great flexibility and freedom of thought and He never committed Himself on subjects which were outside the scope of verification by human intelligence.

The second reason is that the scientific spirit can be found in the Buddha's approach to spiritual Truth. The Buddha's method for discovering and testing spiritual Truth is very similar to that of the scientist. A scientist observes the external world objectively, and would only establish a scientific theory after conducting many successful practical experiments.

Using a similar approach 25 centuries ago, the Buddha observed the inner world with detachment, and encouraged His disciples not to accept any teaching until they had critically investigated and personally verified its truth. Just as the scientist today would not claim that his experiment cannot be duplicated by others, the Buddha did not claim that His experience of Enlightenment was exclusive to Him. Thus, in His approach to Truth, the Buddha was as analytical as the present day scientist. He established a practical, scientifically worked-out method for reaching the Ultimate Truth and the experience of Enlightenment.

While Buddhism is very much in line with the scientific spirit, it is not correct to equate Buddhism with science. It is true that the practical applications of science have enabled mankind to live more comfortable lives and experience wonderful things undreamed of before. Science has made it possible for humans to swim better than the fishes, fly higher than the birds, and walk on the moon. Yet the sphere of knowledge acceptable to conventional, scientific wisdom is confined to empirical evidence. And scientific truth is subject to constant change.

This is because, ultimately science does not know the Ultimate Truth. As it gropes about in semi-darkness, it has to constantly shift its positions, as it discovers new Truths it had never thought possible before. As yet, science cannot give human beings control over their mind and it certainly cannot offer moral control and guidance. Despite its wonders, science has indeed many limitations not shared by Buddhism.

Limitations of Science

often one hears so much about science and what it can do, and so little about what it cannot do. Scientific knowledge is limited to the data received through the sense organs. It does not recognise reality which transcends sense-data. Scientific truth is built upon logical observations of sense data which are continually changing. Scientific truth is, therefore, relative truth not intended to stand the test of time. A scientist, being aware of this fact, is always willing to discard a theory if it can be replaced by a better one.

Science attempts to understand the outer world and has barely scratched the surface of humanity's inner world. Even the science of psychology has not really fathomed the underlying cause of human mental unrest. when a person is frustrated and disgusted with life, and the inner world of this person is filled with disturbances and unrest, science today is very much ill-equipped to help him or her. The social sciences which cater for human environment may bring a certain degree of happiness. But unlike animals, humans require more than mere physical comfort and need help to cope with their frustrations and miseries arising from their daily experiences.

Today so many people are plagued with fear, restlessness, and insecurity. Yet science fails to help them. Science is unable to teach the people to control their minds when they are driven by the animal nature that burns within themselves.

Can science make human beings morally better? If it can, why do violent acts and immoral practices increase in countries which are so advanced in science? Isn't it fair to say that despite all the scientific progress achieved and the advantages conferred on humans, science leaves their inner selves unchanged: it has only heightened their feelings of dependence and insufficiency? In addition to its failure to bring security and confidence to mankind, science has also made everyone feel even more insecure by threatening the world with the possibility of mass destruction.

Science is unable to provide a meaningful purpose of life. It cannot provide humanity with clear reasons for living. In fact, science is thoroughly secular in nature and unconcerned with their spiritual goal. The materialism inherent in scientific thought denies the psyche goals higher than material satisfaction. By its selective theorizing and relative truths, science disregards some of the most essential issues and leaves many questions unanswered. For instance, when asked why great inequalities exist among people, no scientific explanation can be given to such questions which are beyond its narrow confines.

Learned Ignorance

The transcendental mind developed by the Buddha is not limited to sense-data and goes beyond the logic trapped within the limitation of relative perception. The human intellect, on the contrary, operates on the basis of information it collects and stores, whether in the field of religion, philosophy, science or art. The information for the mind is gathered through our sense organs which are inferior in so many ways. The very limited information perceived makes our understanding of the world distorted.

Some people are proud of the fact that they know so much. In fact, the less we know, the more certain we are in our explanations; the more we know, the more we realize our limitations.

A brilliant scholar once wrote a book which he considered as the ultimate work. He felt that the book contained all the literary gems and philosophies. Being proud of his achievement, he showed his masterpiece to a colleague of his who was equally brilliant with the request that the book be reviewed by him. Instead, his colleague asked the author to write down on a piece of paper all he knew and all he did not know. The author sat down deep in thought, but after a long while failed to write down anything he knew. Then he turned his mind to the second question, and again he failed to write down anything he did not know. Finally, with his ego at the lowest ebb, he gave up, realizing that all that he knew was really ignorance.

In this regard, Socrates, the Athenian philosopher of

the Ancient World, had this to say when asked what he knew: 'I know only one thing—that I do not know'.

Beyond Science

Buddhism goes beyond modern science in its acceptance of a wider field of knowledge than is allowed by the scientific mind. Buddhism admits knowledge arising from the sense organs as well as personal experiences gained through mental culture. By training and developing a highly concentrated mind, religious experience can be understood and verified. Religious experience is not something which can be understood by conducting experiments in a test-tube or examined under a microscope.

The truth discovered by science is relative and subject to changes, while that found by the Buddha is final and absolute: the Truth of Dharma does not change according to time and space. Furthermore, in contrast to the selective theorizing of science, the Buddha encouraged the wise not to cling to theories, scientific or otherwise. Instead of theorizing, the Buddha taught mankind how to live a righteous life to discover Ultimate Truths. The Buddha pointed the way through which we can discover within ourselves the nature of life by living a righteous life, by calming the senses, and by casting off desires. And as a result the real purpose of life can be found.

Practice is important in Buddhism. A person who studies much but does not practise is like one who is able to recite recipes from a huge cookery book without trying to prepare a single dish. His hunger cannot be relieved by book knowledge alone. Practice is such an important prerequisite of enlightenment that in some schools of Buddhism, such as Zen, practice is put even ahead of knowledge.

The scientific method is outwardly directed and modern scientists exploit nature and the elements for their own comfort, often disregarding the need to harmonise with the environment and thereby polluting the world. In contrast, Buddhism is inwardly directed and is concerned with the inner development of humans. On the lower level, Buddhism teaches the individual how to adjust and cope with events and circumstances of daily life. At the higher level, it represents the human endeavour to grow beyond oneself through the practice of mental culture or mind development.

Buddhism has a complete system of mental culture concerned with gaining insight into the nature of things which leads to complete self-realization of the ultimate Truth – Nirvana. This system is both practical and scientific, it involves dispassionate observation of emotional and mental states. More like a scientist than a judge, a meditator observes the inner world with mindfulness and objectivity.

Science Without Religion

Without having moral ideals, science poses a danger to all mankind. The bullet and bomb are gifts of science to the few in power on whom the destiny of the world depends. Meanwhile the rest of mankind waits in anguish and fear, not knowing when the nuclear weapons, the poisonous gases, the deadly arms – all fruits of scientific research designed to kill efficiently – will be used on them. Not only is science completely unable to provide moral guidance to mankind, it has also fed fuel to the flame of human craving.

Science devoid of morality spells only destruction: it becomes the draconian monster man discovered. And unfortunately, this very monster is becoming more powerful than man himself. Unless man learns to restrain and govern the monster through the practice of religious morality, the monster will soon overpower him. Without religious guidance, science threatens the world with destruction. In contrast, science when coupled with a religion like

Buddhism can transform this world into a haven of peace and security and happiness.

Never was there a time when the co-operation between science and religion has been so desperately needed in the best interest and service of mankind. Religion without science is blind, while science without religion is crippled.

Tribute to Buddhism

Albert Einstein paid a tribute to Buddhism when he said in his autobiography: 'If there is any religion that would cope with modern scientific needs, it would be Buddhism'. Buddhism requires no revision to keep it 'up-to-date' with recent scientific findings. Buddhism need not surrender its views to science because it embraces science besides going beyond science. Buddhism is the bridge between religious and scientific thoughts by stimulating man to discover the latent potentialities within himself and his environment. Buddhism is timeless!

Religion of Freedom

This is a religion of freedom and reason for human beings to lead a noble life.

*B*UDDHISM does not prevent anyone from learning the teachings of other religions. In fact, the Buddha encouraged His followers to learn about other religions and to compare His Teachings with other teachings. The Buddha says that if there are reasonable and rational teachings in other religions, His followers are free to respect such teachings. It seems that certain religionists try to keep their followers in the dark; some of them are not even allowed to touch other religious objects or books. They are instructed not to listen to the preachings of other religions. They are enjoined not to doubt the teachings of their own religion, however unconvincing their teachings may appear to be. They believe that the more they keep their followers on a one-track mind, the more easily they can keep them under control. If anyone of them exercises freedom of thought and realises that he or she had been in the dark all the time, then it is alleged that the devil has possessed their mind. People are given no opportunity to use their common sense and education. Those who wish to change their views on religion are taught to believe that they are not worthy to be allowed to use free will in judging anything for themselves.

According to the Buddha, religion should be left to one's own free choice. Religion is not a law, but a disciplinary code which should be followed with understanding. To Buddhists true religious principles are neither a divine law nor a human law, but a universal law.

In actual fact, there is no real religious freedom in any part of the world today. People have no freedom even to think freely. Whenever they realise that they cannot find satisfaction through their own religion to which they belong, which cannot provide them with satisfactory answers to certain questions, they have no liberty to give it up and to accept another which appeals to them. The reason is that religious authorities, leaders, and family members have taken that freedom away from them. People should be allowed to choose their religion which is in accordance with their own conviction. One has no right to force another to accept a particular religion. This is particularly obvious when people from two different religions fall in love. Some people surrender their religion to get married, without a proper understanding of their partner's religion. Religion should not be changed to suit a person's emotions and human weaknesses. One must think very carefully before changing one's religion. Religion is not a subject for bargaining; one should not change one's religion for emotional, personal, material gains. Religion is to be used for spiritual development and for self-salvation.

Buddhists do not try to influence other religionists to come and embrace their religion for material gain. Nor do they try to exploit poverty, sickness, illiteracy and ignorance in order to increase the number of Buddhists in the population. The Buddha advised those who indicated their wish to follow Him, not to be hasty in accepting His Teachings. He advised them to consider carefully His

Teaching and to determine for themselves whether it was practical or not for them to follow. This is why there has never been a ritual baptism to be performed before one is "converted to Buddhism".

Buddhism teaches that mere belief or outward rituals are insufficient for attaining wisdom and perfection. In this sense, outward conversion becomes meaningless. To promote Buddhism by force would mean pretending to propagate justice and love by means of oppression and injustice. It is of no importance to the followers of the Buddha whether they call themselves Buddhists or not. Buddhists know that only through their own understanding and exertion will they come nearer to the goal preached by the Buddha.

Amongst the followers of religions there are usually some fanatics. Religious fanaticism is dangerous. A fanatic is incapable of guiding himself by reason or even by the scientific principles of observation and analysis. According to the Buddha, Buddhists must be free. People must have an open mind and must not be subservient to anyone for their spiritual development. They seek refuge in the Buddha by accepting Him as a source of supreme guidance and inspiration. The devotee seeks refuge in the Buddha, not blindly, but with understanding. To Buddhists, the Buddha is not a saviour nor is He an anthropomorphic being who claims to possess the power of washing away others' sins. Buddhists regard the Buddha as a Teacher who shows the Path to salvation.

Buddhism has always supported the freedom and progress of mankind. Buddhism has always stood for the advancement of knowledge and freedom for humanity in every sphere of life. There is nothing in the Buddha's Teaching that has to be retracted in the face of modern, scientific inventions and knowledge. The more new things that scientists discover, the closer they come to the Buddha's explanation of the universe and how it operates.

The Buddha emancipated human beings from the thralldom of religion. He also released them from the monopoly and the tyranny of priestcraft. It was the Buddha who first advised people to exercise their reason and not to allow themselves to be driven meekly like dumb cattle, following the dogma of religion. The Buddha stood for rationalism, democracy and practical, ethical conduct in religion. He introduced this Teaching for people to practise with human dignity.

The followers of the Buddha were advised not to believe anything without considering it properly. In the KALAMA SUTRA, the Buddha gave the following guidelines to a group of young people:-

'Do not accept anything based upon mere reports, traditions or hearsay, Nor upon the authority of religious texts, Nor upon mere reasons and arguments, Nor upon one's own inference, Nor upon anything which appears to be true, Nor upon one's own speculative opinions, Nor upon another's seeming ability, Nor upon the consideration: 'This is our Teacher.'

'But, when you know for yourselves that certain things are unwholesome and bad: tending to harm yourself or others, reject them.

'And when you know for yourselves that certain things are wholesome and good: conducive to the spiritual welfare of yourself as well as others, accept and follow them.'

Buddhists are advised to accept religious practices only after careful observation and analysis, and only after being certain that the method agrees with reason and is conducive to the good of one and all.

True Buddhists do not depend on external powers for their salvation. Nor do they expect to get rid of miseries through the intervention of some unknown power. They must try to eradicate all their mental impurities to find eternal happiness. The Buddha says, 'If anyone were to speak ill of me, my teaching and my disciples, do not be upset or perturbed, for this kind of reaction will only cause you harm. On the other hand, if anyone were to speak well of me, my teaching and my disciples, do not be overjoyed, thrilled or elated, for this kind of reaction will only be an obstacle in forming a correct judgement. If you are elated, you cannot judge whether the qualities praised are real and actually found in us.' (BRAHMA JALA SUTRA) Such is the unbiased attitude of a genuine Buddhist.

The Buddha upheld the highest degree of freedom not only in its human essence but also in its divine qualities. It is a freedom that does not deprive human beings of their dignity. It is a freedom that releases one from slavery to dogmas and dictatorial religious laws or religious punishments.

Buddhist Missionaries

'Go forth, O Bhikkhus, for the good of the many, for the happiness of the many, out of compassion for the world, for the good, benefit, and happiness of gods and men.' (THE BUDDHA)

WHEN we turn the pages of the history of Buddhism, we learn that Buddhist missionaries spread the noble message of the Buddha in a peaceful and respectable way. Such a peaceful record should put to shame those who have practised violent methods in propagating their religions.

Buddhist missionaries do not compete with other religionists in converting people in the market place. No Buddhist missionary or monk would ever think of preaching ill will against so called 'unbelievers'. Religious, cultural and national intolerance are unbuddhistic in attitude, to people who are imbued with the real Buddhist spirit.

Aggression never finds approval in the teaching of the Buddha. The world has bled and suffered enough from the disease of dogmatism, religious fanaticism and intolerance. Whether in religion or politics, people make conscious efforts to bring humanity to accept their own way of life. In doing so, they sometimes show their hostility towards the followers of other religions.

Buddhism never interfered with the national traditions and customs, art and culture of the people who accepted it as a way of life but allowed them to exist and encourage further refinement. The Buddha's message of love and compassion opened the hearts of people and they willingly accepted the Teachings, thereby helping

Buddhism to become a world religion. Buddhist missionaries were invited by independent countries which welcomed them with due respect. Buddhism was never introduced to any country through the influence of colonial or any other political power.

Buddhism was the first spiritual force known to us in history which drew closely together large numbers of races which were separated by the most difficult barriers of distance, language, culture and morals. Its motive was not the acquisition of international commerce, empire-building or to follow the migratory impulse and occupy fresh territory. Its aim was to show how people could gain more peace and happiness through the practice of Dharma.

A sparkling example of the qualities and approach of

a Buddhist missionary was Emperor Asoka. It was during Emperor Asoka's time that Buddhism spread to many Asian and western countries. Emperor Asoka sent Buddhist missionaries to many parts of the world to introduce the Buddha's message of peace. Asoka respected and supported every religion at that time. His understanding about other religions was remarkable. One of his scripts engraved in stone on Asoka Pillars, and still standing today in India, says:

'One should not honour only one's own religion and condemn the religion of others, but one should honour others' religions for this or that reason. In so doing, one helps one's own religion to grow and renders service to the religions of others too. In acting otherwise one digs the grave of one's own religion and also does harm to other religions. Whosoever honours his own religion and condemns other religions, does so indeed through devotion to his own religion, thinking, ' I will glorify my own religion. 'But on the contrary, in so doing he injures his own religion more gravely, so concord is good. Let all listen, and be willing to listen to the doctrines professed by others.'

Around 268 B.C., he made the doctrines of the Buddha a living force in India. Hospitals, social service institutions, universities for men and women, public wells and recreation centres sprang up with this new movement and the people thereby realised the cruelty of senseless wars.

The golden era in the history of India and the other countries of Asia was the period when art, culture, education and civilisation reached their zenith. These occurred at the time when Buddhist influence was strongest in these countries. Holy wars, crusades, inquisitions and religious discrimination do not mar the annals of the history of Buddhist countries. This is a noble history mankind can rightly be proud of. The Great Nalanda University of India which flourished from the second to the ninth century was a product of Buddhism. It was the first university that we know of and which was opened to international students.

In the past, Buddhism was able to make itself felt in many parts of the East, although communication and transport were difficult and people had to cross hills and deserts. Despite these difficult barriers Buddhism spread far and wide. Today, this peace message is spreading in the West. Westerners are attracted to Buddhism and agree that Buddhism is the only religion that is in harmony with modern science.

Buddhist missionaries have no need or desire to convert those who already have a proper religion to practise. If people are satisfied with their own religion, then, there is no need for Buddhist missionaries to convert them. They give their full support to missionaries of other faiths if their idea is to convert the wicked, evil, and uncultured people to a religious way of life.

Buddhists are happy to see the progress of other religions so long as they truly help people to lead a religious way of life according to their own faith and enjoy peace, harmony and understanding. On the other hand, Buddhist missionaries deplore the attitude of certain missionaries who disturb the followers of other religions, since there is no reason for them to create an unhealthy atmosphere of competition for converts if their aim is only to teach people to lead a religious way of life.

In introducing the Dharma to others, Buddhist missionaries have never tried to use imaginary exaggerations depicting a heavenly life in order to attract human desire and arouse their craving. They did not create fear in people s minds by saying that they would go to hell if they did not follow the Buddha. Instead, they have tried to explain the real nature of human and divine life as taught by the Buddha.

WAR AND PEACE

WE are living in a world of really amazing contradictions. On the one hand, people are afraid of war; on the other hand, they prepare for it with frenzy. They produce in abundance, but they distribute miserly. The world becomes more and more crowded, but people become increasingly isolated and lonely. They are living close to each other as in a big family, but each individual finds him or herself more than ever before, separated from his or her neighbour. Mutual understanding and sincerity are

lacking very badly. One person cannot trust another, however good the latter may be.

When the United Nations was formed after the horrors of the Second World War, the heads of Nations who gathered to sign the charter agreed that it should begin with the following preamble: 'Since it is in the minds of men that wars begin, it is in the minds of men the ramparts of peace should be erected'. This very same sentiment is echoed in the first verse of the Dhammapada in which the Buddha states: 'All [mental] states have mind as their forerunner, mind is their chief, and they are mind-made. If one speaks or acts, with a defiled mind, suffering follows one even as the wheel follows the hoof of the draught-ox.'

The belief that the only way to fight force is by applying more force has led to the arms race between the great powers. And this competition to increase the weapons of war has brought mankind to the very brink of total self-destruction. If we do nothing about it, the next war will be the end of the world where there will be neither victors nor victims—only dead bodies.

'Hatred does not cease by hatred; by love alone does it cease.' Such is the Buddha's advice to those who preach the doctrine of antagonism and ill will, and who set men to war and rebellion against one another. Many people say that the Buddha's advice to return good for evil is impractical. Actually, it is the only correct method to solve any problem. This method was introduced by the great Teacher from His own experience. Because we are proud and egoistic, we are reluctant to return good for evil, thinking that the public may treat us as cowardly people. Some people even think that kindness and gentleness are effeminate, not 'macho'! But what harm is there if we settle our problems and bring peace and happiness by adopting this cultured method and by sacrificing our dangerous pride? Many people cannot be satisfied without taking revenge for the mistakes done to them by others.

Tolerance must be practised if peace is to come to this earth. Force and compulsion will only create intolerance. To establish peace and harmony among mankind, each and everyone must first learn to practise the ways leading to the extinction of hatred, greed and delusion, the roots of all evil forces. If mankind can eradicate these evil forces, tolerance and peace will come to this restless world.

Today the followers of the most compassionate Buddha have a special duty to work for the establishment of peace in the world and to show an example to others by following their Master's advice: 'All tremble at punishment, all fear death; comparing others with oneself, one should neither kill nor cause to kill.

Peace is always obtainable. But the way to peace is not only through prayers and rituals. Peace is the result of achieving harmony with our fellow beings and with our environment. The peace that we try to introduce by force is not a lasting peace. It is an interval in between the conflict of selfish desire and worldly conditions.

Peace cannot exist on this earth without the practice of tolerance. To be tolerant, we must not allow anger and jealousy to prevail in our minds. The Buddha says, 'No enemy can harm one so much as one's own thoughts of craving, hate and jealousy.

Buddhism is a religion of tolerance because it preaches a life of self-restraint. Buddhism teaches a life based not on rules but on principles. Buddhism has never persecuted or maltreated those whose beliefs are different. The Teaching is such that it is not necessary for anyone to use the label "Buddhist" to practise the Noble Principles of this religion.

The world is like a mirror and if you look at the mirror with a smiling face, you can see your own, beautiful smiling face. On the other hand, if you look at it with a long face, you will invariably see ugliness. Similarly, if you treat the world kindly the world will also certainly treat you kindly. Learn to be peaceful with yourself and the world will also be peaceful with you.

Human kind is given to so much self-deceit that they do not want to admit their own weakness. They will try to find some excuse to justify their action and to create an illusion that they are blameless. If one really wants to be free, one must have the courage to admit one's own weakness. The Buddha says:

'Easily seen are other's faults; hard indeed it is to see one's own faults.'

Can We Justify War?

The difference between a dogfight and a war between two groups of people is only in its preparation.

THE history of mankind is a continuous manifestation of people's greed, hatred, pride, jealousy, selfishness and delusion. During the last 3,000 years, we have fought 15,000 major wars. Is it a characteristic of humans? What is our destiny? How can we end this senseless destruction of one another?

Although human beings have discovered and invented many important things, they have also made great advances towards the destruction of their own kind. This is how many human civilisations have been completely erased from this earth.

Modern human beings have become so sophisticated in the art and techniques of warfare that it is now possible for them to reduce entire cities to ashes within a few seconds. The world has become a storehouse of military hardware as a result of a game called 'Military Superiority.'

We are told that the prototype of a nuclear weapon more powerful than the atomic bomb which was dropped at Hiroshima Japan in August, 1945 is being planned. Scientists believe that a few hundred thermonuclear weapons will chart the course towards universal destruction. Just see what we are doing to our world! Think what sort of scientific development it is! See how foolish and selfish we are! People should not pander to their aggressive instincts. They should uphold the ethical teachings of the religious teachers and display justice with morality to enable peace to prevail.

Treaties, pacts and peace formulae have been adopted and millions of words have been spoken by countless world leaders throughout the world who proclaim that they have found the way to maintain and promote peace on earth. But for all their efforts, they have not succeeded in removing the threat to mankind.

The reason is that we have all failed to educate our young to truly understand and respect the need for selfless service and the danger of selfishness. To guarantee true peace, we must use every method available to us to educate youths to practise love, goodwill and tolerance towards others.

The Buddhist Attitude

Buddhists should not be the aggressors even in protecting their religion or anything else. They must try their best to avoid any kind of violent act. Sometimes they may be forced to go to war by others who do not respect the concept of the brotherhood of humans as taught by the Buddha. They may be called upon to defend their country from external aggression, and as long as they have not renounced the worldly life, they are duty-bound to join in the struggle for peace and freedom.

Under these circumstances, they cannot be blamed for becoming soldiers or being involved in defence. However, if everyone were to follow the advice of the Buddha, there would be no reason for war to take place in this world. It is the duty of every cultured person to find all possible ways and means to settle disputes in a peaceful manner, without declaring war to kill his or her fellow human beings. The Buddha did not teach His followers to surrender to any form of evil power be it a human or supernatural being.

Indeed, with reason and science, humanity has been able to conquer nature, and yet they have to secure their own lives. Why is it that life is in danger? While devoted to reason and being ruled by science, people have forgotten that they have hearts which have been neglected and left to wither and be polluted by passions.

If we cannot secure our own lives, then how can world peace be possible? To obtain peace, we must train our minds to face facts. We must be objective and humble. We must realise that no one person, nor one nation is always wrong. To obtain peace, we must also share the richness of the earth, if not with equality then at least with equity. There can never be absolute equality but surely there can be a greater degree of equity.

It is simply inconceivable that five percent of the world's population should enjoy fifty percent of its wealth, or that twenty-five percent of the world should be fairly well-fed and some overfed, while seventy-five percent of the world is always hungry.

Peace will only come when nations are willing to share and share equitably, the rich to help the poor and the strong to help the weak, thus creating international goodwill. Only if and when these conditions are met, can we envision a world with no excuse for wars.

The madness of the armaments race must stop! We must try to build schools instead of air force jets, hospitals instead of nuclear weapons. The amount of money and human lives that various governments waste in the battlefield should be diverted to build up the economies to elevate the standard of living.

The world cannot have peace until people and nations renounce selfish desires, give up racial arrogance, and eradicate egoistic lust for possession and power. Wealth cannot secure happiness. Religion alone can effect the necessary change of heart and bring about the only real disarmament—that of the mind.

All religions teach people not to kill; but unfortunately this important precept is conveniently ignored. Today, with modern armaments, we can kill millions within one second, that is, more than so called "primitive" tribes did in a century.

Very unfortunately some people in certain countries bring religious labels, slogans and banners into their battlefields. They do not know that they are disgracing the good name of religion.

'Verily, O monk,' said the Buddha, 'due to sensual craving, kings fight with kings, princes with princes, priests with priests, citizens with citizens, the mother quarrels with the son, the son quarrels with the father, brother with brother, brother with sister, sister with brother, friend with friend.

We can happily say that for the last 2,500 years there has never been any serious discord or conflict created by Buddhists that led to war in the name of this religion. This is a result of the dynamic character of the concept of tolerance contained in the Buddha's teaching.

Can Buddhists Join the Army?

You can be a soldier of Truth, but not an aggressor.

ONE day, Sinha, a general of an army, went to the Buddha and said, ' I am a soldier, O Blessed One. I am appointed by the King to enforce his laws and to wage his wars. The Buddha teaches infinite love, kindness and compassion for all sufferers: Does the Buddha permit the punishment of the criminal? And also, does the Buddha declare that it is wrong to go to war for the protection of our homes, our wives, our children and our property? Does the Buddha teach the doctrine of complete self-surrender? Should I suffer the evil-doer to do what he pleases and yield submissively to him who threatens to take by violence what is my own? Does the Buddha maintain that all strife including warfare waged for a righteous cause should be forbidden?'

The Buddha replied, 'He who deserves punishment must be punished. And he who is worthy of favour must be favoured. Do not do injury to any living being but be just, filled with love and kindness.' These injunctions are not contradictory because the person who is punished for his crimes will suffer his injury not through the ill will of the judge but through the evil act itself. His own acts have brought upon him the injury that the executors of the law inflict. When a magistrate punishes, he must not harbour hatred in his heart. When a murderer is put to death, he should realise that his punishment is the result of his own act.

With this understanding, he will no longer lament his fate but can console his mind. And the Blessed One continued, 'The Buddha teaches that all warfare in which man tries to slay his brothers is lamentable. But he does not teach that those who are involved in war to maintain peace and order, after having exhausted all means to avoid conflict, are blameworthy.'

'Struggle must exist, for all life is a struggle of some kind. But make certain that you do not struggle in the interest of self against truth and justice. He, who struggles out of self-interest to make himself great or powerful or rich or famous, will have no reward. But he who struggles for peace and truth will have great reward; even his defeat will be deemed a victory'.

'If a person goes to battle even for a righteous cause, then Sinha, he must be prepared to be slain by his enemies because death is the destiny of warriors. And should his fate overtake him, he has no reason to complain. But if he is victorious his success may be deemed great, but no matter how great it is, the wheel of fortune may turn again and bring his life down into the dust. However, if he moderates himself and extinguishes all hatred in his heart, if he lifts his down-trodden adversary up and says to him, 'Come now and make peace and let us be brothers,' then he will gain a victory that is not a transient success; for the fruits of that victory will remain forever.

'Great is a successful general, Sinha, but he who conquers self is the greater victor. This teaching of conquest of self, Sinha, is not taught to destroy the lives of others, but to protect them. The person who has conquered himself is more fit to live, to be successful and to gain victories than is the person who is the slave of self. The person, whose mind is free from the illusion of self, will stand and not fall in the battle of life. He, whose intentions are righteousness and justice, will meet with no failures. He will be successful in his enterprise and his success will endure. He who harbours love of truth in his heart will live and not suffer, for he has drunk the water of immortality. So struggle courageously and wisely. Then you can be a soldier of Truth.'

There is no justice in war or violence. When we declare war, we justify it, when others declare war, we say, it is unjust. Then who can justify war? People should not follow the law of the jungle to overcome human problems.

Mercy Killing

Mercy and Killing can never go together.

ACCORDING to Buddhism mercy killing cannot be justified. Mercy and killing can never go together. Some people kill their pets on the grounds that they do not like to see the pets suffer. However, if mercy killing is the correct method to be practised on pets and other animals, then why are people so reluctant to do the same to their beloved ones?

When some people see their dogs or cats suffer from some skin disease, they arrange to kill those poor animals. They call this action, mercy killing. Actually it is not that they have mercy towards those animals, but they kill them for their own precaution and to get rid of an awful sight. And even if they do have real mercy towards a suffering animal, they still have no right to take away its life. No matter how sincere one may be, mercy killing is not the correct approach. While the consequences of this killing are different from killing with hatred towards the animal, Buddhists have no grounds to say that any kind of killing is justified.

Some people try to justify mercy killing with the misconception that if the motive or reason is good, then the act itself is good. They then claim that by killing their pet, they have the intention to relieve the unhappy animal from its suffering and so the action is good. No doubt their original intention or motive is good. But the misguided act of killing which occurs through a later thought, requires some degree of cruelty or hard-heartedness which will certainly bring about unwholesome results.

Avoiding mercy killing can create inconvenience to many. Nevertheless, the Buddhist religion cannot justify mercy killing as completely free from bad reactions. However, we must add that to kill without any greed, anger or hatred has less bad reaction than to kill out of intense anger or jealousy.

It must be remembered that, a being (human or animal) suffers owing to his or her bad karma. If by mercy killing, we prevent the working out of one's bad karma, the debt will have to be paid in another existence. As Buddhists, all that we can do is to help to reduce the pain of suffering in others.

Killing for Self-Protection

The Buddha has advised everyone to abstain from killing. If everybody accepts this advice, human beings would not kill each other. In the case where a person's life is threatened, the Buddha says even then it is not advisable to kill in self-defence. The weapon for self-protection is loving-kindness. One who practises this kindness very seldom comes across such misfortune. However, people love their lives so much that they are not prepared to surrender themselves to others; in actual practice, most people would struggle for self-protection. It is natural and every living being struggles and attacks others for self-protection but the karmic effect of the aggression depends on their mental attitude. During the struggle to protect himself, if a man happens to kill his opponent although he had no intention to kill, then he does not create bad karma resulting from that death.

On the other hand, if he kills another person under any circumstances with the intention to kill, then he is not free from the karmic reaction; he has to face the consequences. We must remember that killing is killing; when we disapprove of it, we call it 'murder'. When we punish man for murdering, we call it 'capital punishment'. If our own soldiers are killed by an 'enemy' we call it 'slaughter'. However, if we approve a killing, we call it 'war'. But if we remove the emotional content from these words, we can understand that killing is killing.

In recent years many scientists and some religionists have used the expressions like 'humane killing', 'mercy killing', 'gentle killing' and 'painless killing' to justify the ending of a life. They argue that if the victim feels no pain, if the knife is sharp, killing is justified. Buddhism can never accept these arguments because it is not how the killing occurs that is important, but the fact that the life of one being is unnaturally terminated. No one has any right to do that for whatever reason.

The Buddhist Stand on the Death Sentence

The Buddhist concept on the Death Sentence is clear. We must not only respect the law of the country but we must also strictly obey it.

Religion and law can be seen as two different aspects of life. Buddhism, as a religion teaches man to be good, to do good and do no evil. However, as a religion, none of its members have the power to punish anybody who has defied its precepts to commit evil—to steal, to rape, to commit murder or to traffic in drugs. Any Bud-dhist who chooses to defy the law of the country by committing serious crime will have to be punished by the laws of the country and not by the religious body.

As buddhists and as human beings, we are full of compassion for suffering humanity but compassion by itself does not go far enough to be of help. Compassion does not help to restrain a person who has chosen to go against the law of the country. The laws of the country must be respected and upheld to the very letter. If law stipulates that for committing a serious crime you must pay for it by having your life taken away from you, then the process of law must take its course. Buddhism cannot interfere with the normal enforcement of the law. The only line of action, members of our religion can take is to ask for compassion and plead for clemency to be extended to an accused

The laws of our country are democratically enacted by the people themselves through the certain electioneering process. The people elect their representatives to serve as Members of Parliament. In Parliament the Members debate and promulgate laws for the smooth administration of the country. Without specific laws, then we have to revert back to the law of the jungle where might is right. Al-though in effect, Members of Parliament enact the laws, they do so as representatives of the people. If we, the people, enact the laws, we have no choice but to comply implicitly with our laws. If anyone chooses to defy them, then they must pay for it.

This may sounds harsh but laws of such nature existed even in the time of our lord Buddha, well ever two thousand five hundred years ago. In those days there were kings and rulers who had to administer the country where good and bad people existed as they do now.

From time immemorial, human nature being what it is, society consisted of good people. Religion teaches and guides every hu-man being to lead a good and noble life to gain eventual spiritual attainments. Religion does not condone evil. Even though a reli-gionist may infringe a religious precept, religion should not advo-cate harsh punishment. Religion cannot sentence a person to death for any fault but the law can. It was reported that during the Buddha's time, even monks who committed serious crimes, were sentenced to death. The Buddha did not and would not interfere with the normal enforcement of the law.

The Buddha's view was that if a ruler failed to carry out his functions to punish a criminal for committing a serious offence, the ruler would not be considered as one fit to administer the country. Similarly if a ruler was to be indiscriminate and punishe his subjects who were innocent with-out good reason, he would also be considered as one who would be unfit to rule. These qualifications were given a long time ago but the advice and injunctions given by the Buddha stand good even for the present day.

Buddhism does not subscribe to the taking of a life, human or animal, under any circumstances but if someone chooses to trans-gress the established laws of a country he or she has to pay the penalty – even if the penalty is a death sentence. One of the impor-tant moral codes of Buddhism is to obey the laws of a country.

If the law decrees that a war is on and that all able-bodied men are to be conscripted as soldiers to the country, a Buddhist must comply with the law. If as a Buddhists, we feel strongly enough that we should saves lives and not to destroy lives, the channel open for us is the democratic process to approach political leaders to cause the affected laws to be amended but if the consensus was against any change, we have no choice but to obey the law. The law is supreme. Of course, f we do not wish to join the army, the other option is for us to become monks and nuns and retire into to a monastery and work for our spiritual advancement. If we choose to remain in society, then we must be prepared to sacrifice ourselves for the good of that society.

The Origin of the World

There are three schools of thought regarding the origin of the world. The first school of thought claims that this world came into existence by nature and that nature is not an intelligent force. However, nature works on its own accord and goes on changing.

The second school of thought says that the world was created by an almighty God who is responsible for everything.

The third school of thought says that the beginning of this world and of life is inconceivable since they have neither beginning nor end. Buddhism is in accordance with this third school of thought. Bertrand Russell supports this school of thought by saying, 'There is no reason to suppose that the world had a beginning at all. The idea that things must have a beginning is really due to the poverty of our thoughts.'

Modern science says that some millions of years ago, the gradually cooled earth was lifeless and that life originated in the ocean. Buddhism has never claimed that the world, sun, moon, stars, wind, water, days and nights were created by a powerful god or by a Buddha. Buddhists believe that the world was not created once upon a time, but that the world has been created millions of times every second and will continue to do so by itself and will eventually by itself.

According to Buddhism: world systems always appear, change, decay and disappear in the universe in a never-ending cycle. H.G. Wells, in A Short History of the World, says 'It is universally recognised that the universe in which we live, has to all appearances, existed for an enormous period of time and possibly for endless time. But that the universe in which we live, has existed only for six or seven thousand years may be regarded as an altogether exploded idea. No life seems to have happened suddenly upon earth.' The efforts made by many religions to explain the beginning and the end of the universe are indeed ill conceived. The position of religions which propound the view that the universe was created by God in an exactly fixed year, has become a difficult one to maintain in the light of modern and scientific knowledge. Today scientists, historians, astronomers, biologists, botanists, anthropologists and great thinkers have all contributed vast new knowledge about the origin of the world. This latest discovery and knowledge is not at all contradictory to the Teachings of the Buddha. Bertrand Russell again says that he respects the Buddha for not making false statements like others who committed themselves regarding the origin of the world. The speculative explanations of the origin of the universe that are presented by various religions are not acceptable to the modern scientists and intellectuals. On the other hand, even the com-mentaries of the Buddhist Scriptures, written by certain Buddhist writers, cannot be challenged by scientific thinking in regard to this question. The Buddha did not waste His time on this issue although He did make passing references to the magnitude of the cosmos. His main aim was to help His disciples escape from suffering in Samsara. The reason for His silence was that this issue has no religious value for gaining spiritual wisdom. The explanation of the origin of the universe is not a spiritual concern. Such theorizing is not necessary for living a righteous way of life and for shaping our future lives. However, if one insists on studying this subject, then one must investigate the sciences, astronomy, geology, biology and anthropology. These sciences can offer more reliable and tested information on this subject than can be supplied by any religion.The purpose of a religion is to cultivate the life here in this world and hereafter until liberation is gained and not merely to satisfy our curiousity about the operation of the universe. To the Buddha, the world is nothing but Samsara – the cycle of repeated births and deaths. To Him, the beginning of the world and the end of the world is within this Samsara. Since elements and energies are relative and inter-dependent, it is meaningless to single out anything as the beginning. Whatever speculation we make regarding the origin of the world, there is no absolute truth in our notion. "Infinite is the sky, infinite is the number of beings, Infinite are the worlds in the vast universe, Infinite in wisdom the Buddha teaches these, Infinite are the virtues of Him who teaches these." one day a man called Malunkyaputta approached the Buddha and demanded that He explain the origin of the Universe. He even threatened to cease to be His follower if the Buddha did not reveal this. The Buddha calmly retorted that it was of no consequence to Him whether or not Malunkyaputta followed Him, because the Truth did not need anyone's support. Then the Buddha said that He would not go into a discussion of the origin of the Universe. To Him, gaining knowledge about such matters was a waste of time because a man's task was to liberate himself from suffering. To illustrate this, the Enlightened one related the parable of a man who was shot by a poisoned arrow. This foolish man refused to have the arrow removed until he found out all about the person who shot the arrow. By the time his attendants discovered these unnecessary details, the man was dead. Similarly, our immediate task is to attain Nirvana, not to worry about the beginning or the end of the world.

BIBLIOGRAPHIES

A useful bibliography of journal articles is Yushin Yoo's *Buddhism: A Subject Index to Periodical Articles in English, 1728-1971* (Metuchen, N.J.: Scarecrow Press, 1973).

Bandaranayake, S. *Sinhalese Monastic Architecture: The Viharas of Anuradhapura.* Leiden: E.J. Brill, 1974.

Brown, R.L. *The Dvaravati Wheels of the Law and the Indianization of South East Asia.* Leiden: E.J. Brill, 1996.

Buddhadasa, Bhikkhu, *Teaching Dhamma by Pictures.* Bangkok: Social Science Association Press of Thailand, 1968. This book presents a traditional Thai manuscript that illustrates the Buddhist Path, with commentary on its symbolism.

Bussagli, Mano, *Painting of Central Asia.* Geneva: Editions d'art Albert Skira, 1963. Magnificent Buddhist paintings from the rich finds of Central Asia.

Dagyab, Loden Sherap, *Tibetan Religious Art.* Wiesbaden, Germany: Otto Harrassowitz, 1977. Excellent two-volume work, the first introducing the art, the second showing it in color plates.

Dallapiccola, Anna, ed., *The Stupa: Its Religious, Historical, and Architectural Significance.* Wiesbaden: Franz Steiner Verlag, 1980.

Fickle, Dorothy H., *The Life ot the Buddha: Murals in the Buddhaisawan Chapel National Museum, Bangkok, Thailand.*

Bangkok: Fine Arts Department, 1972. Includes color illustrations of one of the better examples of Thai mural art.

Fontein, Jan, *The Pilgrimage of Sudhana: A Study of Gandavyuha Illustrations in China, Japan, and Java.* The Hague: Mouton, 1968. The Pilgrim's Progress of Buddhism in art and literature, spanning several civilizations.

Freeman, Michael and Roger Warner, *Angkor: The Hidden Glories.* Boston: Houghton Mifflin, 1990.

Ghosh, A., ed., *Ajanta Murals.* New Delhi: Archaeological Survey of India, 1967. Beautiful illustrations, sensitively interpreted.

Ginsberg, Henry. *Thai Manuscript Painting.* Honolulu: University of Hawai'i Press, 1989.

Hisamatsu, Shin'ichi, *Zen and the Fine Arts.* Tokyo: Kodansha International, 1971. Large selection of Zen-related arts.

Karmay, Heather, *Early Sino-Tibetan Art.* Warminster, England, 1975.

Krom, N. I., *The Life of Buddha on the Stupa ot Barabudur According to the Lalitavishtara Text.* The Hague: Martinus Nijhoff, 1926. An excellent retelling of the biography with photographs of the episodes from the great Javanese stupa.

Lyons, Islay, *Gandharan Art in Pakistan.* New York: Pantheon, 1957. Records an important phase of Buddhist art, the product of Indo-Greek culture. Read with Sharma, cited below.

Marshall, Sir John, *The Monuments of Sanchi.* London: Probsthain, 1940. A study of one of the most important remaining Indian Buddhist stupas.

Index